The Per

Problems, Image.   Alternatives

The Persistent Prison

Problems, Images and Alternatives

Edited by Clive Emsley

With a Foreword by Martin Narey
Chief Executive of the National Offender
Management Service

Francis
Boutle
Publishers

First published by Francis Boutle Publishers
272 Alexandra Park Road
London N22 7BG
Tel/Fax: (020) 8889 7744
Email: info@francisboutle.co.uk
www.francisboutle.co.uk

ISBN 1 903427 24 X

Printed by Interprint Ltd., Malta

Acknowledgements

We would like to thank Tim Newburn, editor of *Criminal Justice*, for permission to reprint the article by Andrew Millie, Jessica Jacobson and Mike Hough 'Understanding the growth in the prison population in England and Wales', which first appeared in in that journal in 2003 (*Criminal Justice* 3 (4), pp. 369–387). Acknowledgement is due to the Esmée Fairbairn Foundation for the funding that brought together the individuals respsonsible for this volume and for some of the costs of publication. Thanks are also due to Valerie Humphrey for her formidable organisational skills and for her efficiency, both well beyond the call of duty.

Contents

List of illustrations

Contributors

Ivo Aertsen is Professor in the Department of Criminal Law and Criminology at the Catholic University of Leuven.

Rob Allen is Director of the Rethinking Crime and Punishment programme for the Esmée Fairbairn Foundation.

Alyson Brown is Lecturer in History at Edge Hill College of Higher Education, Liverpool.

Emma Clare is Research Officer with the Extern Organisation in Northern Ireland.

Clive Emsley is Professor of History and Co-Director of the International Centre for Comparative Criminological Research at the Open University.

Marie Gillespie is Senior Lecturer in Sociology at the Open University.

Mike Hough is Professor of Criminal Policy and Director of the Institute for Criminal Policy Research at King's College, London.

Jessica Jacobson is an independent consultant.

René Lévy is a Research Director of the Centre national de la recherche scientifique working at the Centre de recherches sociologiques sur le droit et les institutions pénales (CESDIP) (CNRS and Justice Department, Guyancourt, France).

Eugene McLaughlin is Professor of Criminology at the City University.

Vivien Miller is Principal Lecturer in American Studies at Middlesex University.

Andrew Millie is a Research Fellow at the Institute for Criminal Policy Research at King's College, London.

Pieter Spierenburg is Professor of History at Erasmus University, Rotterdam.

David Wilson is Professor of Criminology at the Centre for Criminal Justice Policy and Research at the University of Central England.

Foreword

Martin Narey

I very much welcomed the Open University's initiative in organising a conference on the prison in December 2003, an event which led ultimately to this collection.

I have argued strongly, and did so at the conference, that imprisonment can be beneficial in the right circumstances. For a young man leading an utterly chaotic life, deeply addicted to drugs, unemployed and unemployable as well as being homeless, prison can provide a vital respite and a chance to start again. As investment in making imprisonment more constructive has arrived, more frequently than ever before prisons have discharged prisoners free – temporarily at least – from drug abuse and perhaps with their first educational qualifications and the realistic prospect of employment and a place to live.

I make no apology for persisting in this unfashionable view that imprisonment can work. And because it is the only possible sentence for some offenders we must make it work. We have an economic but also a moral obligation to do so. But the progress made in recent years in improving the nature of imprisonment, driving forward decency and providing more constructive activity, fuelled by generous Government investment has been reduced by the seemingly inexorable growth in the size of the prison population. A prison population which shocked commentators when it breached 50,000 as recently as 1995 has now grown to 75,000 and Home Office projections, which have never previously exaggerated the growth of prisoner numbers, suggest the population will reach 93,000 by 2009.

The challenge we face is preventing the population from growing so dramatically. The prize for success will be the ability to concentrate investment from the 2004 spending review – which I expect to be considerable - in supervising offenders in the community. But the alternative is that investment will once again be substantially invested in providing more and more prison cells to accommodate many more prisoners, substantial numbers of which will be serving short and inevitably ineffectual sentences.

I am optimistic that we can succeed. First of all we have, despite media interpretations which frequently mislead, a Home Secretary who has made plain that dangerous and persistent offenders should spend longer in custody but who has made it plain that for other offenders, custody should only be used when no other penalty will suffice. Secondly, we have in the newly established Sentencing Guidelines Council, a body, chaired by the Lord Chief Justice, which is tasked with issuing guidelines which take account of effectiveness and value for money in using correctional resources. Thirdly, rather than indulging largely in rhetoric about the greater effectiveness of community penalties we have begun genuinely to make them more effective than short sentences of imprisonment. The Intensive Supervision and Change Programme, the adult equivalent, the Intensive Control and Change Programme and the Drug Testing and Treatment Order, all provide encouraging evidence of effectiveness in reducing offending. Fourthly we have the bringing together of Prison and Probation under the National Offender Management Service, a unique opportunity to bring real coherence to how we supervise and support offenders in and out of custody and equip them to change their lives.

The challenge is very great but as I write this, in August 2004, there is already evidence of success on the sentencing front. A prison population, which should have grown by more than 3,000 since the end of April, has fallen by a few hundred. This may be fragile progress but it is significant nevertheless and encourages me to believe that the goal of a decent prison system, caring for those for whom prison is the only alternative and better resourced supervision and support of offenders in the community can reduce re-offending, draw individuals out of social exclusion, change their lives and in doing so protect our communities.

Introduction

The Persistent Prison

Clive Emsley

It is difficult to conceive of a society that does not have some system to deal with those who break its norms. In the contemporary world the prison is popularly regarded as the means of punishing and reforming serious offenders who break laws. The prison has a long history, yet it is really only since the Enlightenment, and particularly since the end of the eighteenth century, that it has been perceived as the best and principal means of dealing with offenders. It is only since the last third of the twentieth century that the numbers in prisons in the western world have begun to soar to bursting point.

The scale of increase in prison populations in recent years has been enormous. In England and Wales the numbers incarcerated have risen steadily from 45,817 (or 90 per 100,000 of the population) in 1992 to 75,324 (143 per 100,000) in mid-2004. Across the channel in France the numbers have moved up and down between 48,113 (84 per 100,000) in 1992, to 51,623 (89 per 100,000) in 1998, to 46,376 (78 per 100,000) in 2001, to 56,957 (95 per 100,000) in mid-2004. In the United States, the world leader for contemporary prison population, the figures rose from 1,295,150 (505 per 100,000) in 1992 to 2,033,331 (701 per

100,000) in mid-2004 (International Centre for Prison Statistics). Moreover, almost ten percent of all inmates in state and federal prisons at the latter date were serving life sentences; in the states of California and New York the percentage of such prisoners was almost twenty percent. The increases in prison populations during the 1990s continued when, statistically, the amount of crime began to level out and even drop (*New York Times*, 12 May 2004). The general public of different countries was, and continues to be assured by polemicists in the press and by many politicians currying popular favour and hanging on to the polemicists' coat tails, that 'prison works'. More sober reflection forces the questions – in what ways? and how? and what alternatives are there? These issues constitute an undercurrent in the chapters that follow, together with the key question of how, today, people understand the prison and what it might stand for.

The late eighteenth- and early nineteenth-century legal reformers urged that every individual accused of a criminal offence should face an identical legal process that left no space for allegations of, or opportunities for, arbitrariness or partiality. They also urged that the prison was a humane replacement for brutalities inflicted on the body of the convicted offender. Cesare Beccaria, whose 1764 pamphlet *Dei Delitti e delle Pene* (On Crimes and Punishments) encapsulated the emerging penal reform ideas of the Enlightenment, posed the question succinctly: 'Who, in reading history, can keep from cringing with horror before the spectacle of barbarous and useless torments, cold-bloodedly devised and carried through by men who called themselves wise?' (Beccaria, 1963: 42). It was not just grisly executions that the public was able to view such as, for example, the extended sufferings of the offender as he or she choked on the rope at Tyburn Tree or was beaten to death on a wheel in *la Place de la Grève*. Offenders were also publicly whipped, branded, had their ears or noses slit or were exposed in the pillory. Indeed, for anyone in England who had particularly offended the populace by his offence, the pillory itself could be a death sentence, or at best a sentence that might lead to severe injury at the hands of the crowd.

From the early modern period there were experiments in using incarceration to reform those among the poor accused of being idle or work-shy – 'sturdy beggars' in the parlance of the day. Nevertheless the prison at the time that

Beccaria was writing, and as Pieter Spierenburg notes in the opening chapter below, was used largely as a place to hold those awaiting trial, awaiting execution or some other form of punishment. Generations of historians who, during the nineteenth and early twentieth centuries, wrote of changes in the penal system followed the reformers' lines of argument stressing the brutal, barbaric and 'medieval' nature of pre-Enlightenment and pre-the-prison punishment. They adopted what has been characterised as the Whig view of historical development. This view portrays penal reform since the eighteenth century as progressive, the work of far-sighted reformers pushing through humanitarian changes in the teeth of conservative and blinkered opposition. Whig historians wrote with assumptions of progress and credited the reformers with sharing a vision of this progress. The Whig interpretation of penal development also began at a time when crime statistics in the European world generally appeared to be falling, or at least levelling out. Furthermore, in spite of the appalling blood-letting of the First World War and the Depression, people in liberal democratic societies kept faith with humanitarian progress and continued to observe relatively steady crime rates. Indeed, such thinking continued to predominate for many years after the horrors of the Second World War. The change in historical approach and understanding appears to have come in the last third of the twentieth century. It is during this latter period that David Garland has charted a broad swing away from policies that had evolved over the preceding century, policies that he defines as penal welfarism – 'the legal liberalism of due process and proportionate punishment [combined] with a correctionalist commitment to rehabilitation, welfare and criminological expertise' (Garland, 2001: 27).

The Whig historians' stress on the physical punishments of the old regime ignored the mental punishment of the new prison. Michel Foucault played a key role in emphasising the shift from a physical assault on the body of the convicted offender to the attempt to confine the body and to allow experts boasting new forms of knowledge to work on the mind of a prisoner. The prison was only one part of what Foucault (1977) identified as a broad strategy of bodily confinement that was developed from the Enlightenment onwards. His sombre vision has inspired much new research. A series of critics, however, have emphasised that Foucault identified a shift in policies without identifying either the actors responsible or their motivations (see for example the essays in

Perrot, ed., 1980)). Michael Ignatieff (1978) looking at the English context, challenged Foucault's perspective for its denial of any alternative vision. Ignatieff located the motives of the reformers in their respective personality traits and their desire for a controlled and obedient workforce for the burgeoning industrial economy. At the same time he stressed the terrible impact of the strategies of anonymity and silence imposed in the early penitentiaries. These strategies often prompted suicide or mental breakdown. Moreover, and looking beyond Ignatieff's work, while prison authorities may have made enormous claims for the way that they treated their charges, there were several instances when prisoners considered that the only way to make their problems known and to get them resolved was through insurrection (Brown, 2003).[1] And even in the days of penal welfarism, the treatment of prisoners itself could involve physical violence both unofficial and official. It was possible for a sentence of flogging to be awarded to a male prisoner by a Board of Visitors in a British prison for mutiny, incitement to mutiny or gross personal violence against an officer until 1967.[2] This was nineteen years after a Criminal Justice Act had abolished corporal punishment in the courts of England and Wales.

Foucault's contribution to the debate on the development of the prison, like the old Whig interpretation, stressed the violence of old regime punishments. In so doing it has helped perpetuate ignorance about the prevalence of the fine as a punishment, or as a means of resolving a conflict under the old regime. In some respects the fine was a vestige of the old system of an arrangement that was perpetuated in the infrajudicial policies pursued by small, generally inward-looking communities who appeared to ignore formal law. Many European explorers, missionaries, colonists and jurors insisted that the indigenous peoples that they met had no legal system. Justice Burton of New South Wales, for example, condemned Aboriginal practices as 'only such as are consistent with a state of darkness and irrational superstition' (quoted in Reynolds, 1996: 62). At the same time the more thoughtful and inquisitive Europeans recorded and seriously assessed systems whereby conflicts were resolved through agreements mediated by acknowledged leaders within the indigenous communities. Father Brébeuf of the mission to the Huron in New France explained their practices in 1636.

[I]f laws are like the governing wheel regulating communities ... it seems to me that, in view of the perfect understanding that reigns among [the Huron], I am right in maintaining that they are not without laws. They punish murderers, thieves, traitors and Sorcerers; and ... the little disorder there is among them in this respect makes me conclude that their procedure is scarcely less efficacious than is the punishment of death elsewhere; for the relatives of the deceased pursue not only him who has committed the murder, but address themselves to the whole village, which must give satisfaction for it, and furnish, as soon as possible ... as many as sixty presents, the least of which must be the value of a new beaver robe (Quoted in Brown, 2002: 380).

In New Zealand the Maori had no distinction between civil and criminal offences; they resolved 'wrongs' usually with a hearing in a communal meeting house that was intended to restore social equilibrium. Restoration generally meant a mixture of compensation and mediation, though on occasions this involved the right to raid and plunder the offender and his kin. The lack of a formal agreement following a 'wrong' could result in a feud (Pratt, 1992: 34-8). These 'primitive' systems of compensation and mediation had echoes in the societies from which earliest European explorers and colonists had come. Blood feuds as a means of resolving conflicts continued in parts of southern and south eastern Europe into the nineteenth and, in some instances, well into the twentieth century (see for example, Boehm, 1984; Wilson, 1988; Gallant, 2000). In eighteenth-century France and England disputes, which might involve theft, assault, even rape, were still being settled outside the formality of the law through the resolution of an individual or individuals who exercised power and authority by virtue of their position within the community. In France this might be a *curé* or an estate manager. In England it could be a justice of the peace, sitting in petty sessions in a pub or even his own home, but choosing to seek an arrangement rather than invoking the weight and majesty of the law (see for example, Garnot, 2000; King, 2004). Such infrajudicial resolution, however, was not something that could survive the legal systems and practices of the bureaucratic states that emerged in the nineteenth century. Other developments in these states also contributed to the rise of the prison.

Secure prisons designed to hold large numbers of convicted offenders for any length of time require a significant financial outlay, first to establish the institution and then to run and maintain it. This requires political ability, political will and political decision. Only gradually did the states of Europe seek and acquire the ability to raise funds to meet these requirements. The decision to build the first national penitentiary in Britain was made when the government was raising enormous sums to fight Revolutionary and Napoleonic France, and the costs of the wars delayed the building of what became Millbank Penitentiary. But, at the same time, the wars gave the government the administrative experience of prison management as a result of the need to keep secure thousands of French prisoners of war. The iconic Dartmoor Prison was a product of these wars, being built initially to house French prisoners. But even with financial resources, management experience and the political will, other systems were tried often in tandem with the prison.

Banishment was one alternative with a long European and extra-European pedigree. On continental Europe the formal banishment of an offender from the town or community in which he or she lived continued from the medieval period into the nineteenth century. In the seventeenth century the British began to experiment with a system of banishment that involved the transportation of convicted felons to the colonies. This was formalised at the beginning of the eighteenth century largely to provide an alternative to executing large numbers of those convicted of felony. Transportation to the American colonies effectively ended with the Declaration of Independence. The claiming of New South Wales for the British Crown, however, enabled the system to continue to the mid-nineteenth century. The French experimented with transportation for political offenders from the great revolution of the 1790s and through the subsequent revolutions and coups of the nineteenth century. In the 1880s they established transportation for criminal offenders and this continued into the twentieth century (O'Brien, 1982; Wright, 1983). In the southern states of the United States yet another alternative to the prison was favoured in the late nineteenth century. Convict leasing to the owners of penal farms and workplaces expanded considerably in the aftermath of the Civil War and generally at the expense of the penitentiary system. It has been argued that, since the overwhelming majority of offenders sent to these penal workplaces in the southern states were black, then they were essentially the plantation-slave system reborn to discipline and punish recalcitrant African Americans. Similar accusations have been levelled against the chain gangs (Freedman, 1993: 156-7; and see Miller's chapter below).

The prisons of the old regime rarely made any distinction between those awaiting trial and those awaiting punishment, between men and women, between children and adults, between first offenders and recidivists. The Enlightenment-inspired reformers sought to change this. They were concerned that the old, incorrigible offender would corrupt the juvenile. They also hoped to remould the offender to bring him or her to a recognition of their wrong-doing and of their place in society. Thus the first prisons relied heavily on input from the clergy and on training the convict in the virtue of work. The training, however, was often meaningless drudgery on a hand crank, a treadmill or picking oakum. Only really in some of the establishments set up for juveniles, most notably at Mettray near Tours in France, were significant achievements made in developing work skills. And throughout the early years of the prison-peniten-tiary system the pendulum swung regularly between a predominant focus on the reform of the offender and a focus on punishment.

At the close of the nineteenth century and particularly in the two decades before the First World War many of the principal states of Europe witnessed popular scares about the corruption of their 'race' manifested through different forms of criminality and deviance. At the same time penal experts and reform-ers from across the Europeanised world were meeting in international con-gresses and developing new ideas for the treatment of offenders. Some of the treatments proposed are abhorrent to modern eyes, notably the eugenicist argu-ments for sterilisation. But there was also a strong belief, developed from Enlightenment ideas, in the potential for human progress and it was this that engendered the liberal penal policies that sometimes sat alongside eugenics but that also resulted in Garland's penal welfarism. While crime showed a slight upswing, Britain still felt able to close 15 of its 26 local prisons between 1914 and 1930. The daily average prison population ranged between 9,000 and 13,000 throughout the inter-war period; this was roughly half of what it had been at the beginning of the century. Moreover, this was during two decades noted for economic recession and when there was a strong belief that much acquisitive crime was the product of economic hardship. In the same period there were attempts to soften the tough prison regimes in the United States. Clinton Duffy, for example, took over as warden of the California State Prison of San Quentin in 1940. He abolished the notorious punishment area of 'Siberia', sacked the guards who were known to have participated in beatings, expanded the education department and sought to boost rehabilitation by a mixture of education, psychiatry, religion and sport (Cummins, 1994: 11-12).

The liberal policies of men like Duffy appeared initially to meet with success. Prisoners astonished many, for example, by manifesting their loyalty for America during the Second World War by giving blood, buying bonds and even offering to serve as human torpedoes. But, by the late 1960s, the progressive educational policies in American prisons were being used by some prisoners, and especially by some young African American inmates, to develop revolutionary ideologies and demands. This created disquiet. The climax came with the revolt in the Attica Correctional Institution in New York State in September 1971, a revolt that was suppressed by a thousand National Guards and police and that resulted in the deaths of thirty-two prisoners and eleven staff. Serious rioting in British prisons was twenty years away and the worst trouble, that at Strangeways in Manchester in 1991, was neither as serious nor as bloody as that at Attica or elsewhere in America. The shift away from an understood, generally progressive policy of rehabilitation was also possibly slower in Britain, but the pendulum still swung in the same direction as that in America with calls for more prisons, longer sentences and, in the tabloid and mid-level press particularly, less 'soft' treatment.

Much of the tabloid and mid-level press continues with its shrill exposés of 'soft' regimes in which offenders are 'molly-coddled'. Some of the press stories about Maxine Carr, the unfortunate and foolish girlfriend of the child killer Ian Huntley who provided him with an alibi, offer a good example. Foston Hall Prison in Derbyshire, to which she was transferred at the end of her sentence, was described as 'cushy' by the *Daily Mirror* (28 April 2004) and like a 'holiday camp' that pampered its inmates by the *News of the World* (25 April 2004). The *Mail on Sunday* used her move to Foston Hall as an opportunity to condemn the whole system: 'Our modern courts fear to hand out strong penalties. And our modern prisons are nothing like austere enough, with their in-cell TVs, pool tables, tolerated drug dealers and near powerless warders' (2 May, 2004). These demands raise questions about from whence the general public get their ideas about the inside of prisons and the 'softness' of the regimes; and also where they get there ideas about who is actually serving prison sentences.

Former prisoners have published autobiographies describing their experiences. A few have played upon the traditional fears of prison being a university for criminals and of the regimes not being particularly harsh (for example, Hill, 1955). Yet while there are bound to be opportunities for discussing 'dodges' and various forms of illegal behaviour, the overall experience of the prison rarely appears to have been positive. In their chapter Alyson Brown and Emma Clare chart a series of continuities in the prison experience since the nineteenth century; continuities largely of deprivation and of a negative impact on self-esteem. The thrust of their chapter is that the implementation of penal policy can produce outcomes that are often the opposite of the aspirations. Prison autobiographies are rarely best sellers and rarely reach the same mass-market as cinema and television. David Wilson moves out from prisoner biography to the representation of prison in films and on television. Aside from the jolly roguery of the long-running and endlessly repeated television series *Porridge*, he notes how films can highlight the negative, often brutal and degrading effects of prison. Other evidence, some of which is presented by Rob Allen and by Mike Hough and his colleagues, suggests that few of those currently in British prisons are major league criminals. Moreover, unlike the number of long-term inmates in American penal institutions, few in Britain are incarcerated for a particularly long period, though the number of these is rising.

Knowledge of the bleak, often counter-productive world of the prison is not confined to academics or those with experience of prison as, particularly, the media representations described by Wilson demonstrate. The knowledge that many of those in prison are not major league criminals but petty offenders often with poor educational achievement is, perhaps, less well-known. McLaughlin and Gillespie's chapter notes how the media creates a restricted image of violent crime and criminals. They explain also how most crime genres rarely discuss the backgrounds and motivations of criminals, and that most media representation rarely extends beyond the conclusion of a court case. However, their work also suggests that when people are pressed, they often recognise that real difficulties exist in sentencing and admit that alternatives to prison should

be tried. So why does no-one seek to press them? And why is there so little challenge to the fierce populist trope of longer prison sentences and harsher
regimes?

It is possible that an awareness of the failure of prison to solve the crime
problem is beginning to affect penal policy at state level in the United States.
Since the turn of the millennium a range of opinion polls have shown concerns
about crime to be declining; education, healthcare, the economy and sometimes
terrorism are more important issues for the public. At the same time the
economies of the individual states are in poor shape with many running enormous deficits. The result is increasing pressure on state governments to find
alternatives to the building of more and more correctional facilities and to the
incarceration of large numbers of non-violent offenders. These pressures, in
turn, appear to be encouraging elected state governors, even those on the
extreme right, and state bureaucrats to look for alternatives in cheaper and,
possibly more effective systems of parole and treatment. But this, of course, is
the situation at state level; the federal government has a rather different dynam-
ic, at least for the moment (Jacobson, 2005). And similarly with the central governments in Europe that have also experienced the massive upsurge in their
prison populations over the past thirty years or so.

The chapters that follow focus primarily on the contemporary British experience. Pieter Spierenburg begins with a broad survey of the origins of the
prison, but then a succession of chapters explore the experience and representation of incarceration in Britain, the increase in the prison population and
public awareness of the problems. At this point there is a switch to some overseas experiences of alternatives to incarceration, notably American experiments with forced labour and the emerging use of electronic monitoring in
France. From here the focus returns to the prison with a discussion of the
restorative justice programme pioneered within Belgian prisons. The final
chapter rounds off the collection with a broad discussion of who is currently in
British prisons and an evaluation of some of the current alternatives that are
being developed and deployed.

Notes

1. Brown's book finishes before the great Dartmoor mutiny of January 1932.
2. Such sentences were subject to ratification by the home secretary, and while boards continued to award such sentences, none were confirmed after 1962.

References

Beccaria, Cesare (1963) *On Crimes and Punishments.* (translated and with an introduction by Henry Paolucci) Indianapolis and New York: Bobbs-Merrill

Boehm, Christopher (1984) *Blood Revenge: The Anthropology of Feuding in Montenegro and Other Tribal Societies*, Lawrence, Kan.: University Press of Kansas

Brown, Alyson (2003) *English Society and the Prison: Time, Culture and Politics in the Development of the Prison, 1850-1920.* Woodbridge: Boydell

Brown, D.H. (2002) ' "They Punish Murderers, Thieves, Traitors and Sorcerers": Aboriginal Criminal Justice as Reported by early French Observers', *Histoire Sociale/Social History*, xxxv, no. 70 (2002) pp. 363-91

Cummins, Eric (1994) *The Rise and Fall of California's Radical Prison Movement.* Stanford, Cal.: University of California Press

Foucault, Michel, (1977) *Discipline and Punish: The Birth of the Modern Prison.* London: Allen Lane (English translation of *Surveiller et punir: naissance de la prison* Paris: Gallimard, 1975)

Freedman, Lawrence M. (1993) *Crime and Punishment in American History.* New York: Basic Books

Gallant, Thomas W. (2000) 'Honor, Masculinity and Ritual Knife-Fighting in Nineteenth-Century Greece', *American Historical Review*, 105 (2000) pp. 359-82

Garland, David (2001) *The Culture of Control: Crime and Social Order in Contemporary Society.* Oxford: Oxford University Press

Garnot, Benoît, (2000) 'Justice, infrajustice, parajustice et extrajustice dans la France d'Ancien Régime', *Crime, histoire et sociétés/Crime, history and societies*, 4, 1, pp. 103-20

Hill, Billy (1955) *Boss of Britain's Underworld.* London: Naldrett Press

Ignatieff, Michael (1978) *A Just Measure of Pain: The Penitentiary in the Industrial Revolution 1750-1850.* London: Macmillan

International Centre for Prison statistics, King's College, London: http://www.kcl.ac.uk/depsta/rel/icps

Jacobson, Michael (2005) *Downsizing Prisons: How to Reduce Crime and End Incarceration.* New York: New York University Press

King, Peter (2004) 'The Summary Courts and Social Relations in Eighteenth-Century England', *Past and Present*, 183, pp. 125-72

O'Brien, Patricia (1982) *The Promise of Punishment: Prisons in Nineteenth-Century*

France. Princeton, NJ: Princeton University Press

Perrot, Michelle, ed., (1980) *L'impossible prison: recherches sur le système pénitentiaire au XIX siècle*. Paris: Seuil

Pratt, John, (1992) *Punishment in a Perfect Society: The New Zealand Penal System 1840-1930*. Wellington, NZ: Victoria University Press

Reynolds, Henry (1996) *Aboriginal Sovereignty: Reflections on Race, State and Nation*. St. Leonards, NSW: Allen and Unwin

Wilson, Stephen, (1988) *Conflict and Banditry in Nineteenth-Century Corsica*. Cambridge: Cambridge University Press

Wright, Gordon (1983) *Between the Guillotine and Liberty: Two Centuries of the Crime Problem in France*. New York: Oxford University Press.

Chapter One

The Origins of the Prison

Pieter Spierenburg

The origins and historical development of imprisonment constitute a vast subject and within the confines of this contribution no more than the principal lines of development can be sketched. I will endeavour to introduce the subject to non-specialist readers and students of the contemporary penal system. But I trust that I may be allowed to begin with a personal anecdote. Some ten years ago I had a conversation with a specialist in prison architecture, who got very excited upon hearing that Haarlem was my native town. As it happens, Haarlem has one of the few remaining full panoptic prisons, built in the late nineteenth century and still functioning today. My conversation partner envied me for having been able to see that prison during my whole youth. I had to disappoint him. As a child, I had no idea yet of the building's unique character and I simply would have assumed that all prisons in the whole world looked just like that one. The moral of this story, if any, is that without historical knowledge it is easy to take any institution's present shape for granted, while in fact institutions develop and their character and function change over time. This is certainly true for the prison.

There has even been some debate on what exactly to call a prison. Clearly, not every form of incarceration or restriction of a person's freedom can reasonably be termed imprisonment. For example, we would consider the workers who built the Egyptian pyramids as slaves rather than prisoners. The first generation of historians who made a serious study of imprisonment considered the early nineteenth century as the major turning point. For them, the building of penitentiaries in this period and the extension of the penalty of imprisonment to cover most criminal offences, marked the beginning of prison history (Major studies are Rothman 1971, Ignatieff 1978 and, to a certain extent also Foucault 1975, but he did recognise the penitentiary's precursors). Some historians, on the other hand, are inclined to categorise even medieval jails as prisons. Thus, the author of a recent book on pardons criticises me for positing that punitive imprisonment did not start until the mid-sixteenth century (Kesselring 2003: 27). In England in the middle ages, the incarceration of convicted offenders indeed seems to have been a little less uncommon than on the Continent. (Cf. Pugh 1970. On Venice: Scarabello 1979). That was indeed my argument, more or less, in earlier publications and I still believe it to be valid (Spierenburg 1991a. This was the 'other half of a thesis on the long-term evolution of punishment, first outlined in Spierenburg, 1984).

The point about medieval jails is not that they never housed convicted offenders or persons to be chastised without having received a criminal sentence, but that, in large majority, the inmates were either incarcerated because they were standing trial or to force them to pay back their creditors. By contrast, a new type of carceral institution emerged after the middle of the sixteenth century. This historical sequence allows me to make an analytical distinction between jails and prisons. The prison is, first of all, a punitive institution: the inmates, although not necessarily all felons, are there to be chastised or corrected in some way. Note the word 'punitive', which is different from 'penal'. The correction the inmates are subjected to can have been imposed as a criminal sentence or as a measure of administrative law or otherwise. Second, the prison has a specific regime: forced labour, for example, or a system of solitude, or even a rehabilitation program. The inmates are not simply left to themselves.

According to this definition, prisons appeared on the European scene for the first time in the second half of the sixteenth century. There is no better proof of the institution being recognised as novel than the fact that it got a new generic name everywhere. In England prisons were first called bridewells, after the London one opened in the former royal palace of Bridewell. Later, house of correction became their generic name. Identical words were used in the Netherlands, Germany and Scandinavia: *tuchthuis, Zuchthaus, tukthus*. Figure 1 (*overleaf*) shows the Dutch name on the reverse of a prison coin. Obviously, contemporaries realised that something new had appeared, in particular the regime of forced labour and the accompanying notion that hard work served the inmates well.

Although this model was developed first in England, it was elaborated more fully in the newly created Dutch Republic. For example, whereas the sentences to be served in English houses of correction were usually counted in weeks well into the eighteenth century, most Dutch terms amounted to one year or more. Dutch prison administrators also were more active in securing the continuity of a labour programme. The Amsterdam *tuchthuis*, soon popularly named the rasphouse, was opened in 1596 and from the beginning it attracted numerous visitors to the city. Sebastiaan Egberts was one of its founding fathers. We may call him a reformer, like John Howard or Beccaria, if we take 'reformer' in the neutral sense as someone who changes things and gives them another form. Although it would be foolish to account for penal change by only looking at the activities of such individuals, their views of imprisonment tell us something about the social climate in which they operated. Dr. Sebastiaan (Egberts is merely his patronym) was also the city's physician. He saw the prison as, among other purposes, an alternative to capital punishment. This did not mean that he advocated imprisoning those guilty of capital crimes instead of executing them. Rather, he believed that imprisonment and forced labour could turn some thieves away from a career in crime, so that they would avoid receiving a capital sentence later in their lives. The idea that malefactors can be reformed, then, certainly was around at the end of the sixteenth century, but the usual expectation was that only some offenders, in particular young thieves, could be reformed.

This alerts us to the fact that the prison originated as a non-judicial institution. 'Real criminals' would sooner or later end up on the scaffold, perhaps first to receive a corporal penalty and eventually to be executed. Prisons were not for hardened felons. During the early years of the institution's existence, beggars

Figure 1. The reverse of a Dutch prison coin showing the word for prison
Reproduced by permission of Amsterdams Historisch Museum

and vagrants constituted the majority of inmates in most places. Indeed, prisons were partly seen as a kind of poor-relief institution and, in several cases, it was the supervisors of the poor that had taken the initiative to open a prison. Beggars and vagabonds were simply rounded up by special teams appointed to catch them (on measures against vagrants: Küther 1983; Beier 1985). Although technically they had contravened the laws against vagrancy and unlicenced begging, their imprisonment followed upon an administrative measure, with no criminal trial whatsoever. Next to beggars and vagrants, the early prisons often housed disobedient children or recalcitrant spouses, upon the request of their families and also without a criminal trial. We might say that, in origin, the prison functioned as an alternative to criminal sanctions. Imprisonment was a kind of diversion.

Nevertheless, prisons became judicial and penal institutions later on. Already in the second half of the seventeenth century several Dutch *tuchthuizen* housed a significant number of convicts who were serving a term as part of a criminal sentence. From 1654 onward the Amsterdam rasphouse was a purely criminal prison, in the sense that all inmates served a term imposed by the court after a trial. The Hamburg spinhouse, opened in 1669 and contrary to what its name suggests having female and male inmates, was the second purely criminal prison in Europe (on the Hamburg spinhouse, Streng 1890 is still valuable). In Germany and some other countries, convicts became a major category among prison inmates in the course of the eighteenth century (on German prisons of the early modern period, most recently: Harrington 1999). Obviously, these historical developments were part of the longer-term process by which the prison became the principal penal institution. The fact that it originated as a non-penal institution, may give rise to some scepticism about present-day programmes concerning alternative sentences or keeping offenders out of the judicial machinery.

Because of its regime of forced labour, the typical prison of the early modern period can be designated more specifically as the prison workhouse. Although the principle of deprivation of personal liberty for punitive purposes made it akin to modern carceral institutions, the early modern ones also had distinct characteristics. Some of these were peculiar to the Dutch model, others were more widely spread over Europe. The architectural structure of the *tuchthuis* was probably typical for the Netherlands. The centrality of the inner courtyard highlights its resemblance to other asylum institutions such as orphanages, old people's homes, or, as in the case of the Amsterdam rasphouse (Figure 2. *opposite page*) the convent out of which it was created through rebuilding. Early modern prison workhouses usually had conspicuous ornamental façades, often adorned with statues and reliefs. Again, the Amsterdam rasphouse is an excellent example. The statue on top of the gate represented *Castigatio* with two chained prisoners. A relief showed a driver whipping the wild animals who were drawing his waggon; the wild animals represented the prisoners to be tamed, while the waggon was loaded with logs of dyewood. It has been argued that such ornamental buildings, together with the equally conspicuous charitable institutions, testified to the civic spirit of the Dutch urban elites. Whereas Italian patricians and aristocrats invested money in family palaces, the Dutch elites did so in buildings which served their city's common well-being (for example, Burke 1974. See also Schama 1987). For the appreciation of this argument, however, it should be realised, first that prisons abroad, like the Bremen *Zuchthaus*, also had ornamental façades (see Reinkingk 1659: 842). Second, conspicuous display characterised not only prison workhouses but the entire penal system, public executions above all, throughout early modern Europe. The confiscation of a Catholic convent in order to make room for the rasphouse can hardly be called an investment and even then Sebastiaan Egberts wrote in a secret memo that it was better not to reveal the costs to the Amsterdam town council.

Commissioning group portraits was another habit which prison administrators had in common with the administrators of other institutional homes (on these portraits: Muller 1985). Usually we see only the members of the administrative college itself, but on one of the oldest pictures in this genre, Cornelis van der Voort's The Regents of the Amsterdam Rasphouse of 1618, the 'indoor father' is visible as well. The term 'indoor father' needs a little explanation. In all, four groups of people had dealings with prisoners in the early modern period. On top were the magistrates who had instituted the prison and, as judges, sent new offenders there. The magistrates also judged serious infractions of the prison order such as violence among inmates or rioting. The board of administrators – the regents as they were called in the Netherlands – constituted the

Figure 2. An overview of the Amsterdam rasphouse, from Dapper 1663

second level in the hierarchy. They met in their room in prison once a week and they were the first to be informed if inmates seriously misbehaved. They were authorised to impose punishments of their own for misbehaviour. The daily managers at the third level had the most intensive contacts with the prisoners. They provided them with work, food and discipline, these tasks divided in one way or the other. Whatever the division of tasks, however, the daily managers were always assisted by their wives and being married was a necessary condition to qualify for the job. A paternalistic terminology prevailed, exemplified by terms like indoor father and mother. The prison workhouse was seen as a substitute for the family. The inmates – the pseudo-children – were a kind of journeymen and maidservants, together with their counterparts at the fourth level, the real servants of the managing couples. This arrangement meant that early modern prisons did not entirely approach Goffman's model of the total institution (Goffman 1961). Goffman posited a rigorous distinction between inmates and staff, the latter having their leisure-time social life outside the institution. By contrast, early modern indoor fathers and mothers actually lived in the institution. Their office, during the period in which they held it, largely determined their life experience, not unlike the inmates' situation.

And unlike in the case of these managing couples, the boards of prison administrators were usually all male. This reflected the fact that the prison workhouses of most towns housed inmates of both sexes though, as a rule, in separate wards. According to contemporary opinion, only institutions exclusively for women might need a female board. Amsterdam was the major exception, with the rasphouse for male and the spinhouse for female offenders. The Amsterdam spinhouse had a board of women regents (who also came to administer the workhouse for juvenile and minor offenders of both sexes), whose portrait was painted by Philip van Dijk in 1728. The black and white illustration regrettably cannot show the bright colours of their dresses, according to the fashion of the day, but these may well have been coloured with dye produced in the male prison.

The fabrication of dyewood was the main prison trade until the early eighteenth century. The production process involved is no longer familiar to us. Before the age of chemical industry the colours for dying or painting were obtained mostly from vegetable and mineral sources. For a long time it was difficult to produce dye and paint on a mass scale. This was one reason for the fashion of plain black clothes, which we see on many portraits of the early seventeenth century. Red, blue or yellow colours could be obtained from certain trees, but the trunks had to be pulverised or at least chopped to little pieces. The pieces were then boiled with the textiles to be dyed. Soon after the opening of the Amsterdam *tuchthuis*, it was suggested that prisoners might rasp dyewood with a many-bladed saw. That was the origin of rasping, which gave the prison its popular name (Figure 3. *Overleaf*). This form of labour was even represented on a prison coin which the inmates could earn through extra work and spend in the institution's canteen. Incidentally, the coin itself is the only extant source through which we know that special coins were in use. Rasping was soon adopted, as forced labour for male inmates, by most prison workhouses on the European Continent. At almost the same time, however, its economic function was eroded by the invention of a rasping mill. Prison workhouses in Holland held out for some time, because the Estates of the province forbade rasping in mills. This was done clandestinely nevertheless. By the early eighteenth century most towns had substituted the fabrication of cloth or some other product as prison trade (on rasping and the economic functions of early modern prisons more elaborately: Spierenburg 1991b), but preparing dyewood was revived in a few Saxon prisons at the end of the century. The wood was milled, but the water movement which supplied the mill's energy was created by a treadmill operated by prisoners (Wagnitz 1791–1794: *passim*). Thus, the 'useless' treadmills of the nineteenth century were preceded by economically productive ones.

The prison workhouses of the early modern period originated in and remained largely confined to Northern Europe, at least until about the middle of the eighteenth century. The main reason for this was simple. And to understand this, it should be noted that the prison is only one penal option among a broader category of punishments which involve severe restrictions upon the convict's freedom of movement. We may call that category (penal) bondage. Other forms of bondage were originally preferred to the south of the prison's core zone and soon in England as well. Significantly, these penal options also involved some type of forced labour. Public works, such as labour in mines, for example, or going from house to house to empty latrines, were among them. Galley servitude was practiced widely in the countries bordering on the

Figure 3. Prisoners rasping dyewood, an occupation that gave prisons their popular name 'rasphouse'

Mediterranean Sea. In England, where the prison model soon stagnated, transportation became the principal form of penal bondage. As a consequence, the prison developed more slowly in France, Spain, Italy and England (Pike 1983, Spain; Beattie 1986, England; Zysberg 1987, France. But eventually, toward the end of the early modern period, the prison acquired greater prominence in these countries too.

It may be concluded that the prison only gradually became the principal institution for depriving offenders of their freedom of movement. In the end the others all had major disadvantages, in particular their vulnerability to shifts in military methods or to different forms of decolonisation. Prisons were relatively more impervious to economic and political change.

Thus, prisons have been with us for some four hundred and fifty years, including most of the early modern period. Nevertheless, early modern Europe knew various alternative types of conflict solution or social control. The harshest and most conspicuous type was the traditional theatre of the scaffold. Throughout Europe, the public infliction of corporal and capital punishment was reserved for the most serious crimes. The offenders in question constituted a minority among all persons sentenced by the various courts, but scaffold punishments were the most visible manifestation of the power of justice and the state. Executions were elaborate ceremonies and they always drew large crowds, as with the decapitation of the notorious J.B.F. van Gogh, who had stabbed his sweetheart to death after she had rejected him, in Amsterdam in 1778 (on this case: Spierenburg 2004: chapters 6-9). Throughout the Continent, but less so in England, the corpses of those capital convicts whose crimes had been particularly heinous, were hanged anew or put upon a wheel at a specially designated spot. This spot, the gallows field or gallows hill, was usually just outside the town, along an incoming route. The Amsterdam gallows field lay just across the waterway from the harbour, where all incoming and outgoing ships passed. In winter, when the harbour was frozen, citizens could skate or walk to the other side and parents took the opportunity to point out the corpses to little children (Figure 4. *Overleaf*). In this way, capital punishment served an educative function as well. Note also the lions proudly showing the city's arms with the three St Andrew crosses. These, too, were meant to show that Amsterdam was a 'city of law' which did not tolerate robbers, burglars and killers.

Figure 4. The Amsterdam gallows field, where parents visited with their children

The prison, then, did not simply replace the theatre of the scaffold. These two forms of punishment coexisted for more than two centuries. Although their purposes were different, personal honour played a role in both of them. Honour was very important for early modern Europeans and almost everything connected with official justice tended to be regarded as a mark of infamy. The authorities usually proclaimed prison workhouses to be 'honourable institutions', but often the public saw this differently. The infliction of corporal punishment on the scaffold dishonoured the person subjected to it. A somewhat milder form of infamy came with the shaming punishments imposed for lesser offences or upon juvenile or pregnant offenders. They could be exposed at the scaffold's railing or on the pillory, with a sign denoting their offence or, as in the case of male bigamists, carrying two distaffs. Shaming punishments also could take the form of a parade on horseback, as was done especially in England into the seventeenth century and beyond (Ingram 1997). Shaming punishments like these parades were related to popular sanctions such as the charivari for a husband beaten by his wife or the posting of horns at a cuckold's door.

Social control certainly did not emanate from the state alone. Several institutions were active in this respect, while local communities also had control functions (on the spectrum of social control in early modern Europe: Roodenburg and Spierenburg, eds. 2004). Institutional controls may be termed semi-formal, because they were often supplementary to state controls. This applies in particular to the English Church Courts, which operated largely from above and whose jurisdiction was clearly demarcated from that of the secular courts (see especially Ingram 1987). Other ecclesiastical agencies were relatively independent from the secular authorities, foremost among them the Calvinist consistories and presbyteries in various parts of Europe. Consistorial discipline was aimed, rather than at retribution, at reconciliation of the sinner with God and the church community. It was to keep this community 'pure' (a recent collection on this subject: Schilling, ed. 1999). From a modern point of view, religious discipline has distinct disadvantages. First of all, it works only for members of that faith community, with excommunication often being the ultimate penalty. Second, its targets were essentially the control of a large part of personal conduct, in particular religious beliefs and sexual behaviour. Nevertheless, consistories also engaged in such activities as the mediation of conflicts between husbands and wives. A study of discipline in the Dutch towns of Rotterdam and Delft, for example, shows that, by the mid-seventeenth century, consistory meetings censured men for beating their wives (van der Heijden 1998).

Informal types of social control included, among other things, the regulatory functions of guilds. In this case, too, controls only applied to members. Another example, already alluded to, is the popular shaming of the charivari, usually applied for a breach of informal norms related to marriage. Communal controls also involved the handling of behaviour that might have been prosecuted as a crime. The so-called infra-judiciary system referred to a repertoire of private reconciliation, mediation, or direct handling between criminal and victim within local communities. Originally, even manslaughter fell within its purview. Well into the sixteenth century, men who had inadvertently killed their opponent in a fight were reconciled with the victim's family in an elaborate ritual involving publicly asking for forgiveness and the payment of a compensation (de Waardt 1996; Vrolijk 2001). After the sixteenth century, this reconciliation practice was no longer recognised by state courts and hence repressed. The private handling of thefts continued for a longer time. Within local communities people often knew who had stolen their goods and they simply demanded them back, whether or not with a beating. Alternatively, a priest, a neighbourhood official or another authority figure offered his mediation. Usually we know of such cases because persistent thieves were officially prosecuted in the end. A famous English case concerns a certain John Aston from Myddle in Shropshire, whose chronicle was written in the seventeenth century. After his twentieth theft or so, the inhabitants of Myddle finally prosecuted Aston, but they did not want him to hang (Gough 1981: 145-6).

Why did this early modern variety of social controls disappear? Within the confines of this brief contribution, an answer can only be given very summarily. In fact, the two principal developments involved – the growth of the state and broad socio-cultural change – were interrelated. The first development was already manifest with the coming of the prison. To some extent, imprisonment replaced banishment. Banishment implied that the crime problems of one locality were simply moved on to the next, but within increasingly unified states this was no longer acceptable. This applied equally to the relatively decentralised Dutch Republic, whose towns were conscious of constituting an interdependent urban network. When the Leiden magistrates opened a prison workhouse in 1598, they stated that the spread of imprisonment meant that the Dutch towns would no longer 'banish offenders upon each other's backs' (Spierenburg 1991a:36). Throughout the early modern period, the growth of state power affected the system of social control. Gradually, justice from above overtook informal and ecclesiastical controls. Centralisation and the growth of state influence were especially marked during the French revolutionary period, as Alexis de Tocqueville noted nearly two centuries ago. Admittedly the entire spectrum of social control never became solely a state matter. Industrial discipline and charity projects, for example, were important in this respect in the nineteenth and early twentieth centuries. Nevertheless, the role of private resolution of conflicts declined significantly when compared to the early modern period (on the spectrum of social control in modern Europe: Emsley, Johnson and Spierenburg, eds. 2004).

Next to the growth of state power, broad socio-cultural change, involving the rise of new sensitivities, played a part in the shift in social control. The suffering of unknown others, even criminals, became increasingly unpleasurable. This was an element in the 'civilising process' postulated by Norbert Elias (see especially, among other works, Elias 1969). If not done away with, customs that had become unpleasurable were at least concealed; hence the disappearance of public executions and most punishments involving the infliction of pain. Thus, the Amsterdam gallows field, the use of which had been discontinued in 1798, was pictured anew, after an older drawing, around 1860 (Figure 5. *Overleaf*) Apart from the eerie atmosphere which the artist tried to convey, he did not realise that lions with the city's arms had been on top of the gallows. He turned them into vultures. In the first half of the nineteenth century, the new sensitivity also affected the prison regime. It turned away from forced labour and placed the emphasis on trying to reach the convict's mind. At the same time, the prison became the only form of punishment for most felonies.

The change in prison regimes was already announced in the late eighteenth century by experiments and plans for new architectural models. An intriguing prison model, in the form of a tower, was designed in the German town of Lübeck in the 1760s (Figure 6. *Page 44*). It might have become a competitor to

Figure 5. The Amsterdam gallows field depicted in 1860 after the abolition of public executions

Jeremy Bentham's famous Panopticon, but it was forgotten until I unearthed it from Lübeck's archive in the late 1980s. The story of the Panopticon, on the other hand, is well-known. Surveillance from one central point was to assure that the inmates interiorised the discipline expected from them. The panoptic principle was seldom practiced in its most extreme form, but the system of solitary confinement was common in Europe by the middle of the nineteenth century. Notably Michel Foucault emphasised that it meant that discipline was not aimed solely at the prisoner's mind but also at his or her body – in the latter case not by inflicting pain but through orderly movements, a precise timetable and related measures (Foucault 1975). Solitary confinement was based on the illusion that inmates could reform themselves, by being left alone, apart from occasional contact with a minister of religion. Nineteenth-century institution builders had little notion yet of psychic suffering. For some reason, the system of solitary confinement proved particularly tenacious in the Netherlands.

The twentieth-century emancipation of prisoners, a term coined by Herman Franke, was analysed by him for the Netherlands, but it occurred throughout Europe (Franke 1995). This process followed – immediately or after a short interval – upon the demise of solitary confinement. Solitary confinement had increasingly come to be viewed as cruel, a form of sensory deprivation. When the regime of solitary confinement disappeared, there was no return to forced labour. Routine imprisonment remained. Indeed, the prison stayed in place because of a lack of alternatives. Within the system of routine imprisonment, the emancipation of inmates meant that from passive sufferers they turned into persons whose voice was heard; and eventually they acquired acknowledged rights. Materially, their situation became more comfortable; they could engage in sports and watch television, for example. Emancipation meant that power relations between prisoners on the one hand and guards, officials and magistrates on the other shifted at the expense of the latter. Every additional discomfort, next to the deprivation of liberty, increasingly became problematic, as sensitivity to suffering increased in the wider society. We can explain this again in terms of Elias' theory of of civilising processes. Even partially concealed suffering became an object of concern, especially among groups who doubted the usefulness of imprisonment as a preventive tool against crime or as a means of reforming or rehabilitating offenders.

44

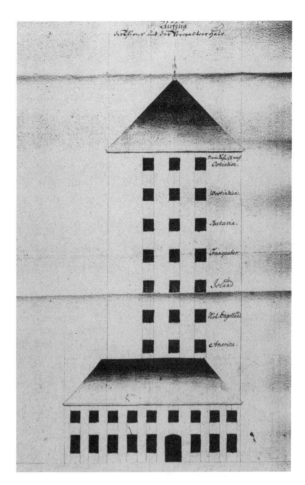

Figure 6. A prison model in the form of a tower,
designed in the German town of Lübeck in the 1760s

By permission of Archiv der Hansestadt Lübeck

These groups are obviously critical of imprisonment or distrustful of the authorities, whose actions they monitor constantly. On the other hand, vindictiveness still remains a powerful emotion in present-day society. David Garland speaks of a continued hostility towards offenders, a concern for less eligibility and a need for deterrence and security. According to him, these vindictive emotions 'have severely limited the extent to which punishments have been mitigated by a process of "civilization" '(Garland 1990: 237). Understandably, this statement primarily concerns the attitudes toward serious crime. Additionally, after some five hundred years of relative indifference, these attitudes tune in to a renewed attention on the victims of crime, in criminology as well as in society generally. In the Netherlands, empathy with the victim was notoriously widespread during the trial, in the fall of 2003, of Volkert van der Graaf, who had shot the popular politician Pim Fortuyn during the previous year. Many people expressed their dissatisfaction when the killer received a sentence of 'only' eighteen years. When the emotion of vindictiveness takes the upper hand, the fact that the prison 'does not work' (or, especially in the USA, that the death penalty does not prevent crime) seems of little concern.

Conclusion: can we do without the prison?
Since there is no obvious relationship between the severity of punishment and the incidence of crime, it can be doubted whether the existence of prisons keeps many people from engaging in unlawful activities. The most promising strategy for reducing the use of the prison, therefore, is the further study of what causes crime. If we can have fewer crimes, then fewer people will go to prison for them. As an example we may consider the cases of revenge for family honour which have taken place among Turkish inhabitants of the Netherlands. The incidence of such cases is not reduced by the threat of imprisonment, but it may be reduced by persuading Turkish people that the maintenance of their honour requires other methods than killing. A similar strategy might be employed with respect to robbery or assault, for example, despite the increased attention for the victim in modern society. One could persuade victims that they can be compensated in other ways than by satisfaction with the perpetrator's suffering. Admittedly, this is probably only possible in case of not too serious offences. As to alternative sanctions, such as cleaning in hospitals, these already exist in

many countries. These, too, are not likely to be extended to serious crimes. Moreover, the origin of the prison as a non-judicial institution warns us that we should take care that alternative punishments do not become institutionalised as just another form of judicial sanction.

Could we learn something, finally, from the system of social control in the early modern period? Ancient shaming rituals, for example, have a parallel in civil law in the form of the collection of debts in India, which is sometimes done by having transsexuals or eunuchs stalking the debtors. In other countries, courts sometimes order to put up a sign in an offender's yard or garden (if he has one!). But again, such punishments have only a limited applicability. They work within the context of a face-to-face community, so perhaps a modern parallel could be to shame offenders on television. Public notoriety, however, easily leads to a kind of fame, as with the men who kidnapped the beer tycoon Freddy Heineken in the early 1980s and who are still known, alive or shot to death, as the former Heineken kidnappers. Historical situations help us to understand present-day problems, but they do not provide ready recipes for solving them.

Bibliography

Beattie (J[ohn] M.), *Crime and the courts in England, 1660-1800*. Oxford 1986.

Beier (A[ugustus] L.), *Masterless men. The vagrancy problem in England, 1560-1640*. London, New York 1985.

Burke (Peter), *Venice and Amsterdam. A study of 17th-century élites*. London 1974.

Elias (Norbert), *Über den Prozess der Zivilisation. Soziogenetische und psychogenetische Untersuchungen*. 2 vols. (2d ed.) Bern, München 1969.

Emsley (Clive), Johnson (Eric) and Spierenburg (Pieter) (eds.), *Social Control in Europe. Vol. 2, 1800-2000*. Columbus (Ohio State UP) 2004.

Foucault (Michel), *Surveiller et punir. Naissance de la prison*. Paris 1975.

Franke (Herman), *The emancipation of prisoners. A socio-historical analysis of the Dutch prison experience*. Edinburgh (Edinburgh UP) 1995.

Garland (David), *Punishment and modern society. A study in social theory*. Chicago (Univ. of Chicago Press) 1990.

Goffman (Erving), *Asylums. Essays on the social situation of mental patients and other inmates*. Garden City, NY 1961.

Gough (Richard), *The history of Myddle*. Edited by David Hey. Harmondsworth (Penguin) 1981.

Harrington (Joel), 'Escape from the Great Confinement: The Genealogy of a German Workhouse' in: *Journal of Modern History* 71,2 (1999): 308-345.

Heijden (Manon van der), *Huwelijk in Holland. Stedelijke rechtspraak en kerkelijke tucht, 1550-1700*. Amsterdam (Bert Bakker) 1998.

Ignatieff (Michael), *A just measure of pain. The penitentiary in the Industrial Revolution, 1750-1850*. New York 1978.

Ingram (Martin), *Church courts, sex and marriage in England, 1570-1640*. Cambridge etc. 1987.

—, 'Juridical folklore in England illustrated by rough music'. in: Brooks (Christopher) and Lobban (Michael) (eds.), *Communities and courts in Britain, 1150-1900*. London (Hambledon Press) 1997: 61-82.

Kesselring (K.J.), *Mercy and authority in the Tudor state*. Cambridge (Cambridge UP) 2003.

Küther (Carsten), *Menschen auf der Strasse. Vagierende Unterschichten in Bayern, Franken und Schwaben in der zweiten Hälfte des 18. Jahrhunderts*. Göttingen 1983.

Muller (Sheila D.), *Charity in the Dutch Republic. Pictures of rich and poor for charitable institutions*. Ann Arbor 1985.

Pike (Ruth), *Penal servitude in early modern Spain*. Madison, London 1983.

Pugh (Ralph B.), *Imprisonment in medieval England*. Cambridge 1970.

Reinkingk (Theodorus), *Tractatus de regimine seculari et ecclesiastico (...)*. Francofurti ad Moenum (Johannes Martinus Porssius) 1659.

Roodenburg (Herman) and Spierenburg (Pieter) (eds.), *Social Control in Europe. Vol. 1, 1500-1800*. Columbus (Ohio State UP) 2004.

Rothman (David J.), *The Discovery of the Asylum. Social Order and Disorder in the New Republic*. Boston, Toronto 1971.

Scarabello (Giovanni), *Carcerati e carceri a Venezia nell' età moderna*. Roma 1979.

Schama (Simon), *The Embarrassment of Riches. An Interpretation of Dutch Culture in the Golden Age*. London (Collins) 1987.

Schilling (Heinz) (ed.), *Institutionen, Instrumente und Akteure sozialer Kontrolle und Disziplinierung im frühneuzeitlichen Europa/Institutions, Instruments and Agents of Social Control and Discipline in Early Modern Europe* (Ius Commune, Sonderheft nr. 127). Frankfurt a.M. (Vittorio Klostermann) 1999.

Spierenburg (Pieter), *The Spectacle of Suffering. Executions and the Evolution of Repression: from a Preindustrial Metropolis to the European experience*. Cambridge (Cambridge UP) 1984.

—, *The prison experience. Disciplinary institutions and their inmates in early modern Europe*. New Brunswick, NJ (Rutgers UP) 1991 (1991a).

—, 'Early Modern Prisons and the Dye Trade: The Fate of Convict Rasping as Proof for the Insufficiency of the Economic Approach to Prison History'. in: *Economic and Social History in the Netherlands 3* (1991): 1-17 (1991b).

—, *Written in Blood: Fatal Attraction in Enlightenment Amsterdam*. Columbus (Ohio State University Press) 2004.

Streng (Adolf), *Geschichte der Gefängnisverwaltung in Hamburg von 1622-1872*. Hamburg 1890.

Vrolijk (Marjan), *Recht door gratie. Gratie bij doodslagen en andere delicten in Vlaanderen, Holland en Zeeland, 1531-1567*. (diss. Nijmegen) 2001.

Waardt (Hans de), 'Feud and atonement in Holland and Zeeland. From private vengeance to reconciliation under state supervision'. in: Schuurman (Anton) & Spierenburg (Pieter) (eds.), *Private domain, public inquiry. Families and life-styles in the Netherlands and Europe, 1550 to the present*. Hilversum (Verloren) 1996: 15-38.

Wagnitz (H[einrich] B[althasar]), *Historische Nachrichten und Bemerkungen über die merkwürdigsten Zuchthäuser in Deutschland. Nebst einem Anhange über die zweckmässigste Einrichtung der Gefängnisse und Irrenanstalten*. 2 Bände, 3 vols. Halle 1791-1794.

Zysberg (André), *Les galériens. Vies et destins de 60,000 forçats sur les galères de France, 1680-1748*. Paris 1987.

Chapter Two

A History of Experience: Exploring Prisoners' Accounts of Incarceration

Alyson Brown and Emma Clare

Introduction

It has been noted elsewhere that explicit links between the work of historians of crime and punishment and that of criminologists remains limited (King, 1999). In 1999, Peter King was still able to state legitimately that 'If the relationship between social history and criminology can no longer be described as a dialogue of the deaf, it is still being conducted very largely in discreet whispers' (King, 1999: 161). Nevertheless, significant advances have been made including a special edition of the *British Journal of Criminology* (1999) devoted wholly to historical subjects and the recent publication of *Comparative Histories of Crime* (Godfrey, Emsley and Dunstall, 2003). This chapter contributes to the growing dialogue between history and criminology through an analysis of the experience of the prison using prisoner autobiographies published since the mid-nineteenth century. To be more specific this can be seen as a dialogue between social history and the sociology of the prison. There are many aspects of the prison and life within it that cannot be discussed in this one chapter. Emphasis is given to those themes and issues that have long permeated the autobiographies of prisoners, and which are representative of wider and long lasting problems within penal institutions.

Numerous prisoner autobiographies have been published since the mid-nineteenth century and this paper by no means utilises them all (see Priestley 1985 and 1989 for an in depth survey). The concentration here is not upon a broad survey of all available texts but an analysis of themes and conflicts that are common within them. Certainly, in the context of a net-widening penal policy and overcrowded penal institutions of the early twenty-first century it seems appropriate to re-emphasise the extent to which the experience of the prison can be psychologically and physically damaging. Such an analysis also highlights that through all the changes in policy and practice during the nineteenth and twentieth centuries, the experience of imprisonment is one more marked by continuity than change.Hence, reflecting the themes and concerns of prisoners' autobiographies this chapter focuses on the deprivations of prison life, the impact on status, autonomy and identity and also the nature and consequences of the institutional staff-prisoner relationship.

Prisoners' subjective accounts of imprisonment offer an important tool in attempting to understand and untangle the impact prison policy and its implementation has on the lives of prisoners, and those working in the prison environment. More specifically, they offer insights about unintended consequences of policy implementation, which are often absent from both historical and contemporary official sources. Certainly, investigations into the sociology of the prison have long highlighted the disparity that can exist between the rhetoric of policy and the lived experiences of prisoners (Clemmer, 1940; Cohen and Taylor, 1972; Irwin, 1970; 1985; Sykes, 1958). Furthermore, Clemmer and Irwin have debated the extent to which prison cultures develop as an adaptation to prison life itself or are an adaptation by prisoners to their lives as a whole and which they bring into prison with them (Clemmer, 1940; Irwin, 1970; 1985). These writers were able to use interview material generated by their research projects. However, to examine the lives of those imprisoned further back in time, for example during the nineteenth and early twentieth centuries, other sources must be utilised. The most important subjective source available which gives insight into prisoners lives in the past as well as the present are prisoners'

autobiographies. Davies (2001) argues that these prisoner writings are significant as they generate alternative knowledges about the prison; it is this alternative knowledge that has been sought in this chapter.

Nineteenth-century prison punishment was developed to be socially distant
and experientially remote, although this was achieved much more fully with
long-term prisoners than with those who experienced the 'revolving door' of
short-term local imprisonment. The theory of penal incarceration centred upon
the creation of socially divisive, isolating and disciplined space. The apogee of
this kind of thinking was the highly deterrent and punitive regimes operating
in English prisons from the 1860s to roughly the end of the century. By the
1960s, prison conditions as a whole, and facilities to enable prisoners to communicate with their families and friends outside, had in most cases improved.
In addition, the social space of the prison had become somewhat more accessible (but not less divisive) to the public principally via the media as well as
through scholarly and popular discourses of the social sciences. However, since
the end of the twentieth century, political and social developments have resulted in complex discourses of the prison being increasingly marginalised once
more. In the continued politicisation of crime, the claim 'prison works' has
dominated prison discourse whilst also engaging with concerns surrounding
the re-emergence of an 'underclass'. As constructive activities in prison were
reduced, prisoners themselves struggled to find a purpose 'beyond containment
and punishment' (James, 2003: 96). In addition, since the late 1970s, neo-liberal rhetoric and policy has undermined welfarism and tolerance toward offenders. Within this broad context, the intricacies of prisoner writings provide an
important reminder of the tensions surrounding the shifting usage of images
and representations of both the prison and the prisoner. While discourses on
the purpose of imprisonment have diversified in the twentieth century, imprisonment is still predominately portrayed as a rational and rigorous punishment
for offenders deserving of penalty. Prisoners' own autobiographies present
much more complex and contentious dynamics. As Davies (2001: 429) points
out, prison writings present the institution both 'as an aberrant social formation with its totalitarian character and attendant brutality and at the same time
as a stable community of individuals who try to live normal lives' (also see for
example, Chevigny, 1999).

The writing of prison autobiographies has served a variety of purposes and as such offers a diverse source of information. For example, an autobiographical account may be a means of coming to terms with the experience of a long prison sentence or an act of resistance against a routinised mass prison existence. As Freeman (1993: 29) has observed, 'Memory ... often has to do not merely with recounting the past but with making sense of it'. So, these accounts, often written some time after release, comprise a combination of selectivity and interpretation (Stanley, 1993; also see Burnett, 1982: xii) but also a process of inner assimilation, a working through, or working out of the prison experience. However, even a superficial examination of some of the asserted motives for writing prisoner autobiographies reveals the extent to which many of the authors of these texts are not representative of the general prison population. These motives include a chance to protest innocence (Maybrick, 1905), to promote a political cause (Lytton, 1914), to campaign for prison reform (Davitt, 1972), to begin or enhance a literary career (Phelan, 1940), to warn the young against glamorising violence and crime (Boyle, 1977). This, however, does not mean that these sources offer an insurmountable bias and therefore should not be used. To look at this issue from another perspective may be enlightening. The calls for prison reform by Stephen Hobhouse, a Quaker and conscientious objector during the First World War, were criticised by contemporaries on the basis that his pamphlet edition of *An English Prison From Within* stated 'Prisons were never meant for him ... prisons are meant for real criminals' (preface by Murray, 1918: 5-6). Yet, political and academic attempts to identify 'real criminals' or a 'criminal class' have proved seriously flawed and often counter-productive. We may not be able to define effectively a 'real criminal' but we can locate a 'real' prisoner identifiable by their experience of penal confinement. Should we really suggest that an individual's experience of his incarceration is less relevant or legitimate or indeed less 'real' because of his or her social class?

Over the last century and a half, the English prison system has spawned prisoner autobiographies as a significant form of literary testimony. Similarly, academic research has increasingly incorporated prisoner perspectives through interviewing. These 'subjugated knowledges' (Foucault, 1980: 81) or 'documents of life' offer an important source to understanding the complexities of social order within the prison environment. Although still under-utilised, there is a growing interest from historians, criminologists and analysts of literary forms in prisoner accounts and the perspectives they can provide (Brown, 1998 and 2003; Forsythe, 1991; Grass, 2003; Morgan, 1999; Pratt, 2002; Priestley, 1985 and 1989). This emphasis on perspective is important since it cannot be asserted that autobiographies offer some kind of objective truth, clearly they are about experience and personal recollection; an admitted attempt to describe *their* reality from a purely subjective approach (Cockshut, 1984: 216-7). Nevertheless, this personal view of the prison can contribute to understanding the lived experience of imprisonment when compared to the official rhetoric about the effects of imprisonment.

Prison life and deprivation
One important aspect of the official rhetoric about the prison is that it has emphasised humanitarian intentions whilst sanitising the deprivations of prison life, the 'distasteful ugliness associated with imprisonment' (Pratt, 2002: 97). For prisoners it has been the deprivations of prison life that have been felt most keenly – the disabling isolation, the rigid routine, the boredom, the monotony of the food, the lack of dignity in the reception process. One conscientious objector described his feelings during his imprisonment during the First World War in the following way:

> The dull monotony, the weary repetition of commands, the regular meal times, the same rotation of food, and the systematic working of all departments, work their depressing ravages upon prisoner and warder alike. Initiative, self-assertion, individuality, are crimes – nay, almost impossibilities (Mason, 1918: 135).

At a similar time, a suffragette commented about the food, that it was 'good and well-cooked but the absolute monotony of the fare was a great trial to some of the prisoners' (Lytton, 1914:101) while another prisoner emphasised the 'natural repulsiveness of the prison clothes' (Scott Duckers, 1917: 149). For one prisoner in the 1990s, it was the experience of 'slopping out' that provoked the most indignation and humiliation:

> I was so angry, I wanted to grab whoever was responsible for dragging

this disgusting, inhuman practice into the 1990s by the scruff of the neck and throw them headlong into this filth (Hoskison, 1998: 29).

As these examples suggest, questioning the legitimacy of the prison as punishment does not form the focus of most prisoners' accounts. Prisoners in general accepted that prison punishment as a concept was appropriate. It is the nature of prison regimes, the lack of status, conditions, the perceived rights and wrongs that preoccupy those who have recorded their prison experiences as well as those who have been asked about their experiences by others. These preoccupations have been recurrent in prisoners' accounts regardless of the seriousness of their offence/s.

It is often the mundane aspects of prison life that have pervaded the accounts of prisoner writings. For example, the quality and quantity of prison food has long been a source of discontent and conflict. So, William Lovett, for example, would not eat the gruel after he took up a black beetle in about the first spoonful (1876: 229). In the particularly harsh penal climate of the second half of the nineteenth century, it was also asserted that the effects of the prison diet 'of hunger and torment of mind' could be seen on the convicts at Chatham Convict Prison. 'The first part visibly affected was the neck. The flesh shrinks, disappears and leaves what looks like two artificial props to support the head (Bidwell, 1895: 456). Conflict over food is further illustrated in the following example from the 1870s:

> A man is discontented with his dinner, and thinks he has not got his quantity, he appeals to the warder. The officer takes him to the cookhouse, when the dinner is weighed; if deficient, the quantity is made up, if it is alright, the man is reported and punished for giving unnecessary trouble (Anon (Callow) 1877:199).

However, almost a century later, Robert Sykes, convicted amongst other things for robbing a post office, objected to the standard of the food, specifically the quality of the skilly which was

> made from Canadian Grade A pig-meal so old that it smells musty, and often flavoured with a generous sprinkling of black garnish of mouse

dirt – six ounces of bread, and a pat of margarine the size of a penny (Sykes, 1967: 133).

Little improvement appeared to be witnessed in the prison food throughout the 1970s and 1980s: 'One of the things that caused me to go crazy at times was the food, because it was filthy, like pulp' (Conlon, 1990: 154). In part, what is expressed in these accounts of imprisonment is a criticism, commentary and reaction to the internal organisation and the practical provisions of the prison as it relates to the individual's experience.

In the subjective sense, prisoners, whether representative or not, knew and understood their environment better than anyone else since they were so dependent upon it. In this respect many prisoners understood most clearly the intricacies and insecurities of prison life, and the persistent condemnation of particular aspects of prison regimes reflects the slow pace of reform. Later accounts in particular commented, for example, on the unwritten and informal social hierarchies and systems that came into operation when prisoners requested items from prison officers. Writing in the late 1990s, Hoskison observed that when he had run out of toilet roll or toothpaste in prison he had to ask an officer for more. By having to do this, the prisoner was assuming the role of a supplicant. The relationship soon became clear to him, 'I would come to realise that the officers responsible for handing out items used their power to cause maximum humiliation' (Hoskison, 1998: 22). A similar mechanism was noted by another prisoner writing in the 1970s:

> To give a random example: if a prisoner wants to cut his toe-nails, it is necessary to make an official application in the morning, which is then processed by whatever bureaucracy grinds away in the depths of the wing, and results in an officer solemnly coming to your cell carrying one of the wing's pairs of scissors, which then has to be returned immediately after use (Caird, 1974: 31).

Prisoners themselves judged the effectiveness of reforms or indeed whether the reforms claimed in official documentation and/or the newspapers had taken place at all. The level of discretion held by prison staff and the extent of autonomy and categorisation within individual prisons has meant that historically regimes and systems of privileges and punishments have varied considerably both over time and between prisons.

In the early twentieth century, there were clear, if slow, incremental improvements in prison life, part of what Bailey (1997) has termed the amelioration of imprisonment. This refers to a decline in the use of imprisonment as a punishment for offenders but also to the reforming of some of the prison practices that had been the subject of particular criticism. Therefore, in 1921 the close cropping of convict's hair was abolished and from March 1922 older prison uniforms were gradually phased out; the new ones had the broad arrow stencilled on the inside (B.2.15, 1924: 183; Bailey, 1997: 299-300). Nevertheless, reforms were not always what they appeared to be when reported by the Prison Commission or in the press. Official information on the pace of change has in many cases jarred with the experience of prisoners themselves. Such a case in point was the regulations regarding talking. The gradual alleviation of silent regimes was evident from the early twentieth century for 'political' offenders. Thus, as early as 1914, Constance Lytton, an imprisoned suffragette, noted 'We were not supposed to talk to each other, but we were allowed to communicate to a certain extent in whispers' (Lytton, 1914: 95). In 1918 'talking exercise'[1] was introduced for those conscientious objectors to war who were in prison for a year or more, although it was also noted that some warders more or less 'wink[ed]' at discrete talking between prisoners (Hobhouse, 1918).

An autobiography published in 1925 highlighted the use of the discretion to punish talking being used as an everyday control mechanism. It states:

> no man is reported for talking unless he has continued to talk after he has been told to stop. They all talk, and will continue to talk, and no earthy power can stop them, and the officers know it. But they must stop talking when they are told to, and when a principal, the chief warder, or the governor is within sight or hearing, otherwise the warder he gets into trouble (Jervis, 1925: 118).

Several other writers later remarked that while reports of the Prison Commissioners claimed that talking was permitted in prisons, and therefore not subject to punishment, their own communications were restricted. Speaking of his imprisonment during the inter-war period, Phelan observed:

No man was punished for talking in all my time in the English jails: it was illegal to punish people for such acts. What happened was that a man spoke, a warder told him to stop, he spoke again, and was reported: not for talking, but for disobeying an order (Phelan, 1940: 16; also see Macartney, 1936: 78; Sykes, 1967: 50).

Similarly, this writer also complained: 'I have read in newspapers, dozens of times that I was being allowed to smoke when I wasn't, just as I often read that I was allowed to talk when I wasn't' (Phelan, 1940: 47). Prisoner autobiographies suggest that the formal, and crucially discretionary, introduction of the privilege to talk had altered little in practice – the use of discretion whether to punish talking continued to be used as a control mechanism whatever the regulations formally stated. One conscientious objector remarked on this tendency in prison administration. He observed: 'It is remarkable how efficiently the official mind can neutralise reforms intended to benefit prisoners, so that the prisoner continues to suffer that which the reform was intended to remove' (Mason, 1918: 210-11). This prisoner, Mason, was speaking from grim experience following his solitary confinement for considerably longer than the regulation first 28 days of his sentence. In his case instead of working in the company of prisoners, associated labour was defined as working alone in his cell with the door open.

Similar evidence regarding other aspects of prison conditions should therefore also be subject to scrutiny, for instance the claim by prison authorities throughout the twentieth century that prisoners locked in their cells could call for assistance. One suffragette account recalls, however: 'Every cell has an electric bell for summoning a wardress, but frequently no notice is taken of such a summons and the bells are often out of order and do not work' (Lytton 1914: 182). Indeed, it was the highlighting of such disingenuous practices within prison regimes by suffragettes imprisoned before the First World War that helped to bring about pressure to reform (also see *English Prisons Today*, 1922). Nevertheless, a woman writer who worked as a prison officer during the 1930s could still assert: 'Each cell has a bell, and the occupant can ring it if she wants to be unlocked to go to the lavatory. But bells very often are out of order. More often still, it takes so long before it is answered that the woman gives up in despair' (McCall, 1938: 32).

Such seemingly minor issues make it clear that in some cases when reforms were introduced there were institutional tendencies to ignore or contravene them or alternatively to allow them to lapse or break down. One important point to take into account when considering this is that given the extensive rules and regulations it was practically impossible for prison officers to detect and punish all offences. Inherent in the practical policies that regulated the administration of prisons was an unvoiced acceptance of the discretionary treatment of prisoners and by association individual prison cultures. Thus in his autobiography published in 1998, Hoskison (1998: 92) railed: 'The rules at Wandsworth were not the problem. They were all understandable. It was the way they were enforced that led to the extreme bitterness felt by all inmates.'

Prisoner autonomy, identity and self-esteem

Prisoners' lives within modern prisons are structured by such schemes as Incentives and Earned Privileges, behaviour programmes and the basic requirements of feeding, clothing and housing large numbers of people. It is however, the manner in which these systems are operated that impinge most often on the prisoners' perceptions of fairness, willingness to co-operate or not, and on the prisoners' sense of self as autonomous individuals, albeit imprisoned ones. Historically, the emphasis upon control in prison has been to ensure that it is the prison authorities and decisively not the prisoners who determine the nature of their confinement (for example Gordon, 1922). In the prison context, then, the flexibility to make choices and control one's surroundings does not exist. Sparks et al (1996) – drawing on Gidden's (1984) theory of structuration – argue that it is the prisoners' struggle to maintain agency in the face of such custodial constraints that is the source of a powerful motivation to speak out or to resist in ways which at times seem wholly self-defeating.

In their review of recent evidence pertaining to the effects of imprisonment Bonta and Gendreau (1990) found that the health risks associated with imprisonment provided inconclusive evidence regarding the 'pains of imprisonment'. But evidence did point to the importance of individual differences in adapting to incarceration, an emphasis that has a long history in prisoner autobiographies and was discussed at length in the major study published in 1922, *English Prisons Today*. Bonata and Gendreau's conclusion was that it was time to re-examine the effects of incarceration with special attention being given to the specific conditions of confinement.

The responses of individuals to incarceration and the regimes they experience whilst imprisoned are recurrent themes within prisoner autobiographies (also see Goffman, 1961 for groundbreaking work on the effects of confinement in asylums). Prisoners observe the ways in which they themselves and other prisoners attempt to maintain autonomy and self-esteem in the face of prison regimes and prison officer authority. These reflections provide useful insight into the often counter-productive and self-destructive behaviour that has been commonly displayed amongst prisoners. Prisoners' accounts illustrate diverse behaviour, ranging from the secreting of prohibited items to aggressive challenging of the regime and staff to the infliction of harm upon the self. These are often reactions to, or coping mechanisms for dealing with, the prison environment in which they find themselves incarcerated:

> And in prison, which otherwise would crush him, he saves his ego from entire defeat by the secret possession of a nail or a pin or a pencil, anything so long as it is forbidden. The mania for doing wrong things simply because they are prohibited and involve punishment if discovered arises from this craving of the convict to delude himself as to his own powers and freedom (Mason, 1918: 141).

> For some of them, breaking occasional rules (or every rule in the book) becomes a part of the basic survival kit, a means of keeping one's head above the mire of institutionalisation (Caird, 1974: 62).

> Unless you've been in prison its difficult to imagine how grimly a prisoner will fight for any liberty he has won for himself, and the threat of having even these trivial freedoms taken away amounted to an attack on our identity (McVicar, 1979: 39).

> As some men resist the system by violence and hunger strike so others resist by self-inflicted wounds and suffering (Macartney, 1936: 75).

Therefore, within the prison environment the meanings attached to particular forms of behaviour and the specific contexts in which it occurs require close scrutiny.

What is also clear from prisoner testimonies is that action and experience outside of the routine involved considerable emotional intensity; an emotional intensity which is often absent from official and academic discourse on imprisonment. Equally, however, difficult prison environments can also create contexts in which seemingly ordinary behaviour is perceived to be problematic or the behaviour of a troublesome individual. Prisoner accounts capture how behaviour that might appear inconsequential outside the parameters of the prison may have far-reaching practical and emotional consequences when expressed within the boundaries of its walls. One late twentieth century prisoner noted:

> It does seem petty, a lot of gripes of the prisoner to someone on the street would seem really petty .... I mean for you to go into a cell and somebody to slam the door, if you're not a prisoner, it's just somebody slamming the door, right? But if you're a prisoner and slams the door then it's a different, there's different connotations all round, you know what I mean? (prisoner quoted in Clare and Bottomley, 2001: 150).

Echoes of such concerns can be located in this prisoner's observations: 'What in normal circumstances would at the very worst would be a harmless neurosis turns into dynamite in a three'd-up cell' (Caird, 1974: 26). A prison chaplain in the 1920s observed this distortion of perception and interpretation of behaviour on the part of prisoners. In his opinion a long sentence convict's 'thoughts are concentrated upon himself, and every little thing is magnified into an injury done to *him*. You have no idea how cranky and touchy and suspicious men get in a convict-prison' (Jervis, 1925: 240). Conversely, behaviour that seems important outside of the prison might become less so. One woman imprisoned during the 1980s had intended to be doubly scrupulous about keeping up her personal standards, but when confined felt that

> it did not really seem worth the trouble. So I ate peas with my knife, and dropped sugar all over me from my bread, and I understood the fragility of the hold that a civilised being has on civilisation, and how much easi-

er it is to relapse. And I understood how people can give up washing (Peckham, 1985: 112).

It is important to recognise that the regime and culture within any prison represents an accommodation between the prisoners and the institution that renders the prison manageable. It would be inaccurate, therefore, to suggest that the relationships between inmates and the prison establishment revealed in the transcripts of prisoner's accounts merely depicted the powerless *versus* the powerful. As Sparks et al (1996) note, 'prisoners do not passively *undergo* imprisonment but rather *live* it'. Nevertheless, in the context of differential powers of interpretation, disproportionate meaning is attached to the actions of different actors. This is not to say that the behaviour of prisoners has inevitably been interpreted in a negative light, but that the flexibility to interpret behaviour lay predominantly with prison staff albeit that such discretion is constrained by working relations and the nature of the specific prison's regime.

The sociological study of the prison especially asserts the strength of prison cultures and how resistant they have been to change (see, for example, Finkelstein, 1993). These issues are also reflected upon in prisoner autobiographies. Jim Phelan (1940: 121 and 209) claimed that the 'worst traditions in the world' persisted in prison and noted that 'I have seen many jail-governors try in vain to break a tradition, good or bad'. Whilst exhibiting commonalities, prisons also developed individual practices and reputations. For instance, a reputation for toughness was identified with Strangeways in 1950s Manchester (Sparks, 1961: 48): 'Strangeways is probably different now, but in those days when a new screw arrived at any prison in England, if the convicts knew he had come from Strangeways they went pale.' This reputation was still intact 20 years later. One prisoner talking of his imprisonment during the 1970s and 1980s observed: 'Anybody who'd ever done a day's remand knew that the two hardest prisons in the system were Manchester's Strangeways and London's Wandsworth' (Conlon, 1990: 136; also see James, 2003: 72). Individual prisons have long appeared to gain particular reputations as indicated by this early doggerel discovered by Irish nationalist, Michael Davitt (1885/1972: 161-2) on the bottom of a dinner-can in Millbank as far back as the 1880s:

Millbank for thick shins and graft at the pump;
Broadmoor for all laggs as go off their chump;
Brixton for good toke and cocoa with fat;
Dartmoor for bad grub but plenty of chat;
Portsmouth a blooming bad place for hard work;
Chatham on Sunday gives four ounce of pork;
Portland is worst of the lot for to joke in –
For fetching a lagging there is no place like *Woking*.
        CRUTCHY QUINN, 10 and ticket

Davitt states in his autobiography that he met 'CRUTCHY' and that he believed him to have actually spent some time in seven of the prisons included in the account. The history of a prison can continue to impact upon the day-to-day activities of its contemporary life (Liebling, et al., 1997). It would appear that imprisonment induces long memories in both prisoners and staff. Grievances and perceived misbehaviour on the part of staff and prisoners can be carried throughout their careers and opportune moments are looked for where 'respect' could be restored:

> I never forgot a screw who upset me, and, as the years went by, opportunities usually presented themselves. This sort of thing helped to save one's self-respect. To know that it is in one to hit back, even if it is to be years, – yes decades – after, is a good indication of the amount of vitality available to draw on. As one's indifference to indignity and injury increases, so the will to live declines (Macartney, 1936: 69).

> I did not expect to escape but wanted to take any chance there was...It is very touching how upset they get when you happen to leave them for a few minutes. ... They swilled me off the roof with a hosepipe and when they got hold of me, one of them said: 'A pity about that serious fall Sparks!' I said: What serious fall? 'The one you're just going to have', he said, and they booted me like a sack of spuds down every prison landing and stairway (Sparks, 1961: 49-50; also see O'Donovan Rossa, 1991; Boyle, 1977; McVicar, 1979).

Conclusions about individual prison cultures on the basis of prisoner autobiographies would be tentative at best. What prisoner autobiographies do, however, is highlight the impact of these prison cultures and create a counter-discourse to that of the 'official' prison. They also reveal the more closed areas of prisons, such as segregation, and expose them to critical scrutiny that, until recent years, has often been absent in official discourse. An example of this type of counter-discourse is that related to explanations for prison disturbances and acts of individual prisoner rebellion. Prisoner accounts are likely to express awareness of the impact of the prison environment, and those managing that environment, upon them and their behaviour.

> One poor fellow who had not been able to stand the strain smashed everything on which he could lay his hands. Within a few minutes from cell to cell the nervous storm spread; every prisoner appeared to be thundering at his door in a fury of pent-up emotions which swept reason away. I had the greatest of difficulty in not joining in. I stood at my door, my fists clenched within an inch of it, my whole body tense, my arms vibrating, my teeth clenched, a bursting pressure in my head. The warders came running along the corridors and dragged off prisoners to the padded cells (Fenner Brockway, 1947: 1003-4).

> The exercise of one hour a day – half an hour in the morning and half an hour at 4.15 – is not enough, and yet most of us detested it. It was an awful business, this walking round in a circle, silent. Continual admonition to keep three feet from the man in front, and to stop talking, even when one had not uttered a word since the exercise began, was very tiresome. All this shouted –for jailors always shout – at one for hour is irritating to the point of frenzy, and assaults on jailors were a feature of the exercise ring. Men's nerves would give under the continual nagging, and a convict, exasperated beyond control, would step out of the circulating ring and belt the life out of the jailor (Macartney, 1936: 86 and 92).

> [It is the] petty, unnecessary indignities that infuriate the lags and spark off trouble, far more than the major hardships of being in gaol. It could all be avoided if there was any intelligent prison administration in this country (Skyes, 1967: 63).

However, official discourse has often precluded analyses of the impact of the environments in which prisoners exist. More traditionally, the influence of individual prisoners is given greater attention than the influence of the environment. For example, the May Committee (1979) wrote of the 'toxic mix' of prisoners instigating disturbances. In the past, 'difficult prisoners' have been identified much more often than 'difficult environments' or regimes. This practice continues to be reflected in more modern policies for dealing with 'disruptive' prisoners, and informed the development of Close Supervision Centres in the late 1990s (Clare and Bottomley, 2000). This was also the philosophy on which the use of smaller units for 'difficult prisoners' was based (Bottomley et al., 1994). This emphasis on individual over environment or circumstance has occasionally been identified in prisoner autobiographies: 'authorities are greatly obsessed with ringleaders and always look round for one to make an example of' (McVicar, 1979: 55).

Staff and prisoner relations
Bonta and Gendreau (1990), in their review of the effects of imprisonment, concluded that when inmates are dealt with capriciously by management or individual custodial officers, psychological stress can be created in even the most humane of prison environments. There is immediate staff discretion governing every aspect of prison life. Prison officers have been historically, and remain, the mediators of all schemes and systems within the prison environment and as such they have been identified as one of the most important mechanisms of order and control within the prison. The long-used term for a prison officer, 'screw' has been a reflection of the power of custodial staff and the pressures they could impose. Historically, in autobiographies, prison officers have been seen as powerful determinants of the harshness or otherwise of life for prisoners as well as of the cultures of different prisons (for example, Willis Fletcher, 1884: 329; No.7, 1903: 113; B.2.15, 1924).

In the most obvious sense, power, or at least potential power, influence or pressure, could be based on numbers and in the general prison context prisoners always outnumber prison staff. This situation is reversed in restricted or segregated areas of the prison, and it is often such locations that have gained a reputation for brutality. Again and again prisoner accounts written in the nineteenth and twentieth centuries assert that assaults took place, or were believed by prisoners to have taken place, in the punishment cells. One prisoner describes the experience of his first shower in the segregation block in Wakefield during the 1970s thus:

> It was oppressive, degrading – wherever your eyes went, you could see the blood. I couldn't help looking at the screws, thinking am I going to add to this blood. You knew the reputation of the block and how brutal the screws were. Fortunately, I never got beaten up in the shower (Conlon, 1990: 156).

Another prisoner records the helplessness experienced by prisoners who listen to the violence being done to others in the punishment cells:

> I lay in solitary for four months awaiting trial and experienced moments of downright despair listening to the screws beating up guys who were being brought into the solitary block (Boyle, 1977: 174).

Some prisoner accounts have therefore recorded helplessness experienced in the face of staff aggression and the limited choices prisoners had in terms of defending themselves against it. Prisoner autobiographies commonly observed that a prisoners' word would never be taken over that of an officer (for example, Anon (Callow) 1877: 251 and 293; Willis Fletcher, 1884: 329; Sykes, 1967: 134). It was maintained that this turned the adjudication of prison offences into a 'farcical ceremony' (Sykes, 1967:134).

> Most governor's, if they feel doubt about the prisoner's guilt, will merely caution him – thereby saving everyone's face, except that of the prisoner, who still has a finding of guilt placed on his record (Caird, 1974: 51-54).

> One of the guys, who had been brutalised and had complained by petition, was charged for making false allegations and was put in front of the Visiting Committee and they took a month's remission from him. This was enough to frighten others from petitioning or complaining (Boyle, 1977: 175).

A minority of prisoner autobiographies asserted that the only recourse was to meet violence with violence (for example, Sparks, 1961; Boyle, 1979; McVicar, 1979). The autobiography of Jeremiah O'Donovan Rossa, an Irish nationalist imprisoned during the 1860s, records the cycle of aggression and counter-aggression that also occurred in the nineteenth century. The culmination of this was his being illegally handcuffed for thirty-five days (not nights) with his hands behind his back, except for meal times (O'Donovan Rossa, 1991). From the perspective of the prisoner, violence was judged to have been instigated by prison officers. Yet even in this extreme case, Rossa also recognised acts of kindness on the part of prison officers. On one occasion an officer offered him two 'cakes':

> As I took them into my manacled hands, whatever blood was in my body seemed to rush to my face. I had an urge to throw them at him or out of the window. But another impulse overrode that, for I sensed that the man was going against orders. There was kindness in his act, and the last thing I should do would be to hurt the feelings of a man who didn't mean to hurt mine (O'Donovan Rossa, 1991: 148).

The complexity of the relationship between prisoners and prison officers is clearly discernible in the autobiographies written by those who have been confined, with this sometimes extended to an acceptance of the system itself as a determining factor. The only criticism that one prisoner felt he could make of the officers who had imposed his daily discipline was that 'they remain in a profession in which daily actions of direct or indirect harshness to their fellow-beings are inseparable from the routine of duty' (Hobhouse, 1918: 29-30).

In contrast it has been the importance of staff confidence and their ability to achieve and maintain control that has been recognised and highlighted in numerous studies and official reports (for example, Home Office, 1984; Dunbar,1986; Woolf, 1991; Sykes, 1958; Thomas, 1972).

> At the end of the day, nothing else that we can say will be as important as the general proposition that relations between staff and prisoners are at the heart of the whole prison system and that control and security flow from getting that relationship right. Prisons cannot be run on coercion: they depend on staff having a firm, confident and humane approach

that enables them to maintain close contact with prisoners without abrasive confrontation (Home Office, 1984: para. 16).

The similarities between this statement by the Home Office made in 1984 and the following assertion made in 1861 by, Joshua Jebb, the head of the Convict Prison Directorate following a large-scale riot in Chatham Convict Prison are evident.

> [P]risoners shall be treated with kindness and humanity, &c. It is by firmness and decision, united with consideration for the men, who will, of course, long continue to remember and feel the humiliation of such a defeat as they experienced, that a right and proper feeling between warders and prisoners will be re-established' (*Returns Relating to the recent Convict Disturbances at Chatham*, pp 1861 (125) III.3: also see Brown, 2002).

Prisoner accounts, in contrast to official discourse until recent times, have also captured the manner in which the prison regime imprisons the staff also. These accounts depict the inconsistency between the official rhetoric of valuing staff and the staff's actual experience. There is an awareness of the contradictory status of an officer as being powerful over the prisoners, but also being powerless in relation to their own management and officials:

> The want of confidence in the prisoners is accompanied by a corresponding want of confidence in the warders. These officers are also spied upon by the Chief Warder and Governor; and such us the fear of collusion or bribery, that a warder is forbidden to engage in 'familiar' conversation with a prisoner, and is not supposed to say anything to him that does not bear upon his work or the prison rules (Hobson, 1918: 29) .

> It is necessary for prisoners to learn that, as warders watch them, so they themselves are subject to being watched. Every person in a prison, in fact, comes under the regulations: the System dominates all (B.2.15, 1924: 166).

Conclusion

Given the susceptibility of the recording of memory to selectivity and interpretation, relying on prisoner accounts will always be vulnerable to criticism and accusations of bias. Whilst acknowledging these factors, and the extent to which prisoner autobiographies each present an 'individual theory' of prisons (Foucault, 1977: 209), analysis of a range of autobiographies reveals the consistency and persistence of certain sentient experiences, reference points and anxieties. These consistencies form a subjective counter-discourse of the prison, of which 'an alternative reading of the identity of prisoner' is an important aspect (Morgan, 1999: 231), and lend credibility to autobiographical sources for analysis of the impact of imprisonment. That the impact of the prison has to an extent been similar among the greater part of prisoners who experienced it, irrespective of their social background etc, has been asserted by a few who left autobiographies of their experiences. Stephen Hobhouse, who was imprisoned during the First World War for his conscientious objection to war, observed that in terms of 'the main tendencies of the system ... [its] general effects on character and mentality, seemed to me to be sufficiently clear, and to be of a similar nature for all prisoners involved' (Hobhouse, 1918: 21).

Prisoners' accounts can help to highlight areas in which policy has been inappropriate or where the subjective impact of the policy on what it means to be a prisoner has been absent, either deliberately or unintentionally (see Cohen, 2001; Liebling et al, 1996). This has often resulted in far-reaching unintended consequences for prisoners, staff or the prison system as a whole. Prisoner autobiographies can be an important medium for illustrating how the implementation of policy can produce outcomes contrary to original aims.

One could argue that with the emergence of managerialism and actuarial approaches to imprisonment and crime control, what Feeley and Simon (1992) term 'the new penology', these discourses against institutionalised power are all the more salient. Similarly, *in the wake of* political willingness to resurrect the 'less eligibility' debate (Sparks, 1996; 2000) *prisoner representations* take on a greater significance. Bauman (1989), amongst others, has noted that the tendency of all bureaucracies is to lose sight of the original goal and to concentrate on the means instead; the means which turns into the ends. Bauman goes on to argue that the dehumanisation of people starts at the point where the objects at which the operation is aimed can, and are reduced to a set of quantitative measures. If, as Feeley and Simon (1992) amongst others argue, the new penology is neither about punishment nor about rehabilitating individuals, but about identifying and managing unruly groups and managing offenders as risk-factors to be calculated rather than autonomous individuals, the personalised accounts of prisoners and other offenders offer an important reminder of the lived realities and consequences of such policies (Simon, 1996; Dash, 1997).

Prisoner accounts capture the intricacies of imprisonment; its multiple functions, its unintended consequences and its contradictory nature for the individuals imprisoned and for those who manage the system. They have revealed a consistency and persistence of experience, reference points and anxieties in relation to incarceration. To allow these analyses of the complexity of imprisonment to be lost, or ignored, undermines the all-important debate about what we are trying to achieve through imprisonment, how, and why.

Note

1. Talking in pairs while walking in the exercise yard for 40 minutes a day.

References

Anon [Callow]. (1877) *Five Years' Penal Servitude by one who has endured it*. London.

Anon [S.Roe]. (1864) 'A Convict's Views of Penal Discipline', *The Cornhill Magazine* 10: 722-33.

B.2.15. (1924) *Among the Broad-Arrow Men*. London: A & C Black.

Bailey, V. (1997) 'English Prisons, Penal Culture, and the Abatement of Imprisonment, 1895-1922', *Journal of British Studies*, 36: 285-324.

Balfour, J.S. (1907) *My Prison Life*. London: Chapman & Hall.

Bauman, Z. (1989) *Modernity and the Holocaust*. Cambridge: Polity Press.

Bidwell, A. (1895) *From Wall Street to Newgate*. Hartford, Conn: Bidwell Publishing Co.

Bonta, J. and Gendreau, P. (1990) 'Reexamining the Cruel and Unusual Punishment of Prison Life', *Law and Human Behaviour*, 14 (4):347-372.

Bottomley, A.K. (1998) 'Prison Privatisation and the Remand Population: Principle Versus Pragmatism', *Howard Journal* 37 (3): 223-233.

—, Leibling, A., and Sparks., R. (1994) *An Evaluation of Barlinnie and Shotts Units*. Scottish Prison Service Occasional Paper No.7. Edinburgh: Scottish Prison Service.

—, James, A., Clare, E., and Liebling, A. (1997) *Monitoring and Evaluation of Wolds Remand Prison and Comparison with Public-Sector Prisons, in particular HMP Woodhill*. London: Home Office Publications Unit.

Boyle, J. (1977) *A Sense of Freedom*. London: Pan Books.

Brown, A. (1998) '"Doing Time": the extended present of the long-term prisoner', *Time & Society* 7 (1): 93-103.

—, (2002) 'Legitimacy in the Evolution of the Prison: The Chatham Convict Prison Outbreak 1861', *Criminal Justice History* 18.

—, (2003) *English Society and the Prison*. Woodbridge: The Boydell Press.

Burnett, J. (1982) *Destiny Obscured, Autobiographies of Childhood, Education and Family from the 1820s to the 1920s*. London: Routledge.

Caird, R. (1974) *A Good and Useful Life, Imprisonment in Britain Today*. London: Hart-Davis, Macgibbon.

Chevigny, B.G., ed with Helen Prejean. (1999) *Doing time: Twenty-five years of prison writing*. New York: Arcade Publishing Inc.

Clare, E. and Bottomley, A.K. (2001) *Evaluation of close supervision centres*. Home Office Research, Development and Statistics Directorate (assisted by Grounds, A., Hammond, C.J., Liebling, A., and Taylor, C).

Clemmer, D. (1940) *The Prison Community*. New York: Holt.

Cockshut, A.O.J. (1984) *The Art of Autobiography in 19th & 20th Century England*. New Haven & London: Yale University Press.

Cohen, S. (2001) *States of Denial: Knowing About Atrocities and Suffering*. Cambridge: Polity Press.

—, and Taylor, L. (1972) *Psychological Survival, The Experience of Long-Term Imprisonment*. Harmondsworth: Penguin.

Cook, F. and Wilkinson, M. (1998) *Hard Cell*. Liverpool: The Bluecoat Press

Conlon, G. (1990) *Proved Innocent*. London: Penguin

Dash, L. (1997) *Rosa Lee*. London: Profile Books Ltd.

Davies, A. (2001) 'Writing on the wall: Prisoners on punishment', *Punishment and Society : The International Journal of Penology*, 3 (3), July.

Davitt, M. (1972) *Leaves from a Prison Diary, or Lectures to a 'Solitary' Audience*. Shannon Ireland: Irish University Press.

Dunbar, I. (1986) *A Sense of Direction*. London: Home Office.

Feeley, M. and Simon, J. (1992) 'The New Penology: Notes on the Emerging Strategy of Corrections and its Implications', *Criminology* 30 (4): 449-474.

Finkelstein, E. (1993) *Prison Culture: An Inside View*. Aldershot:Avebury.

Foucault, M. (1977) *Discipline and Punish, The Birth of the Prison*. Harmondsworth: Penguin.

—, (1980) 'Prison Talk' in C.Gordon (ed.), *Power/Knowledge: Selected Interviews and*

Other Writings 1977-84. London: Routledge

Franklin, H.B., ed with Tom Wicker (1998) *Prison writing in 20th century America*. New York: Viking Penguin.

Freeman, M. (1993) *Rewriting the Self, History, Memory, Narrative*. London: Routledge.

Giddens, A. (1984) *The Constitution of Society: Outline of the Theory of Structuation*. Cambridge: Polity Press.

Godfrey, B., Emsley, C. and Dunstall, G. (2003) *Comparative Histories of Crime*. Cullumpton: Willan Publishing.

Goffman, E. (1961) *Asylums, Essays on the Social Situation of Mental Patients and other Inmates*. Harmondsworth: Penguin.

Gordon, M. (1922) *Penal Discipline*. London: Routledge & Sons.

Grass, S. (2003) *The Self in the Cell: Narrating the Victorian Prisoner*. New York & London: Routledge.

Hannah-Moffat, K. (2000) 'Prisons That Empower: Neo-Liberal Governance in Canadian Women's Prisons' *British Journal of Criminology* 40: 510-531.

HM Chief Inspector of Prisons (1993) *Report on Wolds Remand Prison*. London: Home Office.

—, (1999) *Suicide is Everyone's Concern: A thematic review*. London: Home Office

HM Prison Service (1992b) *Model Regime for Local Prisons and Remand Centres*. London: HM Prison Service.

—, (1994a) *HM Prison Service Corporate Plan 1994-97*. London: HMSO.

Hobhouse, S. (1918) 'English prison from within', *The Quarterly Review* 230: 21-37.

—, and Fenner Brockway, A. (1922) *English Prisons Today*. Longman: Green & Co.

Home Office (1979) *Committee of Enquiry into UK Prison Services* (May Committee). London: HMSO.

—, (1984) *Managing the Long-Term Prison System, The Report of the Control and Review Committee*. London: HMSO.

—, (1988b) *Private Sector Involvement in the Remand System*. London: HMSO.

Hoskison, J. (1998) *One Man's Experience of Prison*. London: John Murray.

House of Commons (1981) *Fourth Report from the Home Affairs Committee: Session 1980-1981*. London: HMSO.

Howard, P. (1996) *The Joy*. Dublin: The O'Brien Press Ltd.

Irwin, J. (1970) *The Felon*. Englewood Cliffs, NJ: Prentice-Hall

James, E. (2003) *A Life Inside: a prisoner's notebook*. London: Atlantic Books.

Jervis, E. (1925) *Twenty-Five Years in Six Prisons*. London: T. Fisher Unwin

Leech, M. (1993) *Product of the System: My Life in and out of Prison*. London: Victor Gollancz.

Leibling, A. & Bosworth, M. (1995) 'Incentives in Prison Regimes', *Prison Service*

Journal 98: 57-64.

—, & Taylor, C. *Evaluation of Close Supervision Centres*, Home Office Research Study 219. London: Home Office Research Development and Statistics Directorate.

—, Muir, G., Rose, G. and Bottoms, A. (1997) *Incentives and Earned Privileges for Prisoners – An Evaluation. Research Findings* No.87. Home Office Research, development and Statistics Directorate.

Lovett, W. (1876) *The Life and Struggles of William Lovett*. London: Trubner.

Lytton, C. (1914) *Prisons and Prisoners*. London: Heinemann.

Macartney, W. (1936) *Walls Have Mouths: A Record of Ten Years' Penal Servitude*. London: Gollancz.

Mason, E.W. (1918) *Made Free in Prison. London*: George Allen & Unwin.

Maybrick (1905) *My Fifteen Years Lost*. London.

McCall, C. (1938) *They Always Come Back*. London: Methuen & Co Ltd.

McVicar, J. (1979) *McVicar by Himself*. London: Arrow Books.

Medlicott, D. (1999) 'Researching the Prison: Prisoners as Knowledgeable Agents', paper presented to the British Criminology Conference July 1999.

Morgan, R. (1994) 'An Awkward Anomaly: Remand Prisoners' in Player, E. and Jenkins, M. (eds) *Prisons After Woolf: Reform Through Riot*. London: Routledge: 143-160.

Morgan, S. (1999) 'Prison Lives: Critical Issues in Reading Prisoner Autobiography', *Howard Journal of Criminal Justice* 38 (3): 328-40.

Murray, G. (1918) *Preface to An English Prison From Within*. London: George Allen & Unwin Ltd

No.7. (1903) *Twenty-Five Years in Seventeen Prisons, the Life-Story of an Ex-Convict*. London: F.E.Robinson.

O'Donovan Rossa, J.; (1991) *Irish Rebels in English Prisons*. New York: Sadleir.

Peckham, A. (1985) *A Woman in Custody: A Personal Account of One Nightmare Journey Through the English Penal System*. London: Fontana.

Phelan, J. (1940) *Jail Journey*. London: Secker & Warburg.

Pratt, J. (2002) *Punishment and Civilisation: Penal Tolerance and Intolerance in Modern Society*. London: Sage.

Priestley, P. (1985) *Victorian Prison Lives: English Prison Biography 1830-1914.* London: Methuen.

—, (1989) *Jail Journeys, The English Prison Experience since 1918*. London: Routledge.

Prison Ombudsman. *Annual Report, Independent Investigation of Prisoners' Complaints* (2000) Cm.4730.

Returns Relating to the recent Convict Disturbances at Chatham Convict Prison, PP 1861 (125) 1II.3.

Rickards, Rev. C. (1920) *A Prison Chaplain on Dartmoor*. London: Edward Arnold.

Scott, S. (1924) *The Human Side of Crook and Convict Life*. London: Hurst & Blackett Ltd.

Scott Duckers, J. (1917) *'Handed Over'. The Prison Experience of Mr Scott Duckers*. London: C.W. Daniel.

Sparks, R. (1961) *Burglar to the Nobility: The Autobiography of Ruby Sparks*. London: Arthur Barker Limited.

—, Bottoms, A. and Hay, W. (1996) *Prisons and the Problem of Order*. Oxford: Clarendon Press.

—, (1996) 'Penal 'Austerity': The Doctrine of Less Eligibility Reborn?', in R.Matthews and P.Francis (eds) *Prisons 2000: An International Perspective on the Current State and Future of Imprisonment*. London: Macmillan

—, (2000) 'Perspectives on Risk in Penal Politics' in Hope, T. and Sparks, R. (eds) *Crime, Risk and Insecurity*. London: Routledge.

Stanley, L. (1993) 'On auto-biography', *Sociology* 27: 41-52.

Sykes, G.M. (1958) *Society of Captives, the Study of a Maximum Security Prison*. Princeton: Princeton University Press.

Sykes, R. (1967) *Who's Been Eating My Porridge?* London: Leslie Frewin.

Thomas, J.E. (1972) *The English Prison Officer since1850, A Study in Conflict*. London: Routledge & Kegan Paul.

Von Hirsch and Andrews, A. (eds) (1992) *Principled Sentencing*. Edinburgh University Press.

Willis Fletcher, S. (1884) *Twelve Months in an English Prison*. Boston: Lee & Shepherd.

Windlesham, D. (1993) *Responses to Crime Vol.2: Penal Policy in the Making*. Oxford: Clarendon Press.

Woolf, H and Tumin, S. (1991) *Prison Disturbances April 1990*. Cm.1456. London: HMSO.

Zamble, E., and Porporino, F.J. (1990) 'Coping, imprisonment and rehabilitation: Some data and their implications'. *Criminal Justice and Behaviour*, 17: 53-70.

Chapter Three

The Cinematic Appeal of the Prison

David Wilson

The origins of this chapter lie in three separate places. Firstly, on a personal level, the reality that prison occupies a place in our popular culture and imagination and could generate and hold its audience was brought home to me as a result of my acting as an advisor to the Channel 4 drama series *Buried* which was set in a fictional prison called HMP Mandrake. My experiences on that series, produced by World Productions, made me realise that fictional representations of prison could not only capture large audiences, but also a cross-over interest by that audience and the press into real places of confinement. Frankly *Buried* generated more column inches about gaol and more discussion about what happened to people once they were locked up than any number of Chief Inspector's reports, pressure group investigations, or academic articles, including my own. *Buried* spoke to an audience that would have been suspicious of these reports and articles – if they had read them at all – and instead introduced ideas related to what it means to be locked up through action, character development and the nuances of plot and drama.

Secondly, using this experience of *Buried* as a platform and together with Sean O'Sullivan, I wanted to look more broadly at fictional representations of prison and prisoners, both on television and in film, so as to uncover how prison and prisoners were imagined by film makers over time and in three different countries – Britain, the USA and Australia. In short, we wanted to take seriously the possibility that representations of prison in film and television drama are an important source of people's implicit and common sense understandings of prison. As such our book, *Images of Incarceration* (Wilson and O'Sullivan, 2004), seeks to develop an analysis of some of the main ways in which prison has been represented in film and television drama and to suggest how and why these representations might come to influence people's perceptions of existing prisons.

Finally, and perhaps of greater interest, we wanted to see if those representations had served, or could be used to serve the cause of penal reform, at a time of our highest ever prison numbers and when the case against prison seems to have been all but lost. In this respect, beginning in March 2004 and through sponsorship that we obtained from the Esmée Fairbairn Trust's Re-Thinking Crime and Punishment initiative, we held a series of prison film weekends in London, Glasgow and Birmingham. We wanted to see what happened when the audience for prison drama encounters real prisoners, prison staff and penal pressure groups and organisations, as a way of creating – to misquote Thomas Mathiesen (2000), with whom in this respect I disagree, an 'alternative within public space'. The opportunity for digesting and assessing the results of these meetings remains a little way off. What this chapter does, is to suggest that film provides people with imaginative resources that help them to visualise or imagine the nature of the world. Further, that people are much more receptive to arguments about those things that are outside of their own experience, like imprisonment, if they possess a cultural model or metaphor which helps them to visualise and make sense of those things. Thus, I am going to argue that prison drama can act as an 'imaginative resource' for the viewer in the form of five specific propositions. Namely, that prison drama:

- Helps to set the limits of what we take to be the plausible range of interpretations of the world
- Translates or transcodes ideas and arguments from specialist sources (official reports, social scientific research, experiential writings) into accessible popular forms
- Can commit sins of omission as well as commission: dramatic products

may help create a view of the world as much by what they leave out as through what they include
- Gives people access to models of, or metaphors for other people's experiences which they do not experience themselves directly
- May evoke feelings of empathy and attach sentiment to subjects that cannot be entirely reduced to matters of rational debate.

I will amplify these five propositions by asking you to briefly consider first a quotation and then some quick examples of prison on film or on television. In particular try and bear these propositions in mind as I briefly compare *Porridge* – the long running and endlessly repeated BBC comedy – with Jimmy Boyle's *A Sense of Freedom* and Larry Winters's *Silent Scream*. Thereafter I will focus in a more detailed way on *Buried* and the Australian film *Ghosts of the Civil Dead*. I could equally look at *Oz*, *Bad Girls*, *Scum*, *The Loneliness of the Long Distance Runner*, *Chopper*, *Brubaker* or *The Shawshank Redemption* – voted Channel 4's 'favourite' film of all time and celebrating its tenth anniversary next year – or a whole host of other prison dramas. We all have our favourite prison movie!

Commonsense Expectations, Actual Experience and Dramatic Preparation
In 1993 Sandra Gregory, a British citizen working in Thailand as a teacher, fell ill and subsequently lost her job. As a result, as she explains in her autobiography, she agreed to act as a drug 'mule' so as to be able to afford her plane fare home. However, unsurprisingly – doesn't she watch the movies? – she was arrested at the airport, charged with drug smuggling, eventually convicted and sentenced to 25 years in Lard Yao prison, also known as 'The Bangkok Hilton'. Later, writing of her experiences she commented: 'What I sensed immediately is that prison is not like the movies, or television dramas. It's far more insane, terrible, emotional and disgusting than any of those' (Gregory 2002: 98). These comments are of not of interest to me because they are aimed at the Thai penal or criminal justice systems. But rather because they reflect that her impressions of prison, gained from film and television, did not prepare her for the awful reality of incarceration, whether in Thailand or indeed in Britain, where she completed her sentence. Prison in reality was far more 'insane, terrible, emotional and disgusting', despite the healthy women-in-prison sub-genre of prison

movies, and in particular those in that sub-genre featuring prisons abroad. Prison film, in short, did not prepare her for the reality that she was to experience in either Thailand or in England. For her, film had created a view of imprisonment by what it lacked, rather than what it had included.

There is an argument to be made as to whether film can ever educate us to the reality of prison, so that our entry into the actual and still largely secret world of the prison would not be as much of a culture shock. In one sense what I am describing here is the old chestnut of whether a film will always be only that – a film. After all film – the medium – possesses a necessary degree of artificiality, with the most commonly cited example here in relation to prison films, the difference between the run-time of a film and the run-time of a sentence. Can film really show the extended stretches of boredom that a prison sentence entails? Films have other artificialities too. For example, they tend to use photogenic stars who are likely to be, though not always, atypical of the type of people that one would meet locked up. For these, and for other reasons too, some have dismissed, or discounted 'film-prisons' as bearing no or little useful relation to 'real-prisons' and have insisted that the medium of film and television almost inevitably make it unsuitable to convey the 'awful reality of gaol.

I do not accept that logic and indeed because I do not accept that logic I want more, not less prison films and television dramas. Nor do I think that I am being naïve here, for prison film can push the debate about real prison forward. Look, for example, at the films and television adaptations of the autobiographies and other writings of people who have experienced prison including the autobiography of Sandra Gregory. These are a rarely used source but they contain genuine insight into what prison is like, and are often at variance to what we are officially told what prison is like. Indeed this is the power of Gregory's autobiography, which is claiming a 'truth' which she is denying for other accounts of life inside. She is trying to seduce us by convincing us that her vision and her account is closer to the 'real thing' than anything else that we may have read or seen. And in this respect she is following in an increasingly well-worn tradition, and one highlighted in this volume by Brown and Clare. Moreover, anyone reading or subsequently watching Jimmy Boyle's (1977) account of Scottish prisons in the 1970s could not but help but be struck by the extent to which his version of events portrays a view of prison markedly different to that conveyed by, for example, the BBC situation comedy *Porridge*. And whilst not everyone might agree with Boyle's account of his life and career within the penal system as provided in *A Sense of Freedom*, this merely makes his account a contested one, rather than establishing that his experience is unrepresentable. Boyle's book was adapted for television and screened as a one-off television drama special, and arguably it did succeed in capturing some of the insights provided by his autobiography.

Again the point is not so much that drama can fully capture reality or 'tell the whole story', rather that drama can help set the limits of plausibility and through its inclusion or exclusion of particular issues help to shape perceptions of reality. So to the extent that *Porridge* never showed prison officer brutality, riots or prison suicides, these issues were absent from our screens and to that extent much less visible in popular debate. Thus *A Sense of Freedom* provided a very different account to that provided by the much more popular situation comedy *Porridge* as to what penal reality is like, despite the fact that both were set in and intended to reflect prisons during the 1970s and subsequently. Indeed, I would argue that if more people had had the opportunity to see the TV adaptation of *A Sense of Freedom* rather than endless re-runs of *Porridge* then their understanding of prison would be that much different. Here I am not so much arguing that *Porridge* is 'wrong' or even that it is endlessly repeated, but rather that other representations of prison found it much harder to get made and those that were made were seen less often, thus ensuring that 'real' prisons could hide how they were 'insane, terrible, emotional and disgusting'.

A case in point is the film *Silent Scream* (1990). Briefly *Silent Scream* tells the story of Larry Winters and his experience of the Scottish penal system in the 1960s and 1970s. In 1964 Winters was convicted for the murder of a barman in a London pub but was given a life as opposed to a death sentence, apparently on the basis that he had some kind of psychological or mental instability. Winters found it difficult to cope with the inflexible regimes of the Scottish prison system. His mental health worsened and he became addicted to drugs while in prison. Like other lifers in the Scotland at the time, Winters came into conflict with the authorities about the conditions of his incarceration and was involved in peaceful protests, demonstrating against extended periods of solitary confinement and prison officer brutality. He was also involved in several violent assaults on prison officers.

The film *Silent Scream* presents a fairly sympathetic portrayal of Larry Winters. He is shown to be a disturbed but sensitive young man who could have led a productive life in prison, if accommodated within an appropriate regime. One significant scene in the film comes early on, just as Winters is about to be admitted to the Special Unit at Barlinnie. A small group of prison officers are discussing his impending arrival, with one of them expressing strong reservations about accepting him into the Unit. The officer knows of Winters by his reputation within the system and admits, quite frankly, that he is scared of him. When Winters actually arrives we see a tall, thin, slightly dishevelled man wearing blue and white striped pyjamas, open at the top. Winters appears slightly edgy and somewhat traumatised, but is able to accept a cigarette when it is offered to him. Overall it is clear that he is reasonably non-threatening and has far more to fear from the prison officers than they have reason to fear him.

Silent Scream is not an easy film to watch. It has only a loosely chronological narrative, interspersed with flashbacks, which have no clear order. The overall style of the film is fragmentary, disconnected and impressionistic. Perhaps this is why the film succeeds in conveying the sense of a man whose mental and physical health has been totally wrecked by the prison system; and this in spite the fact that much of its narrative centres on the efforts of the staff in the Barlinnie Special Unit to reconnect Winters with his family, and with reality. The film succeeds not only in showing the harm prison did to Winters, but is also able to suggest that things could have been different. In passing we might also note that the film is possibly too sympathetic to Winters. It shows his original crime more as an act of confusion, rather than malice. Similarly it tends to depict the violence inflicted on Winters, but not the violence inflicted in the opposite direction. But the point is not really whether the film succeeds in telling everybody's version of the story of Larry Winters, for it obviously cannot. Its significance is that it gives a radically different version of imprisonment to that presented in the sanitised comedic prison of *Porridge*, or indeed in the stylised Hollywood, male, action-adventure prison movie. It is an example of the ability of drama powerfully to convey an idea and in so doing to give some insight into reality. I am not simply suggesting that *Silent Scream* is a 'better' or more realistic view of prison than *Porridge*, although it clearly is, but rather that its significance is in its difference. This difference, in turn, adds to the plausible range of representations available from which people can draw on to make sense of prison – the 'reality' of prison.

Using these examples and my quotation from Sandra Gregory I want to suggest that:

- The general public systematically underestimate the reality of imprisonment and just how awful it is, because they lack the necessary experiential knowledge and imaginative resources to make sense of what information that they do have.
- Secondly, that prison regimes are generally worse at any one time than the general public imagines and much worse than they would accept for themselves if they were imprisoned.
- That prisoners, and some members of staff are one of the main sources of information about prison and what happens inside and that their accounts often reveal the irrationality of what happens inside and which is inevitably at variance with official accounts of imprisonment.
- That film can perform a penal reform function when it popularises critical accounts of the penal system, by translating the insight of first hand experience into a wider domain. It does this by benchmarking; revelation; defence; news/memory and humanisation/empathy.

These issues of benchmarking, revelation, defence, news/memory and humanisation/empathy are important for the following discussion of the Channel 4 series *Buried* and the Australian film *Ghosts of the Civil Dead*. Time and space in this chapter does not allow me to describe each of these issues in detail. But by benchmarking I mean how film and television dramas imply model forms, either by connoting the prisons in which the action is set as falling below socially acceptable standards of decency, or by flagging up what they consider to be the characteristics of a good prison or of good staff. Indeed, this benchmarking is often retrospective, so that the prison of the past can be used in films to put pressure on the standards of the present and any number of prison films – including *The Shawshank Redemption*, would fit this category.

Given that the films that I am going to describe were never major box-office, I want to spend a little time outlining their plots.

Ghosts… and *Buried*: An Overview

The narrative of *Ghosts of the Civil Dead* (hereafter simply *Ghosts…*) is concerned with the events that lead up to a riot in Central Industrial Prison – the future of containment. The riot is, however, not seen and the film is presented in a pseudo-documentary style with prisoner identification photographs and long intertitle quotes from a 'Report' which clears the penal authorities from any culpability in the trouble. We are informed that the riot takes place on 25 October and thus we are presented with a series of events that attempt to explain how the disorder came about. We are specifically told that Central Industrial Prison houses 'the prison system's most violent, unmanageable and predatory inmates'. Yet there is little character development and we rarely come to know any of the protagonists in relation to what they did that led to their incarceration or why they might have been involved with crime in the first place. The film begins and ends with one of the characters, Wenzil, played by David Field, first entering the prison and then leaving it after the riot. To this extent we see the story of *Ghosts…* through his eyes.

As Wenzil first enters the gaol we see him naked and being given his prison number, in effect his new administrative identity within Central Industrial Prison. He is also given more informal advice from a fellow inmate: 'Watch your back and stay sitting down for as long as possible.' As Wenzil begins to orientate himself to his new surroundings, so too the viewer comes to see what he is experiencing and what life is like in Central Industrial Prison. In fact, prior to the lock down that precedes the riot, there is initially a great deal of freedom of movement within the unit where Wenzil is located. Everything that the prisoners do, however, is constantly monitored through CCTV, the use of which contributes to the documentary style of the film. As such, we see well-organised gangs of prisoners preying on each other and waging a perpetual war against the guards. In turn, the guards wage war on the prisoners and they are initially concerned that Grezner, a 'guard killer', with a police escort, has been placed on the unit. We see one inmate after another using drugs and watching pornography on televisions in their cells and moving freely from one cell to another.

Thus we are introduced to various other characters apart from Wenzil, including Waychek, who appears to run the informal inmate economy and to his transvestite lover Lilly. The early action centres on Wenzil's desire to buy a tattoo. This costs a carton of cigarettes and thus involves him stealing a radio to pay the tattoo artist, who advises him that 'a man looks a bit funny without tattoos doesn't he?' It is this theft that propels the action forward. Wenzil is caught with the stolen radio by two inmate heavies and is badly beaten up as a consequence. They also tattoo 'cunt' onto his forehead, which means that for most of the remainder of the film Wenzil wears a bandana around his head.

Gradually the staff begin to remove the freedoms and privileges that the inmates have been enjoying and we see prisoners and their cells being searched for drugs and other forms of contraband. When two inmates murder a third, an indigenous prisoner, outdoor recreation is stopped and the prisoners are forced to take their exercise in a locked cage within the unit. The prison authorities also begin to move new prisoners into the units, prisoners who, we are told, are 'the psychos, the dregs of the whole system'. One such psycho, Maynard, played by the singer Nick Cave, enters the unit shouting: 'there goes the neighbourhood. I can see a coon in a cage. Nigger, nigger, nigger.' The new tough, lockdown regime means that drugs are harder to come by and that there is virtually nothing to do, except play dominoes. Old scores are settled and Waychek, no longer controlling the informal economy, is eventually killed when two prisoners pour glue onto him and set him alight, leaving Lilly defenceless. In these changing circumstances the staff become ever more concerned and one at breaking point throws his teacup at the wall crying: 'I'm sick, I'm leaving. It's just a job. You're not supposed to get killed doing your job. I'm leaving. Open the door. I'm out of here.' We later discover that he has shot himself. Similarly the prisoners respond to the new regime by self-harming, lighting cell fires and thirty of them begin a hunger strike.

Towards the end of the film we see a distraught Lilly, no longer able to get access to drugs and without the protection of Waychek being beaten up and killed by Wenzil, whilst all the time being filmed by the guards on CCTV. The murder of one of his fellow prisoners can be seen as symbolic of the 'progress' that Wenzil has made since coming into gaol. However, if Wenzil had hoped that this would have given him some status, he is advised by another inmate:

'you kill a nobody and it makes you a nobody'. The murders do not end here, and we discover Grezner, the 'guard killer', hanged in his cell. These deaths are but a prelude to the horrific murder of a staff member, who is repeatedly stabbed and to the riot itself, which is reported on the television news. As a result thirty prisoners are transferred out of Central Industrial Prison and five – including Wenzil, who had been filmed murdering Lilly – are released back into the community. The film ends with Wenzil leaving an anonymous train station to go home. We watch him standing on the escalator ascending into the world above, as if he is emerging from hell. Yet another intertitle montage advises us that, as a consequence of the riot, the 'Report' also recommends that the Bureau of Prisons immediately begin construction of a new 'super-maximum security facility'. Just in front of Wenzil on the escalator is a woman and as the final credits roll we are left to wonder what he might be about to do to her as they reach the surface.

Buried too is concerned with a penal journey. The episodic nature of the programme allows and for new characters to be introduced and for character development which is not attempted in *Ghosts*…. But in essence the series is concerned with Lee Kingley's progress at the fictional HMP Mandrake. The main narrative of the series concerns Kingley, played by Lennie James, who claims that he is innocent of the offence for which he has just received eight years – shooting and grievously wounding the man who raped his sister. He spends much of his time trying to re-establish inside the reputation that he had on the outside, where he was seen as a hard-working family man. Inside, however, he is naïve and trusting and at the start is able to survive largely because his brother Troy is a Category A prisoner with a fearsome reputation and who is well known within the penal system for attacking staff. Early on Kingley is advised by 'Rollie man', played by Sean McKee, that there is a hierarchy in jail and that he can rank every prisoner based on how long they are serving, how many times they have been in before and how 'hard' they are. Rollie man reckons that Lee could make it all the way to number one and, over the eight episodes, we see Lee rising or falling in that hierarchy, or choosing as best he can to opt out of it. Along the way, we are introduced to other characters, including staff members, such as the psychologist Nick Vaughn (played by Stephen Walters), SO Steddon (Connor McIntyre) and Officer 'DD' played by Jane

Hazelgrove. 'DD' is a strong female character. A particular strength of *Buried* is its attempt to see the drama not just in how the prisoners interact with each other but also how the staff work with each other, as well as with the prisoners. Through his ups and downs, the viewer is asked to identify with Lee, a black man proclaiming his innocence, and to see prison through his eyes, as fellow prisoners abuse each other, smuggle drugs, or mentally collapse as family relationships get destroyed and the outside World gradually disappears from their view. We are asked to question the rehabilitation that is on offer. In *Buried*'s case this is a 'drug-free' unit that is run by Nick Vaughn and which seems to swim against the tide of a sea of drugs available within the prison and which are, we discover, being smuggled in by a member of staff. Crucially, in viewing the world of HMP Mandrake through Lee's eyes, we are also being asked to identify with his demise – his death at the hands of another prisoner. In the final scene in episode eight the camera captures Lee's look of helplessness as he clutches at his stomach, blood oozing through his fingers. He is unable to reach his cell bell to call for staff assistance and his cell-mate incapable of helping either, having slipped into a drug induced stupor.

Ghosts… and *Buried*: Views of Prison as an Institution

Both *Buried* and *Ghosts*… present prison as a failing institution, although *Buried* is less polemical and more measured in its opposition. *Buried*, for example, at least attempts to demonstrate the possibility of rehabilitation through Nick Vaughn's 'drug free' unit. It is clear through discussions with the writers that they had been impressed in their research with what HMP Grendon, which operates as a therapeutic community, had to offer. Indeed, in talking to Erwin James, a former prisoner who writes for the *Guardian*, Kath Mattock, the series producer described HMP Grendon as 'an interesting place, geared to helping people take responsibility for their actions' (*Guardian*, 19 February 2003). It is obvious that they wanted some element of the possibility that people could change for the better in prison brought into the series. However, this possibility for change had to be seen against the backdrop of a penal culture that, for one reason or another, resisted those changes and where survival was a daily reality. In this respect even Vaughn's 'drug free' unit was seen as compromised. Jimmy Gardner, who with Robert Jones wrote seven of the eight episodes, suggested that the character Henry was deliberately introduced into episode three so as to reveal the absurdity of the Prison Service's drug testing programme which encourages prisoners to 'switch' their drug use from cannabis to heroin – a clear example of benchmarking. Indeed *Buried* takes this view to its logical conclusion and shows prisoners being released from HMP Mandrake but being brought back into jail in later episodes after they have re-offended. *Ghosts…* is deliberately more polemical and uncompromising and as such no effort is made at all to show prisoners being offered help in any form. Staff and inmate violence dominate the film and, more than this, the violence is seen as being instigated by the prison authorities so as to justify the building of even more secure prisons – the 'super-maximum security facility' that is recommended in the 'Report' at the conclusion of the riot.

Both in *Buried* and *Ghosts…* the most obvious failures within the prison are the staff themselves. They are consistently presented as ineffectual, corrupt and violent and even those characters who are seen as decent, such as Steddon in *Buried*, are nonetheless still viewed as being incapable of affecting change. *Ghosts…* uses this to the best advantage by not being too concerned with any character development and thus simply presents the staff as archetypes, agents of the state, as much imprisoned by the system as the prisoners themselves. Indeed, this rather Foucauldian analysis is perhaps best exemplified by the fact that in the credits for *Ghosts…* Simon During is credited as 'Foucault authority'. *Buried* is again less polemical than *Ghosts…* and attempts to develop the characters of the staff, revealing them as people with pasts and, sometimes, troubled presents. This is not to imply that *Ghosts…* does not attempt to present some insight into how the staff might respond to the circumstances in which they find themselves. One staff member commits suicide and another repeatedly warns the Governor of the riot that is about to take place, but with little impact. In this respect *Ghosts…* is a development from *Stir* (1980), which routinely presents the staff as moronic bullies and boors who beat the prisoners for their own sadistic pleasure. In one scene, for example, the Principal Officer rips an earring from a prisoner's ear and another deliberately destroys the bread that he finds during a cell search. Indeed the main narrative drive in *Stir* is the personal inability of China Jackson, played by Bryan Brown, to overcome the bullying and intimidation that he faces at the hands of the guards and the collective inability of the prisoners to effect change in a corrupt regime. In *Chopper* (2000) set at Pentridge Prison in 1978 the guards are again seen as ineffectual, although not sadistic and violent, and somewhat in awe of Chopper himself, played by Eric Bana. This is perhaps best demonstrated by the final scene of the film which has two officers sitting on Chopper's bed discussing a news interview that he had given earlier in the day and which is now being shown on television. It is clear that the staff feel that they are in the presence of a celebrity and as they leave one apologetically points out that he is going to have to lock the cell door. Chopper waves his hand, as if to say 'go ahead'.

However the staff's main dramatic role in *Ghosts...* and *Chopper* is to be absent; to be invisible. In short, they are simply not around when the action takes place, and this is in spite of the design principles of 'new generation' prisons. Thus, the prisoners are allowed to create their own world, with their own rules, devoid of staff interference. Chopper is therefore able to stab Keith George repeatedly in the neck at the beginning of the film and, in due course, is stabbed himself by his friend Jim. As the attack starts Chopper observes: 'it's a bit early in the morning for kung-fu, isn't it Jim?' So Jim stabs him a second and then a third time. 'What's got into you?' Chopper asks, as Jim stabs him again. Chopper hugs him and so Jim apologises but stabs him again, once more and then again. 'Jim', suggests Chopper, 'if you keep stabbing me, you're going to kill me.' The point here is the absence of the staff to prevent a long-drawn out attack from taking place, although in passing we should also note the black humour in *Chopper* which is largely absent from the other two films and also from *Buried*. Indeed the humour is apparent even in the opening titles, as images of prison walls flash before the viewer as Frankie Laine sings Don't Fence Me In. This staff absence is all the more confusing in *Ghosts...* given that they sit observing the prisoners all day through CCTV cameras and even film Wenzil's murder of Lilly. Of course the greatest absence is the absence of the various prisons' Governors and when one does appear in *Ghosts...* he simply refuses to speak to the prisoners at all. Here we have a power vacuum that the prisoners are only too keen to fill.

Here too we should also see the three films and *Buried* as presenting prison as a 'closed institution', where the culture of the institution develops from what happens inside and is divorced from the world outside. Thus, the rules that dominate how the prisons will operate have at best only a tangential relationship with how things would work outside and as one prisoner observes in *Ghosts…* 'I've seen people killed over a rumour, a look, or a whisper.' The most dramatic presentation of this culture is the acceptance of situational homosexuality. Thus, Lilly is seen as desirable inside prison and in one very erotic scene slowly and teasingly lies on top of a fellow prisoner and bites his lip. The viewer is left in no doubt about Lilly's desirability in gaol, a desirability that would no doubt disappear if encountered by the same prisoner in the community. Indeed in *Stir* Redfern, an older dominant prisoner, explains these fluctuating desires to China. 'After I've fucked them,' he says, 'I can't stand them for being such weak bastards for letting me fuck them.' So too Barry Shiel in *Buried* is quite happy to use Lucas for sexual favours and suggests, reminding us of the debt that Wenzil gets into at the beginning of *Ghosts…* that he should get some 'tats' to make himself even more desirable. As Lucas leaves Shiel's cell when the reality hits of what is going to be happening to him, Shiel calls out to remind him: 'have a shower before you get up here tomorrow morning.'

Ghosts… and *Buried:* **Views of the Prisoners as Prisoners and as People**

Jimmy Gardner explained that in co-writing *Buried* he was influenced by the cult, American TV series *Oz*, but with one major difference.

> When I watched Oz, I remember thinking that I was really glad that these people were on the inside, locked up and that I was on the outside. I didn't want people to think that about Buried, but rather to see more of the people behind the label 'prisoner' – more of the compassion and the humanity. Not 'them' and 'us'.

In this respect, far more than in *Ghosts…*, *Buried* succeeds in presenting the prisoners as people who, in different circumstances the viewer could quite happily meet in the pub, on the way to or from work, or have as neighbours. The characters in *Buried* are like us, except that they have been imprisoned; as you or I might, they react to the nature and circumstances of their incarceration. As such, they talk about things which you or I might and behave as we all do. Wives and girlfriends are discussed; letters from home cherished, visits from home eagerly looked forward to and photographs of loved ones posted on cell walls. Indeed it was Lee's mistaken belief that Kappa had been secretly masturbating over a stolen photograph of Lee's daughter Amelia that led to his murder. For as these characters are slowly but surely immersed into the prison world, thoughts of home and of leaving jail gradually surrender to institutionalisation, dependency and survival. In this respect, dreadful acts become almost normal and forgivable.

Unlike *Buried*, *Ghosts...* does not allow its characters a past but rather keeps them firmly in the present. They are only what we see before us and as such each violent incident in which they engage merely serves to distance them further and further from the viewer, or at least what the viewer would like to think of him or herself. The characters become aliens: 'them' and definitely not 'us'. In this sense the viewer of *Ghosts...* becomes placed in the same position as the guards who watch the prisoners on CCTV, only the viewer's role is not to police and control but rather more akin to someone visiting a zoo. Thus we marvel at what we see because it is exotic and different, albeit safely caged and at a distance. Even Wenzil, the only character who is given a future, as he ascends the escalator in the train station at the end of the film, leaves the viewer merely anxious and fearful as to what he might be about to do when he reaches the surface.

In *Stir* the prisoners are always presented as badly treated and abused by their sadistic guards. As such it is easy to be on their 'side', although the colour here is so lacking in shade as to render this identification as meaningless. *Chopper*, largely through the character of Chopper himself, is much more ambiguous and the viewer is never quite certain what is true and what is imagined. As Chopper explains, when questioned by one of his guards as to whether what he has just said in a TV interview is accurate: 'never let the truth get in the way of a good yarn'. The viewer here is being asked to suspend disbelief too and go along with the thrill of the 'yarn' that is being spun; to enjoy the moment, whether it is real or imagined. Indeed, many are prepared to do so, for as Chopper explains, almost incredulously: 'I've written a best seller and I can't even bloody spell. It's sold over 250,000 copies and it is still selling! I'm writing another one and I'm semi-literate!' The question being posed here is 'who's fooling who?' And at the same time the film is also asking us to question our own interest in murder and other extreme forms of violence, reduced here to commodities which sell cinema tickets and create best-selling authors out of murderers.

Concluding the Popular Appeal of Prison

All of the films that I have discussed have argued or concluded that there is a kind of madness and insanity to prison. *Ghosts...* possesses an almost surreal quality as the prison drifts into the madness that leads to the riot. In *Chopper* prison is depicted as an insane and irrational institution. Chopper's own violence is completely senseless. Chopper 'bashes people for no reason' and, when asked to explain why his crew are at war with the rest of H Wing, he has no answer. In *Buried*, Lee takes his own personal journey into madness, echoing a journey that his brother Troy has already taken. In *Buried* violence is both 'rational', necessary to run the internal prison economy, and at times just senseless, as when Carter, the man convicted of killing his two children in a car crash, becomes a focus for mob violence.

In *Ghosts...*, *Chopper* and *Buried* violence is one of the main means of identifying the irrationality of the institutions depicted. But this use of violence is, in a sense, a double-edged sword. On the one hand it can serve to undermine the legitimacy of prison. The fiction of prison is that as an institution it should be 'unimpeachably humane, but unremittingly severe', although the reality is that prison is such an unnatural institution that it will always find it difficult to live up to this ambition. Revealing the madness of prison serves a useful function to counter the fiction of severe, but humane punishment. In *Buried*, Lee begins his journey as a kind of 'everyman', a prison innocent determined to avoid being sucked into the power plays and internal politics of prison culture. But the speed with which prison culture overtakes him is frightening and by episode four Lee has bludgeoned a man to death over 'a rumour'. But why do we wish to watch this descent into madness? What accounts for our fascination with seeing inmate culture depicted as a Darwinian struggle for survival? One issue that requires further investigation is the gendered nature of the audience for prison drama. To what extent do dramatisations of the male experience of prison play to male audiences that are drawn to products which celebrate a fascination with the 'hard man'? Do prison drama's have a tendency towards simply using prison as a testing ground for 'cool masculinity'?

In its favour *Buried* certainly expanded the range of relationships that could be represented within prison drama. *Buried* was able to show same-sex activity in prison as both supportive and predatory. It was also able to show relationships across the staff/inmate divide and its representation of the relationship between Lee and his brother Troy was also novel for British television. Whether it could have done more to indicate the potential for reform is unclear. Perhaps if the show had been re-commissioned the opportunities to develop this aspect may have emerged. But if *Buried* becomes available on DVD it will become part of our culture and, as the writer Jimmy Gardner has suggested, prison is an under-dramatised topic and any innovative approach to depicting prison is to be welcomed. If the point of both *Ghosts...* and *Buried* is that prisons and prisoners can too easily become hidden from view, then the significance of their production is to make them visible again, and through that visibility expanding the plausible range of interpretations of what prison is like. In doing so they are able to translate theoretical ideas and specialist arguments about prison into an accessible popular form and in turn allow the viewer to feel empathy for those who are often the most excluded members of our society. And that is why, as academics, we should be delighted in the popular appeal of the prison.

References
J. Boyle (1977) *A Sense of Freedom*, London: Pan Books
S. Gregory (2002) *Forget You Had A Daughter: Doing Time in the Bangkok Hilton*, London: Vision
T. Mathiesen (2000) *Prison on Trial*, Winchester: Waterside Press
D. Wilson & S. O'Sullivan (2004) *Images of Incarceration: Representations of Prison in Film and Television Drama*, Winchester: Waterside Press

Chapter Four

Understanding the Growth in the Prison Population in England and Wales[1]

Andrew Millie, Jessica Jacobson and Michael Hough

Introduction

On 11 July 2003, the prison population in England and Wales topped 74,000 for the first time, an increase of more than 60 percent on 1991 figures. The number of adults in prison – that is, excluding offenders aged 15 to 20 – has increased even more steeply by 73 percent from a daily average of 36,246 in 1991 to 62,838 on 11 July 2003.[2] This unprecedented rate of increase has occurred against a backdrop of gradually declining crime rates since the mid-1990s, according to both recorded crime figures and the British Crime Survey (Simmons and colleagues, 2002).

England and Wales now have the highest prison rate in the European Union at 139 per 1,000 population[3] (Walmsley, 2003). While this is much lower than, for example, the United States at 686 per 1,000 population, the increase has had the effect both of diverting resources from elsewhere in the criminal justice system and in creating strain within the prison system. In particular, constructive rehabilitative work has become increasingly difficult, being hampered both by overcrowding and by the consequent shuffling and reshuffling of inmates from prison to prison. By 2001 the situation in England and Wales was that 11,204 prisoners were held two to a cell designed for one (Home Office, 2003).

There has been little academic or policy debate about precisely why the prison population in England and Wales has increased at such a rapid rate since the early 1990s. The aim of this chapter is to go some way towards filling this gap. It presents the findings of a study that reviewed patterns and trends in adult sentencing and explored sentencers' views. The main elements of the study were:

• An analysis of Home Office sentencing statistics
• Focus groups with magistrates, supplemented by questionnaires distributed to participants
• Semi-structured interviews with senior judges, Crown Court judges, recorders and district judges.

The focus groups and interviews concentrated on the sentencing of adults. They were carried out in areas served by six Crown Court centres in England and Wales. Within each area, two magistrates' benches were identified – wherever possible, one being a high user and the other a low user of custody, and all with annual caseloads of over 350. A total of 80 magistrates took part in 11 focus groups, and 69 questionnaires were returned by the participants. Forty-eight one-to-one interviews were carried out: 17 with Crown Court judges, 12 with recorders and 14 with district judges.[4] Additionally, five members of the senior judiciary were interviewed in London.

The first part of this paper examines statistics on crime and sentencing to provide an explanation for the rise in the prison population. To anticipate the conclusions, we suggest that the rise has nothing to do with crime trends or with court workloads, but is largely a function of increased use of imprisonment. The second part examines what factors underlie sentencers' growing preparedness to use custodial sentences, and when they do so, to pass longer sentences.

Accounting for the growth in the prison population[5]

The most obvious explanation for the rise in the prison population – and one that the 'man in the street' would probably offer – is that crime has increased.

As discussed above, this is clearly not the case. Crime levels, however measured, are lower now than in 1991.

Nor it is a function of increases in court workloads, which could occur even at a time of falling crime. The general trend in the number of convictions has been downward. For 1991 the recorded adult total was 1.2 million (Home Office, 1992: 101). By 2001 the figure was down 11 percent to just under 1.1 million (Home Office, 2002a: 45). Over the same period the number of adults found guilty of indictable offences fell by one percent from 220,000 to 217,400 (Home Office, 1992: 100; 2002a: 44).

One might argue that the overall fall in crime has masked rises in more serious categories of offences. Indeed, as will be discussed, this was a view proposed by many of the sentencers we interviewed. We found little statistical support for this. For example, the proportion of convictions for violence against the person,[6] sexual offences and burglary – all of which tend to attract custody – has fallen substantially. The one notable exception is a large increase in the number of convictions for drugs offences (see also Corkery, 2002).

The use of remands has increased. The adult remand population grew by a third, from 6,665 in 1991 to 8,890 in 2001. However in absolute terms the increase of just over 2,000 is dwarfed by the increase of 16,000 in the sentenced adult population; thus changes in the use of remand cannot be regarded as a significant factor behind the increase in the overall prison population.

This suggests that the main sources of the rise in the prison population are changes either in the proportion of people *sentenced* to prison (the 'flow' into prison) or changes in the length of time that people are *kept there* (which interacts with the 'flow' to create the 'stock' of people in prison). We shall examine explanations relating to stock and flow in turn. We have restricted our analysis to the adult prison population, which accounts for 84 percent of the total.

Changes in courts' custody rates

There have been very marked changes since 1991 in the custody rate – that is, the proportion of those found guilty who are given a custodial sentence. As Table 1 shows, the adult custody rate in 2001 was approaching twice the 1991 level at 28 percent. Over the same period the custody rate for magistrates' courts increased more than three times from five percent to 16 per cent. Use of custody by Crown Courts similarly rose from 46 percent to 64 percent (Home Office 2002a: 118).

Table 1. Adult custody rate at the courts★

Year	Magistrates' courts	Crown Court	All courts
	%	%	%
1991	5	46	17
1996	10	61	24
1997	11	61	25
1998	13	61	25
1999	14	63	26
2000	16	64	28
2001	16	64	28

★Persons aged 21 and over sentenced to immediate custody as a percentage of all persons of relevant age group sentenced for indictable offences.
Source: Home Office (2002a: 118).

These changes are not restricted to the adult courts. Using figures for all offenders, irrespective of age, there have been the following increases in custody rates:

	1991	2001
Burglary in a dwelling:	37%	60%
Burglary not in a dwelling:	21%	37%
Wounding Section 20 – Grievous Bodily Harm:	28%	54%
Wounding Section 47– Actual Bodily Harm:	10%	27%
Driving whilst disqualified (magistrates' courts):	18%	47%

(Figures provided by Home Office RDS)

Length of sentence passed by the courts

There have also been large changes in sentence length, though it is more complex to identify these than might be imagined. The sharp rise in the use of custody means that those who previously might have been given a community penalty are now serving short prison sentences, typically for six months or less. This has effectively masked increases in other sentence length categories. The average length of adult sentences fell from 19 months in 1991 to 15.4 months in 2001 (Home Office, 2003: 93).[7] To identify trends within different sentence length categories Table 2 divides adult sentences into three groups by length.

Table 2. Adult receptions into prison under sentence – by sentence length
(% change on 1991)

Year	Short sentences (less than 1 year)	Middle-range sentences (1 year to 4 years)	Long sentences – (4 years to life)
1991	N=19,311	N=15,112	N=3,889
	% change	% change	% change
1992	-4	-6	+4
1993	+9	-17	-3
1994	+46	-6	0
1995	+71	+1	+13
1996	+81	+10	+36
1997	+100	+16	+50
1998	+120	+20	+46
1999	+136	+17	+49
2000	+142	+14	+49
2001	+139 (N=46,146)	+13 (N=17,116)	+62 (N=6,292)

Source: Home Office (2003: 28).

The rise in prisoners with short sentences was by far the steepest, showing an increase of 139 percent from 1991 to 2001. Those with sentences of twelve months to less than four years increased by 13 percent, while those with four years to life rose by 62 percent (see Home Office, 2003: 28). It would be a misreading of Table 2 to suggest that the rise in the prison population can be attributed largely to increases in short sentences. Even if the number of short-sentence prisoners increased quickly, they may make a smaller contribution to the total prison population than those serving long sentences. A typical lifer will occupy a prison cell for the same amount of time as a hundred short-sentence offenders.[8] Thus the rise of 62 percent in sentences of four years or more will have had a very significant impact on the overall population.

Analysis of Home Office statistics relating to sentence length and offence group revealed a complicated pattern (see Home Office 1993: 85 and 97; 2003: 81). For some offence groups – e.g. theft and handling – short sentences have become proportionately more significant over the last decade. In these cases courts have probably become more likely to impose custodial rather than community penalties. Violence against the person offences showed no real change in sentence length. In this case the rise in custody has likely interacted with an increase in average sentence length, to cancel out any overall change.

Sentences have clearly become longer in cases of rape and other sexual offences. The proportion getting middle-range sentences has shrunk while the proportion getting long sentences has grown. There is a similar pattern for burglary, except that the shift has been from short sentences to middle-range ones. When all offence types are combined, the largest increase has been in long sentences at the expense of middle-range offences.

In terms of the sentencing court the most significant changes were in Crown Court decisions. For example, while the average length of male custodial sentences given by magistrates' courts showed an increase in the early 1990s, by 1997 this was back down to 1991 levels (2.6 months), and even fell slightly below this for 2000 and 2001 (2.5 months). Although magistrates' courts were sending more people to prison, the length of sentence was in fact slightly lower in 2001 than it was ten years before. The average length of custodial sentence given by the Crown Court has generally been increasing over the past decade, but especially from 1995 onwards. The average sentence given to adult males has increased by a third from 20.5 months in 1991 to 26 months in 2001 (Home Office, 2002a: 120-121). Such a large increase in Crown Court sentence length will have been a major factor in increasing the prison population.

Other factors

While the main causes behind the rise in the prison population are changes in custody rates and in sentence length, other factors have also had an impact. As mentioned above, increased use of remand has added around 2,000 to the adult prison population.

Changes in committal procedure have had some effect. The most significant change occurred immediately after introduction of the *plea before venue* procedure introduced on 1 October 1997.[9] Previously, magistrates had to decide on mode of trial without knowing how a defendant intended to plead. From October 1997 defendants charged with offences triable either way had to indicate a plea before the mode of trial decision was taken (Home Office, 1997). The result was reduction in cases sent to the Crown Court for trial, but a threefold increase in the number committed for sentence (see also Ayres and colleagues, 2000). As the Crown Court imposes heavier sentences than magistrates' courts, even when they are hearing equivalent cases (Hedderman and Moxon, 1992); the *plea before venue* procedure will have pushed up the prison population.

There have also been changes in release policy and practice that have affected the prison population. Between 1991 and 2001 the proportion of time served by adult male offenders actually decreased for shorter sentences, but increased for longer sentences. For example, adult males serving up to and including three months served 42 per cent of their sentence in 1991, but 39 per cent in 2001. Over the same period the time served by adult males serving more than ten years but less than life increased from 49 percent to 55 percent (Home Office, 1993: 92; 2003: 94). The effect of the change for longer sentences will have inflated prison numbers much more than the change for shorter sentences will have deflated them. The reasons for the increase in time served for long sentences are complex. They are partly to do with changes in the time at which prisoners became eligible for parole or conditional release (see Hood and Shute, 2000; Parole Board, 1994), and partly to do with sentencers' partial response to a Practice Directive intended to correct for this.

The situation has been further complicated by the introduction of Home Detention Curfews on 28 January 1999. With a few exceptions, most prisoners in England and Wales aged 18 or over, serving sentences less than four years – but more than three months – became eligible for early release on curfew for up to 60 days (Dodgson, Mortimer and Sugg, 2000). This had the effect of reducing the proportion of time served for shorter sentences.[10]

The growth in the use of imprisonment over the last ten years has been at the expense not of community penalty but of the fine. Since 1991 there has been a fall of almost a third in the use of fines. It is unclear whether this reflects declining confidence amongst sentencers about fine enforcement, a real reduction in offenders' ability to pay fines or the expansion of community penalties available to the courts. All three are probably implicated. Whatever the reasons, the decline in the use of fines has indirect but important consequences for the prison population. If offenders now receive community penalties earlier in their criminal careers than ten years ago, they will exhaust the alternatives to imprisonment more rapidly than previously. The proportion of offenders given community penalties that have no previous convictions has steadily risen over the last decade. For example, in 1991 11 percent of those given Community Rehabilitation Orders had no previous convictions. By 2001 this figure was 27 percent. For those given Community Punishment Orders, the figure has risen from 14 percent to 51 percent (Home Office, 2002b: 25).

Explaining sentencers' greater use of custody

We have suggested that whilst there are also other factors at work, the main reasons for the rise in the prison population are that sentencers are sending a higher proportion of offenders to prison, and that when they use custody they are passing longer sentences. Why should this have occurred? There are two competing explanations:

- defendants have longer records or have committed more serious crimes than hitherto
- sentencers have become more severe in their sentencing decisions.

It is hard to test these hypotheses definitively. Assessing whether sentencing has become more severe requires answers to hypothetical questions about the way sentencers would have treated the same cases had they heard them ten years earlier. Evidence is often circumstantial and questions about changes in persistence are hard to answer because of the complexity and relative inaccessibility of the databases needed to test out the possibilities. Also some of the arguments put by many of our respondents that 'crime has got nastier' are often not amenable to statistical measurement. It is clear, however, that the less evidence there is for the first explanation, the more support there is for the second.

Have cases appearing before the courts become more serious?

At the start of this paper we argued that there had been insufficient changes in the 'offence' mix coming before the courts to account for the scale of increase in the prison population. However, both judges and magistrates suggested to us that within particular offence categories cases had become more serious. Arguments were advanced both about the growing severity of cases within any given category of charge and about the growing length of offenders' criminal records – echoing the argument made by Lord Woolf (2001) that more prolific offending is a primary cause of the increased prison population. Both propositions were often linked to the rising prevalence of drug and alcohol misuse.

Published statistics suggest that there has been no growth in the proportion of persistent offenders appearing before the courts. In fact the proportion of court appearances for males where the offender had no previous convictions (for standard list offences) grew from 27 percent in 1993 to 42 percent in 2000 (Home Office, 1994; 2001) – a trend partly accounted for by reductions in the use of police cautions. The proportion of appearances for males with ten or more previous court appearances has fallen from 19 percent to 17 percent; the figure for females was seven percent in both years. However the figures raise as many questions as they answer. Why should there have been such a large increase in first offenders? Are a third of burglary appearances really for first offences? It is possible that a more fine-grained analysis that identified the proportion of offenders with 20 or 30 previous court appearances might shed more light on the issue of whether there is greater persistence of offending within some crime categories. For the time being, it seems that the available evidence is too inconclusive either to rule out or to confirm the hypothesis.

In one crime category – theft and handling of stolen goods – there is some evidence of a growth in persistence: 21 percent of male appearances were for offenders with ten or more previous appearances in 1993, a figure that rose to 26 percent in 2000. The equivalent figure for female appearances were seven percent and 12 percent. As noted above, the custody rate for this offence group has increased sharply. However, the relationship between prolific offending and use of custody for theft and handling is not straightforward, since the increase in the custody rate appears to be disproportionate to the increase in persistence of offending.

Although the published statistics on offenders do not provide definitive answers about the persistence of offending, there is some plausibility to sentencers' claims that they are seeing more offenders with long criminal records before the courts. This is because of the growth in dependent drug use, and the relationship between dependent drug use and offending. Recent research suggests the number of dependent drug users has increased very rapidly over the last ten years, and that there could now be upward of a quarter of a million problem drug users in Britain today (Godfrey et al., 2000; Audit Commission, 2002).[11] The links between dependent drug use and offending are strong – if complex (see Hough, 1996, Hough et al., 2002). Large proportions of arrestees test positive for heroin or cocaine at the time of arrest (Bennett, Holloway and Williams, 2001; MHA Matrix and Nacro, 2003).[12] The increase in persistence of those convicted for theft and handling is consistent with the hypothesis that there is a growing number of drug-dependent persistent offenders – as shoplifting, their preferred fund-raising strategy, is the biggest single crime category in this group of offences.

If it is correct that offending has become more prolific over the past decade, this does not necessarily contradict the observation that the overall crime rate has fallen over the same period, as depicted by the British Crime Survey and other data sources. This is because a larger proportion of crime may now be committed by a smaller pool of more persistent – and more drug-dependent – offenders.

Whether offenders are committing more serious crimes – within the same offence categories – is very hard to test, as the crime figures do not shed any light on this. A study by Lloyd and Walmsley (1989) provides a rare example of research seeking to explore how the nature of an offence – in this case rape – had changed over time and how any changes had been reflected in sentencing practice. The study concluded that in many respects the offence had changed little in terms of its 'nastiness' between 1973 and 1985 (despite the contentions of many judges and police officers that rapes were getting 'nastier'). Sentencing practice over this period had, however, become more severe. A recent paper by Ashworth (2002) on robbery illustrates the complexity of disentangling the various dimensions of this particular offence, and hence of assessing how it has changed over time.

As with arguments about more persistent offending there are reasons for thinking that offenders may be less controlled now than a decade ago – for example, if there is more drug-related offending, and if a great proportion of this offending is linked to crack rather than heroin use. Excessive use of alcohol may also play an increasing part in some crimes, particularly violent crimes. Department of Health research found that the proportion of 16 to 24-year-old men drinking more than 28 units of alcohol per week rose from 22 to 32 percent between 1993 and 2001 (DoH, 2003); and Richardson (2003) et al have observed a strong association between binge drinking and violent offending.

One possibility that deserves serious consideration is that the Crown Prosecution Service has changed its prosecution strategy over time. One way of increasing the number of guilty pleas and of improving conviction rates amongst contested trials is to prosecute under the least serious available charge – for example, prosecuting for Actual Bodily Harm rather than Grievous Bodily Harm. This strategy could clearly lead sentencers to conclude that some sorts of crime are getting nastier. To test this hypothesis one would have to examine trends in convictions for pairs of 'mutually substitutable' offences.

To summarise what can be said about change in the gravity of cases under sentence, there is some reason for thinking that sentencers are now faced with more serious cases – either in terms of criminal record or in terms of the gravity of the instant offence – than ten years ago. Certainly it would be rash and arrogant to reject out of hand sentencers' contention that this is the case. However the statistical evidence is patchy and inconsistent. Some statistics suggests that the reverse may be true. The very absence of conclusive evidence about more serious or more persistent offending suggests that the worsening nature of offending is likely to be, at best, a secondary explanation for the growth in the prison population.

Tougher sentencing
By a process of elimination we have arrived at tougher sentencing as the most probable explanation for the increased use of imprisonment. The evidence is inferential, rather than direct. We have simply demonstrated that other possible explanations are insufficient to account for the size of the rise in the prison population. However we have some confidence in this claim, in that we can point to the various mechanisms that have led to increases in severity of sentence. We shall now examine these.

What has led to tougher sentencing?

Penal commentators have tended to identify two factors that have led to increased severity of sentences (see e.g. Ashworth and Hough, 1996; Dunbar and Langdon, 1998; Hedderman, 2003; Morgan, 2003). There have been changes in the climate of political and public debate about crime and punishment, and changes in the framework of legislative and guidance within which sentencers operate. Inevitably, these have interacted with one another; the climate of opinion is likely to affect sentencers not only directly but indirectly as it results in changes in legislation or guidance.

The climate of opinion

Certainly the recent history of penal policy suggests that the climate of opinion within which sentencers work can affect their practice markedly. In October 1992 the Government implemented key provisions of the 1991 Criminal Justice Act, a piece of legislation whose guiding principle was parsimony in the use of imprisonment for non-violent offenders. Over the following three months the prison population began to fall, as indeed was the legislative intention. However 1993 saw several brutal murders, most notably that of two-year-old James Bulger. Elements of the press depicted the reforms introduced by the 1991 Act as liberal do-gooding at a time when crime was out of control. The prison population began to rise almost immediately.

In the face of such criticism the Government was quick to abandon its decarceral policy, amending the Criminal Justice Act to remove some of the new restrictions on sentencers' powers to pass prison sentences.[13] The amendments took effect in August 1993, but sentencers appear to have anticipated the legislation well before this. By October 1994 the Government had rid itself of all trace of its decarceral policies. The then Home Secretary, Michael Howard, announced a set of 27 'get tough' policies under the banner 'Prison Works'. There was little challenge from New Labour in opposition, which had positioned itself as 'tough on crime, tough on the causes of crime'. No front-bench politician from either of the main political parties has unequivocally advocated the sparing use of imprisonment since Douglas Hurd was Home Secretary in the late 1980s. When Labour took over from the Conservative administration in 1997, the prison population continued to grow.

The five senior judges whom we interviewed were unanimous in their belief both that sentencing severity had increased, and that this was a consequence of changes in the climate of opinion. One, for example, commented that the rise in the prison population had been caused by 'external pressure', that is, the public's desire to see people punished. Another said a punitive political culture has been a factor: 'Undoubtedly all the drivers from all the political parties have been for longer and longer sentences, and that feeds through. The climate is punitive.' It was also suggested that judges, at least in part, are responding to pressures from the media for tougher punishment. These views echo those expressed by Lord Bingham, the then Lord Chief Justice, in 1998: 'Since 1993 the use of custody has increased very sharply, in response (it would seem likely) to certain highly publicised cases, legislation, ministerial speeches and intense media pressure.'[14]

Crown Court judges and recorders similarly referred to greater severity of sentencing, but were more likely than senior judges to claim that the changes were restricted to specific offence categories such as drug supply, sexual offences and causing death by dangerous driving. Several referred to pressures from politicians and the media in terms similar to those of senior judges. For example, one noted that there is a public 'clamour' for custody in relation to street crime. Another commented that sentencing practice has firmed up in response to the efforts by each successive government to demonstrate that it is tougher on crime that those that went before. And a third said that judges may be less lenient than in the past because of fears of criticism in the press:

> I think that there's much more attention in the press to the sentences that are passed. And whereas in the past, perhaps, people might have taken a very lenient course, it may be that fear of attracting extremely bad publicity for taking a lenient course means that sentences that pander to that, to a certain extent, are passed.

Surprisingly, in the light of findings presented earlier in this paper, district judges and magistrates were less inclined than the other sentencers to talk about sentencing practice becoming more severe. (It will be remembered that over the ten years from 1991 the custody rate for magistrates' courts increased more than three times from five percent to 16 per cent.) Only two of the 14 district judges interviewed referred to increased severity, and in most of the magistrates' focus groups there was general agreement that there has been little or no change in sentencing practice by magistrates in recent years. Some of the magistrates insisted that their own practice had remained constant, and pointed the finger elsewhere – at the severity of district judges and of Crown Court sentencers. This latter finding is understandable given the rarity with which lay magistrates *individually* pass custodial sentences: many said that several months could elapse without them doing so. However, magistrates were not unanimous in saying that their practice had remained unchanged; members of one bench were explicit about their growing use of custody, and in two of the other focus groups there was some suggestion that there had been a toughening up of sentencing practice. In general however district judges and magistrates tended to recognise political and media pressures for tougher punishment, whilst claiming that they were well able to resist this pressure.

The legislative framework and sentencing guidance

Sentencing decisions are not made in a vacuum, of course. Many changes in sentencing practice come about as a direct result of changes to the legislative framework or to the guidance given to sentencers.

The maximum sentences for offences are set out in statute; and whilst the maximum is rarely reached, changes to the legislation are taken as an indication of the intentions of the legislature in calling for heavier (or lighter) penalties. Increasingly, legislation is also tending to set out mandatory minimum sentences in specified circumstances. Court of Appeal guideline judgements further shape and contain sentencers' discretion. Finally, the Magistrates Association has since the mid-1990s issued several versions of a manual setting out sentencing guidelines for use in magistrates' courts.

Leaving aside the 1991 and 1993 Criminal Justice Acts, the key relevant legislative changes over the period covered by this study are:

- The extension of prosecutorial appeals against sentence to certain either-way offences in 1994 (following their introduction for indictable only offences in 1988)

- The introduction of the offence of aggravated vehicle taking in 1992, with tougher penalties for 'joyriding'
- The doubling of the maximum sentence for causing death by dangerous driving and related offences in the Criminal Justice Act 1993
- The mandatory minimum prison terms introduced by the Crime (Sentences) Act 1997, and implemented in 1999, for third-time drug traffickers and burglars
- The introduction of automatic life sentences for a second serious violent or sexual assault following the Crime (Sentences) Act 1997
- The introduction of racially aggravated offences in the Crime and Disorder Act 1998
- Raising of the maximum sentence for incitement of racial hatred from 2 years to 7 years.

Most of these changes were targeted on specific offence categories, some of which are numerically small. Moreover, the provisions for mandatory minimum sentences were restricted to those with relevant previous convictions – an even smaller sub-group of offenders. The overall impact on the prison population might thus be thought to be limited. However the changes are likely to have had knock-on effects on other types of crime. The more that sentencers aim to achieve proportionality in their sentencing – with offences of similar gravity and culpability receiving similar sentences – the more marked these knock-on effects will be (cf. Woolf, 2002). It is also significant that all these legislative changes have created pressure in the same upward direction on the prison population.

There were also some significant guideline judgements in the 1990s and the establishment of the Sentencing Advisory Panel in 1999 generated further guideline judgements. Significant ones related to causing death by dangerous driving (in support of the legislative change) and to rape. Prominent recent guidelines include those laid down by the Lord Chief Justice in January 2002 relating to the use of custody for mobile phone robberies.[15] Judgements covering many other types of crime were also made. As has been observed by Dunbar and Langdon, it is generally believed that the Court of Appeal – because of the nature of its workload and the previous experiences of its judges – 'operates the highest tariff of all and ... takes a view of less serious offences that is markedly more severe than the view of the lower courts' (1998: 69).

Of course not all guideline judgements will push up the prison population. Influential judgements by the Court of Appeal in *Ollerenshaw* (1999), *Mills* and *Kefford* (both 2002) and *McInerney* and *Keating* (2002) encouraged judges to use prison sentences sparingly, with reference to prison capacity, and only when the offender had demonstrated by his behaviour that punishment in the community was not practicable.[16] In June 2002, the Home Secretary and Lord Chancellor issued a joint statement in which they 'welcomed guidance from the Lord Chief Justice' which stressed the importance of keeping prison as a last resort, and 'stressed the suitability of alternatives to custody in many cases'.[17]

Changes in legislation and in guideline judgements were often salient in the minds of those Crown Court judges and recorders we interviewed; and a few of the sentencers talked in terms of proofing their decisions against prosecutorial appeals against sentence. It was suggested that guideline judgements, in combination with the possibility of prosecutorial appeal, served to draw lenient judges' decisions up to the guideline level, whilst leaving those of tougher judges unchanged. And as with legislative change, one would expect guideline judgements for specific crime types to have a knock-on effect on other crimes, given the priority placed by sentencers on achieving parity and proportionality.[18] This is likely to happen whether the guideline judgement in question is concerned with the decision to imprison or the decision about sentence length.

Court of Appeal guideline judgements generally have limited relevance for magistrates, and for this reason the Magistrates Association has developed its own sentencing guidelines. These were first introduced in the 1970s for motoring offences, but in 1989 were extended to cover most offences dealt with by magistrates. The guidelines have since been further developed and reissued. Some of the magistrates in the study argued that these guidelines had had an inflationary effect on the prison population. This was partly because some of the 'entry points' – or recommended sentences for typical cases – were higher in the guidelines than in previous practice, or were adjusted upwards as new versions of the guidelines were issued. For example, the starting point for actual bodily harm assaults was raised from community service in the 1993 version of the guidelines to a short custodial sentence in the 1997 guidelines. It is also likely that, as with Court of Appeal guideline judgements, the Magistrates'

Association guidelines draw lenient benches up to the recommended norm, whilst leaving the decisions of tougher benches untouched.

Summary and conclusions

Knowledge about factors driving up the adult prison population remains frustratingly sketchy. It can be said with certainty that the increase is *not* a product of rising crime. Nor are more people passing through the courts now than a decade ago. Rather, sentencers are making greater use of imprisonment than a decade ago and, when they do so, they tend to pass longer sentences.

This article has attempted to analyse whether these trends reflect tougher decision-making, or more serious crimes and more culpable offenders, or both. The evidence is circumstantial but persuasive, nevertheless, that sentencers have toughened up over the last decade – with the result that, as has been observed by Morgan (2003: 14) among others, 'more and more offenders are getting mired deeper and deeper within the criminal justice system for doing less and less'. This is in part a reflection of changes in the climate of opinion in which sentencers work, and partly a function of the legislative framework and guidance within which they operate. Legislation, guideline judgements and sentence guidelines have all had an inflationary effect.

It remains unclear whether the offenders appearing before the courts now tend to have longer criminal careers and commit more serious crimes than a decade ago. The statistical evidence for this is weak, but the views of sentencers themselves are strongly held and convincing to a degree – especially in the light of the growing prevalence of problematic drug and alcohol use. There is probably something in this argument, given the links between dependent drug use and offending, and between excessive alcohol consumption and violent crime; further research is clearly needed to test it out more thoroughly, but we would be surprised if this research were to show that a *large* part of the increase in the prison population could be attributed to changes in the severity of offences or criminal records.

In assessing sentencers' claims that tougher sentences reflect more serious offending, a sceptic would argue that 'they would say that, wouldn't they'. As is discussed in Hough, Jacobson and Millie (2003) sentencers firmly believe that they use custody only as an absolute last resort, and that they are not unduly swayed by the general climate of opinion. From such a viewpoint – claiming consistency of practice – a 'last resort' in 1991 cannot be qualitatively different from one in 2001. Accordingly, sentencers will be inclined to cite changes in crime, rather than changes in their own decision-making and the framework within which this occurs, as the main determinant of sentencing trends.

In summary, the argument presented here is that the rise in the prison population is due to sentencers passing more custodial sentences, and passing longer sentences when they opt for custodial sentences. The main factors behind this are likely to be the following:
- A more punitive climate of opinion
- A more punitive legislative framework
- Guideline judgements and sentencing guidelines that counteract leniency
- Some changes in patterns of offending
- Sentencers' perceptions of changes in patterns of offending.

Can the ever-upward trend in the prison population be halted? Whether the growth of the prison population should be contained is a political decision that falls beyond the boundaries of this study. But if there is some political will to do so, then success in reducing prison numbers will depend on changes both to sentencing practice and to the context in which sentencing is carried out.

One approach that has been tried by successive governments is to provide sentencers with a wider and more attractive range of community penalties. This may go *some* way to reducing prison numbers. However sentencers in this study did not say that they were using prison for want of adequate non-custodial options. The enhancement of community penalties could simply result in 'net-widening' – where the new sentences are used with offenders who would previously have been fined, or served a conventional community penalty.

Encouraging the use of fines could prove a sensible option. This would relieve pressure on the probation service; in terms of outcomes it could at best deflect some offenders entirely from further offending without resort to imprisonment or community penalties; and at worst it could defer the point in their criminal career where prison becomes inevitable.

The analysis presented here suggests that policies to contain the prison population should involve three levels of intervention:

• Adjustment to the legal and legislative framework of sentencing, so as to bring down custody rates and sentence lengths.

• Softening of the climate of political and public opinion on crime and punishment, so that sentencers feel at liberty to make more sparing use of custody, and greater use of the alternatives to custody.

• Improving understanding of the range of non-custodial penalties – including the fine – both among sentencers and the wider public.

However, none of these interventions is likely to meet with much success unless there is clear political will to stop the uncontrolled growth in prison numbers, and visible, consistent, political leadership in stressing the need to do so. As one senior judge neatly expressed it: 'The question for [Government] is pretty clear: do you really want to bring down the prison population – I mean, do you actually want to *do it* as opposed to want to *say that you'll do it?*'

Notes

1. We would like to express our gratitude to the Esmée Fairbairn Foundation, which funded this study under its Rethinking Crime and Punishment programme. Further findings are reported in Hough, Jacobson and Millie (2003).

2. Sources: 1991 (Home Office 2003); 2003 (HM Prison Service, 2003. www.hmprisonservice.gov.uk/statistics).

3. Attempts have been made to compare different countries' use of imprisonment in relation to their crime rates, rather than their overall populations. These show England and Wales in a slightly more favourable light. However this is at least in part because the police in England and Wales tend to record crime more fully than in many other countries, artificially inflating the rate's denominator. The problems in deriving genuinely comparable statistics on this basis are considerable. Research reported in Tonry and Frase (2001) suggested that variations in the imprisonment rate in different countries are to be explained not by variations in crime rates but through differences in sentencing policy and practice.

4. Among the district judges interviewed, four were also recorders, but for the purposes of analysis, these sentencers are included in the district judge category. For full details of methodology see Hough, Jacobson and Millie (2003).

5. A more detailed analysis of the available sentencing and prison statistics is provided in Hough, Jacobson and Millie (2003).

6. Some of this will reflect a charging standard for assault introduced on 31 August 1994 which moved some offences to summary common assault.

7. Figures exclude those sentenced to life imprisonment.

8. Assuming that the lifer serves about 13 years, and that the average sentence in magistrates courts is about three months, with six weeks actually served.

9. Section 49 of the Criminal Procedure and Investigations Act 1996 (with provisions for committal for sentence contained in section 51 of the Crime (Sentences) Act 1997) – Home Office (1997).

10. Practice Statement (Crime: Sentencing) [1992] 1 WLR. This recognised that '…sentences on the 'old' scale would under the 'new' Act result in many prisoners actually serving longer in custody than hitherto'. It recommended an approach where Crown Court sentencers take the 'actual period likely to be served' into

account along with the risk of increasing sentence length following the Act. However, despite this, the average length of sentence given by the Crown Court continued to rise, suggesting no generalised impact from the Practice Statement (see also Henham, 1996).

11. The Audit Commission work draws on Regional Drug Misuse (RDM) data to illustrate this growth. The rise in drug agencies workloads, as reflected by RDM data, will partly reflect an increase in treatment capacity, but the rise is so large that it is unlikely to be a statistical artefact.

12. See also Hammersley, Marsland and Reid, (2003) on substance use among young offenders.

13. The amendments in the 1993 Criminal Justice Act did little more than clarify the law about 'sentencing on record', reverting to the position prior to the 1991 Act; but they had a symbolic importance in signalling a move away from the philosophy of the 1991 Act.

14. *Brewster* [1998] 1 Cr App R (S) 181, at p. 184.

15. Attorney-General's Reference Nos. 4 and 7 of 2002, and Q [2002] 2 Cr App R (SS) 77. The Youth Justice Board Annual Review of 2001/2 notes that there was a significant rise in numbers of young offenders in custody following the Lord Chief Justice's judgement on mobile phone robberies.

16. *Ollerenshaw* [1999] 1 Cr App R (S) 65; *Kefford* [2002] 2 Cr App R (S) 495; *Mills* (unreported 14 January 2002); *McInerney and Keating* [2002] EWCA Crim 3003

17. LCD Press Notices 194/02.

18. The principle of parity means that guideline judgements about sentence length will have an impact on the custody threshold, and judgements about the custody threshold will have an impact on sentence length.

References

Ashworth, A. (2002) 'Robbery Re-assessed', *Criminal Law Review*, November 2002, pp851-72.

—, and Hough, M. (1996) 'Sentencing and the Climate of Opinion', *Criminal Law Review* pp761-848.

Audit Commission (2002) *Changing Habits: The Commissioning and Management of Drug Treatment Services for Adults*, Briefing February 2002, London: Audit Commission.

Ayres, M. and colleagues (2000) *Cautions, Court Procedure and Sentencing England and Wales 1999*. Home Office Statistical Bulletin Issue 19/00. London: Home Office.

Bennett, T., Holloway, K. and Williams, T. (2001) *Drug Use and Offending: Summary Results from the First Year of the NEW-ADAM Research Programme*, Home Office Research Findings 148, London: Home Office.

Corkery, J. (2002) *Drug Seizure and Offender Statistics, United Kingdom, 2000*. London: Home Office.

Department of Health (2003) *Health Survey of England*, http://www.doh.gov.uk/stats/trends1.htm

Dodgson, K., Mortimer, E. and Sugg, D. (2000) *Assessing Prisoners for Home Detention Curfew: A Guide for Practitioners. RDS Practitioners Guide 1*. London: Home Office.

Dunbar, I. and Langdon, A. (1998) *Tough Justice: Sentencing and Penal Policies in the 1990s*, London: Blackstone.

Godfrey, C., Eaton, G., McDougall, C. and Culyer, A. (2002) *The Economic and Social Costs of Class A Drug Use in England and Wales, 2000*. Home Office Research Study 249. London: Home Office.

Hammersley, R., Marsland, L. and Reid, M. (2003) *Substance Use by Young Offenders*, Home Office Research Findings 192, London: Home Office.

Hedderman, C. (2003) 'Why are More Women Being Sentenced to Custody?' In G. McIvor, (ed.) *Women Who Offend*. London: Jessica Kingsley.

—, and Moxon, D. (1992) *Magistrates' court or Crown Court? Mode of Trial Decisions and Sentencing*. Home Office Research Study 125. London: Home Office.

Henham, R. (1996) 'Truth in Sentencing: Some Problems of Enforcement Strategy', *Web Journal of Current Legal Issues*, 1996 (Issue 3), http://webjcli.ncl.ac.uk/1996/issue3/henham3.htm

Home Office (1992) *Criminal Statistics England and Wales 1991*, London: HMSO.

—, (1993) *Prison Statistics England and Wales 1991*, London: HMSO.

—, (1994) *Criminal Statistics England and Wales 1993*, London: HMSO.

—, (1997) *Section 49 of The Criminal Procedure and Investigations Act 1996 and Section 51 of The Crime (Sentences) Act 1997*. Home Office Circular 45/1997. London: Home Office.

—, (2001) *Criminal Statistics England and Wales 2000*, London: HMSO.

—, (2002a) *Criminal Statistics England and Wales 2001*, London: TSO.

—, (2002b) *Probation Statistics England and Wales 2001*. London: Home Office.

—, (2003) *Prison Statistics England and Wales 2001*, London: TSO.

Hood, R. and Shute, S. (2000) *The Parole System at Work: A Study of Risk Based Decision-Making*. Home Office Research Study 202. London: Home Office.

Hough, M. (1996) *Problem Drug Use and Criminal Justice: A Review of the Literature. Drugs Prevention Initiative paper No. 15*. London: Home Office Central Drugs Prevention Unit.

—, Jacobson, J. and Millie, A. (2003) *The Decision to Imprison: Sentencing and the Prison Population*. London: Prison Reform Trust.

—, McSweeney T. and Turnbull, P. (2002) *Drugs and Crime: What are the Links? Evidence to the Home Affairs Committee Inquiry into Drug Policy*. London: DrugScope.

Lloyd, C. and Walmsley, R. (1989) *Changes in Rape Offences and Sentencing*, Home Office Research Study 105, London: Home Office.

MHA Matrix and Nacro (2003) *Evaluation of Drug Testing in the Criminal Justice*

System in Nine Pilot Areas. Home Office Research Findings 180, London: Home
Office.

Morgan, R. (2003), 'Thinking about the Demand for Probation Services', *Probation Journal*, 50 (1), pp7-19.

Parole Board (1994) *Report of the Parole Board for 1993 (HC 450)*. London: HMSO.

Richardson, A., Budd, T., Engineer, R., Phillips, A., Thompson, J. and Nicholls, J.
(2003) *Drinking, Crime and Disorder*, Home Office Research Findings 185,
London: Home Office

Simmons, J. and colleagues (2002) *Crime in England and Wales 2001/2*. Home Office
Statistical Bulletin 7/02.London: Home Office.

Tonry, M. and Frase, R. (2001) *Sentencing and Sanctions in Western Countries*. Oxford:
Oxford University Press.

Walmsley, R. (2003) *World Prison Population List (fourth edition)*, Home Office
Research Findings 188, London: Home Office.

Woolf, Lord (2001) *Restorative Justice*, Speech to the Youth Justice Board, Church
House Conference Centre, London, 25 October 2001.

—, (2002) *Achieving Criminal Justice*, The 2nd Rose Lecture, Manchester Town Hall,
29 October 2002.

Chapter Five

Consuming Crime and Avoiding Punishment: Media Influence in the Shaping of Public Perceptions of Crime and Sentencing

Marie Gillespie and Eugene McLaughlin

Introduction

This chapter is divided into two main parts. In the first part we outline current trends in news media reporting of crime and its relationship to policy-making. We examine current research into crime and the news media, particularly its role in setting the agenda of public and policy debate. We show how news reporting of crime is a highly selective process bound by rituals and conventions. We examine what constitutes 'newsworthy crime' and recent trends towards the 'tabloidisation' of criminal justice issues and policy-making.

Our argument is that the media play an increasingly central role in informing citizens. In western societies we now live in 'media democracies' in which politics and policy are largely debated and negotiated, enacted and performed through, with and by media. News audiences and readerships are constituted as and by 'publics'. However, the phenomenal popularity of crime fiction and the hyper realism of crime on film and television suggest that we need also to examine further their role in shaping knowledge, values and beliefs about the criminal justice system. How crime media are consumed, read and interpreted is highly significant to how public knowledge of the criminal justice system is constructed and acted upon by media consumer-citizens.

The first part of this chapter sets the context and background and part two reports on a small-scale empirical project which addresses precisely the question of how audiences use and interpret crime news. Drawing upon rich empirical data gathered in focus group discussions, we test and challenge some common assumptions about media influence and impact. Our data shows that while consuming crime, in both fictional and factual media, is popular and pervasive, avoiding questions of punishment and ignoring sentencing issues is common. This can be explained partly by the way that the stories are told. As one informant said, 'Crime is sexy, punishment is boring.' It would seem from our data that there is a 'structured absence' of any sustained interest in, attention to or debate about sentencing and punishment except in sensationalised cases of leniency. This has important implications for how public knowledge and debate are constituted and framed, how policy is formed, and how 'media democracies' function.

Part One

Living in a high crime society?

Criminologists have come to the conclusion that high crime rates should be regarded as one of the defining feature of late modern societies, such as the United Kingdom (see, Garland, 2000; Hope and Sparks, 2000; Reiner, 2000; Young, 1999). Although victimisation continues to be unevenly distributed, with the poorest sections of society suffering disproportionately, within a relatively short period of time, 'crime' has become a prominent reality for 'middle England'. Reiner's (2000) examination of crime trends in England and Wales notes that from the 1870s to the early 1920s crime rates remained just under 100,000 offences recorded by the police per annum. Subsequently, recorded crime rates rose relentlessly despite being punctuated by brief periods of slight decline. Since the early 1920s the average increase in the crime rate has been consistently around 5 per cent. By 1950 the police were recording 500,000 crimes per year. Although this fell slightly in the early 1950s, from 1955 the statistics began to record increases almost every year until the 1990s.

The rate of recorded crime grew to unprecedented levels in the early 1990s. By 1971 the annual total was 1.6 million, in 1980 2.5 million and in 1992 it was 5.4 million. This was followed by a period of decline with the recorded crime rate falling from 5.4 million in 1993/4 to 4.5 million in 1997/8. Since then England and Wales has witnessed significant falls in recorded crime. The 2001 British Crime Survey noted that the crime rate in England and Wales fell by 12 per cent in 2000, with the chance of becoming a victim being the lowest recorded for more than 20 years. However, given that the survey estimates that almost 13 million crimes were committed in 2000 a significant cross section of the population have been either personally victimised, witnessed a crime or are aware of family, friends or neighbours who have been victimised. As Garland (2000: 360) notes, 'crime' has ceased to be a statistical abstraction and has taken on 'a vivid meaning in popular consciousness and individual psychology'.

We have also become more aware of new forms and 'mixes' of crime and disorder resultant from social, economic and cultural changes. Late modern societies are witnessing, as Jock Young (1999) has noted, a complicated double movement of increased intolerance and tolerance. The public is increasingly intolerant of violence and this has generated demands for more order. At the same moment there is considerable ambiguity about what constitutes 'crime' and 'deviance'. For example, sections of the public seem more willing to flout the law openly particularly with regard to soft and recreational drug use.

Criminologists have identified the following shifts that have taken place as a result of the shift to a high crime society. First, the issue of crime now occupies a permanent place in electoral politics and is publicly debated in highly emotive terms. The new politics of law and order has politicians protecting themselves from the allegation that they are 'soft on crime' by promising more police and punishment in return for electoral votes. Second, public concern focuses on the experience and needs of crime victims and this has begun to dominate the thinking of both politicians and criminal justice policy makers. Third, there seems to be considerably less public sympathy for the needs of 'the offender'. What Roberts et al (2003) define as 'penal populism' is particularly notable when it comes to public attitudes about what to do with sex offenders and violent criminals. Fourth, the criminal justice system is viewed with ever greater public scepticism especially with regard to its perceived balance and effectiveness. Fifth, an extensive private security and crime prevention market has emerged. Sixth, the fear of crime has become a social problem in its own right and it is not necessarily related to the reality of crime (Altheide and Michalowski, 1999). Finally, a narrative of decline and deep sense of 'the world we have lost' has been constructed around the belief that 'we are safe no more'.

Consequently, the social and psychological investment that individuals have in issues of crime and punishment has expanded considerably (Garland, 2000: 368). 'Crime' and the fear of crime now exercise a significant influence on what we might describe as the 'deepest routines' of everyday life. In addition, fear of and anger about crime and disorder has begun to impact directly upon the possibility or indeed willingness for reasoned, informed public debate on the crime problem.

However, citizens in high crime societies have what could be described as a 'love-hate' relationship with crime. The public's very real fear of crime is accompanied by a fascination with all things criminal (Taylor, 1999). Crime related news stories are amongst the most widely reported and commented upon, providing more column inches and viewing hours than almost any other issue. As we shall see later in this chapter, many of our most popular entertainment shows are constructed directly or indirectly around crime storylines. Beckett (1997) has noted that it is difficult to determine whether the public's enthusiasm for crime stories is a consequence of their ubiquity or whether crime stories are ubiquitous because the public relishes them. What is not in dispute is that, given the extent and nature of the coverage, the news and entertainment media are a primary source of public information about the state of crime and the purpose and functioning of the criminal justice system (see Braak, 1994; Kidd-Hewitt and Osborne, 1995; Surette, 1998; Krajicek, 1998)

The nightmare crimes that set the criminal justice agenda
Given the fact that the vast majority of crimes are mundane and equally significantly unreported what type of crime is deemed to be newsworthy? Research across a variety of jurisdictions indicates that violence dominates news cover-

age. Krajicek (1998) concludes that the majority of news media space devoted to the reporting of crime concentrates on serious crimes such as murder, forcible rape, aggravated assault, and armed robbery; in other words, on crimes that impact viscerally and can lodge in public consciousness. The concentration on comparatively rare violent serious crimes is most pronounced in tabloid and mid-market rather than broadsheet newspapers and on radio and television news (Schlesinger et al 1991). Other kinds of crime such as white collar or political crime are largely ignored by comparison. Although serious crime will attract substantial coverage across all news media outlets, the intensity of coverage will be determined by events 'outside' the crime such as how it connects to other news media concerns and the absence/presence of competing news items. While the majority of serious cases may generate high levels of news media coverage, particularly during the first few days, some serious offences, such as white collar crime and political crime, are not considered newsworthy (Dowden, 2004).

Various factors have been found to influence the intensity of news media interest. First, the characteristics of the offender are important. Serious violent crimes committed by 'strangers' are more likely to be reported than those committed by acquaintances or intimates (Chermak, 1994; Dahlgreen 1998; Chiricos et al, 2000). As a result criminal offenders are typically portrayed as 'dangerous predators' rather than as friends and family members. Research suggests that these 'dangerous predators' have come to be depicted as ever more vicious while their crimes are presented as more violent and unpredictable (Surette, 1998). Cases of sexual violence deemed to be the most 'newsworthy' are almost exclusively ones involving strangers. This coverage reinforces the notion that sex crimes are committed by sick, irrational individuals and both reflect and perpetuate the myth that sexual violence is not committed by known and trusted individuals (Benedict, 1992). Female violence is newsworthy because of the gender of the offender rather than the crime she has committed. It exemplifies everything that challenges not only our conception of crime but dominant notions about gender roles (Howe, 1998; Naylor, 2001).

Second, to achieve sustained sympathetic coverage, victims have to fit a particular stereotype of the 'ideal victim'. The ideal crime victim is white, female and respectable when the statistics tell us that young, working-class males experience the highest rates of victimisation (Reiner, 2000). Tabloid and mid-market anti-drugs campaigns in the UK have been constructed around a similar type of 'young, white, female' victims such as Leah Betts (1995), Lorna Spinks (2001) and Rachael Whitear (2002). Third, access to sensational details of 'the crime' also guarantees coverage. Violent serious crime is most likely to generate such details. This focus means that relatively little attention is paid to contextualising the crime (Reiner, 1997). Highly emotive news coverage of child sexual abuse for example typically ignores issues of gender and power and highlights instead the pathology of individual perpetrators or the failure of social workers in particular cases. Similarly coverage of public disorder and riots tend to depict such disorder as instances of mass criminality and ignore larger structural and political forces. The focus is not on what caused riots but the threat posed and need for condemnation and hard action to prevent reoccurrence.

The news media also stand accused of playing a key role in the racialisation of certain forms of crime (Hall et al 1978; Barlow, 1998; Dixon, 2000; McLaughlin and Murji, 2001; Romer, 1998; 2002) This takes several forms. News stories in which black people are accused of crimes are more likely to be highlighted if they involve violence, sex or drugs. In the USA evidence suggests that black people charged with violent offences are often depicted differently than whites charged with violent offences. The overall effect is to make black people accused of crimes appear more violent and menacing than whites accused of comparable offences. Equally significantly, black crime against whites is much more likely to be reported than white crime against blacks. Coverage of 'street crime' is racialised to such an extent that 'mugging' in the UK now automatically denotes 'black youth'.

There are of course marked variations between different sections of the news media and markets, between print and broadcast media and tabloid, mid-level and broadsheet newspapers. For example, crime stories are more likely to be framed thematically in terms of causes and possible remedies in the broadsheets and commentary sections of newspapers (Sasson, 1995). The tabloids are more likely to opt for single factor 'something must be done now' explanations. In liberal broadsheets we are more likely to see connections being made between crime and social deprivation whereas right wing papers are more likely to focus on family breakdown, poor parenting, gang culture, the permissive society, the role of popular culture in glamorising crime or the failures of the criminal justice policy, such as lenient judges and legal technicalities.

But the overall conclusion of these studies is that the highly selective nature of crime reporting should be a cause for concern just as much as the extent of coverage. Core sections of the news media stand accused of using high profile and sensational crimes to:

- misinform the public on the nature of crime, criminal justice policies, sentencing practices and the realities of prison;
- orchestrate 'moral panics' about particular crimes and categories of offenders;
- create and/or reinforce unwarranted public fears;
- exaggerate the degree of public support for incarceration and opposition to rehabilitation, treatment and alternatives to imprisonment and;
- force politicians to commit themselves to ever increasing expenditure on law and order and punitive sentencing policies.

Constructing newsworthy crime

A key task for criminologists is examining why the news media opts for such a punitive construction of the crime problem. The following factors have been identified as crucial. First, journalists define as 'newsworthy' stories that are out of the ordinary (Ericson, et al 1991; Hall, et al, 1978; Schlesinger and Tumber, 1994) By definition, criminal events, particularly violent serious crimes, lie at the extremes of human behaviour. Because they violate widely held societal norms and values they require a punitive response. Second, the tendency of journalists to rely on law enforcement agents, politicians and government officials for information also influences the framing of crime news. Journalists prefer official sources because they are defined as authoritative and lend legitimacy to the reporting. Official sources are also able to supply journalists with a steady diet of appropriately formatted and timely information; a necessity in the deadline driven world of the news media (Beckett, 1997; Chermak, 1994; Gans, 1979). Increasingly, well-funded, proactive press departments of criminal justice agencies consciously attempt to impose their primary definition of events and incidents (Ericson et al, 1991; Schlesinger and Tumber, 1994). Although not all of their efforts are successful, in the normal course of things official agencies are relatively successful in their attempt to shape the news. The police retain a particularly privileged position in the news media's coverage of crime (Crandon, 1992; 1997; Boyle, 1999; Perlmutter, 2000). A police statement declaring that the criminal justice system is letting down crime victims will receive maximum attention. The reluctance of journalists to depend on non-official sources means that the range of perspectives on crime, criminal justice and sentencing depicted in the news media remains narrow. In privileging the perspective of authorised sources the news media also reinforce a law and order perspective.

Third, news organisations currently operate in a highly competitive, 24/7 environment and are under constant pressure to increase market share and advertising revenue. The provision of information from the press liaison departments of law enforcement agencies means that crime stories can be produced inexpensively, quickly and regularly and on the basis of authoritative, legitimate sources (Schlesinger and Tumber, 1994; Mawby, 1999). The tabloidisation of mainstream news media operations means that crime is no longer confined to the outer or extreme limits of public debate. This shift has changed the conventions of crime reporting from public information to entertainment and created an insatiable appetite for exclusives and new angles and institutionalised fear of being scooped by rivals (Krajicek, 1998). Equally significantly, this tabloid sensitivity has produced a new wave of reality based shows consisting of detailed crime re-enactments and/or live footage of police raids on criminals. The rise of 'real crime' programming has increasingly blurred the boundaries between documentary and drama, public information and mass entertainment (Hamilton, 1998).

The tabloidisation of criminal justice policy making

A constant concern of researchers has been to examine the ability of the news media to not only influence public opinion on crime and punishment but to define the criminal justice agenda (Surette, 1998). There is of course considerable difficulty in constructing a conceptual model that manages to capture the essence of the relationship between news media's portrayal of crime and audience response. The traditional 'effects model' presented a view of the audience more or less uncritically accepting the news media's portrayal of the crime problem. A second version views the news media's representation of crime as enhancing the power of those with a vested interest in the status quo. 'Moral panics' function to exaggerate personal risks, fuel public anxiety and strengthen the case for punitive law and order measures (Hall, et al, 1978; Scheingold, 1995; Thompson, 1998). Empirical research has been dominated by studies examining the relationship between news media coverage of crime and the public's fear of crime. Gerbner's et al (1994) research, for example, coined the term 'mean world' syndrome to describe how heavy viewers of television violence feel that their neighbourhoods are unsafe, state that crime is a serious personal problem and assume that crime is rising irrespective of the facts. As a result they are more willing to support harsh crime control measures.

In this context, there is mounting evidence to suggest that in high crime societies politicians, criminal justice professionals, pressure groups and journalists work on the assumption that the news media not only has a significant impact on the beliefs and attitudes of a heterogeneous public regarding the problem of crime and criminal justice policy and processes, but in certain instances directly represents public opinion. Furthermore, there is a sense in which the tabloids not only set the crime agenda for other newspapers but also the broadcast news media. This 'tabloidisation of crime' also has an influence on the entertainment media. A plethora of ever more realistic crime dramas, documentaries and crime reconstruction shows has been fuelled by the rapid expansion of multichannel television. In addition, in the words of the cultural commentator Julie Burchill (2003), the UK's prime time soaps (*Eastenders* and *Coronation Street*) have been turned into high ratings 'crime capers'. This is why the government is thinking of investing unprecedented resources and time to influence or indeed manage news media coverage of particular crime initiatives and criminal justice policies (Schlesinger and Tumber, 1994; Hough and Roberts, 1999; Roberts et al, 2003). Of particular concern to policy makers and penal reform groups in the UK is the seemingly endless ability of newspapers, particularly the tabloids and mid-market papers, to orchestrate high profile campaigns to mobilise and focus public concern around a particular issue and to pressurise the government of the day to account for its anti-crime policies in very specific ways. In this sense the most populist sections of the news media are not only reporting criminal justice policy and practice but also *making* and *unmaking* it in highly emotive and sensational ways.

A powerful example of what we might call the 'melodramatic excess' of crime reporting is the outcome of the intense tabloid reporting of eight-year-old Sarah Payne's abduction through to the trial of the suspect. The *News of the World* in July 2000 decided to carry, with the support of the parents, a picture of Sarah Payne on its front page next to a pledge to 'name and shame' every convicted child sex offender in the UK. This 'naming and shaming' spearheaded a campaign to pressurise the government to pass legislation ('Sarah's Law') to ensure that violent and sexual offenders are given an automatic life sentence if they posed a threat to the public. The newspaper called off its campaign as a result of the police expressing concern that it would trigger a public witch-hunt for sex offenders. However, in December 2001, in the aftermath of the conviction of Roy Whiting for the murder, the *News of the World* resumed its campaign this time with the support of the Metropolitan Police and a promise from David Blunkett, the Home Secretary, that tougher sentences, stricter monitoring and community participation in decision making would be forthcoming. Those who argued that the murder of children by strangers is exceedingly rare were sidelined by the *News of the World* campaign, as was the fact that most child killing, like most child abuse, is perpetrated by relatives.

In the first months of 2002 the tabloids were at the forefront of an intense campaign to force the government to act decisively against what they defined as 'spiralling street crime'. Relentless news media coverage took the form of melodramatic front pages, outraged editorials and double page specials on rising gun crime, stabbings, muggings, anti-social behaviour, hooliganism and 'new' crimes such as mobile phone thefts and car-jackings. In addition, major newspapers produced 'street crime specials'. The London *Evening Standard*'s 'Fight Street Crime' was accompanied by the *Daily Mirror*'s 'Crime UK/Crime 2002', the *Sun*'s 'Crusade Against Crime', the *Daily Mail*'s 'Wild West UK', and the *Daily Express*'s 'Is Britain safe in 2002?'. As the tabloid crime crisis offensive unfolded, incorporating a range of concerns and incidents, opinion polls indicated that crime had emerged as the single most damaging electoral issue for the government. The Home Office minister John Denham's public admission that he was personally concerned about the increase in street crime in January 2002 was reinforced by David Blunkett's admission that Britain's streets were unsafe.

'Blunkett: Muggers rule our streets' (*Sun*, 18 March 2002)
'Street crime spiralling out of control' (*Daily Telegraph*, 18 March 2002)
'Blunkett: It's not safe to walk the streets' (*Daily Mail*, 18 March 2002)
'Scared to walk the streets' (*Daily Express*, 18 March, 2002)

This ensured saturation coverage of Tony Blair's hastily convened Downing Street 'Crime Summit' on 20 March 2002 and the startling pledge from the Prime Minister in the House of Commons on the 23 April that 'street crime' would be brought under control by the end of September 2002.

What is equally significant for this chapter is that tabloid and mid-market newspaper editorials and commentaries were scathing about the government's list of 'get tough' measures to tame 'unruly kids' and 'feckless' parents and 'reclaim the streets'. Analysis of these editorials and commentaries reveals a very clear demand for not only tough rhetoric but also highly punitive 'prison centred' policy responses summarised in the demands that lawbreakers must be imprisoned. Whilst sections of the tabloid and mid-market news media may concede that imprisonment achieves little or nothing in the way of rehabilitation they operate from a default position that non-custodial sentences for violent or persistent offenders do not constitute punishment or indeed justice and therefore cannot offer adequate public protection.

Imprisonment and harsh sentences are demanded and justified in highly moralistic 'common sense' terms, such as the need for retribution, the deterrent effect and selective incapacitation. The following examples illustrate just how embedded this punitive 'lock 'em up now!' sensibility is. The dramatic official rise in the theft of mobile phones reported in early 2002 as part of the street crime panic should have and did focus attention on the need for manufacturers to improve the security features and for owners to be more careful with their property. However, as the mobile phone panic continued, what really grabbed the headlines was Lord Justice Woolf's announcement in 29 January that the courts should impose stiffer custodial sentences on mobile phone thieves.

As the 2002 'street crime' crisis unfolded, the Home Office announced on the 20 March that emergency measures would be taken to ease overcrowding inside prisons. The package of measures included proposals to extend the home detention curfew scheme to release certain prisoners before the end of their sentences and relaxation of strict risk assessment criteria. The popular newspapers were derisive in their reporting of this decision:

'Releasing prisoners is a crime waiting to happen' (*Sunday Times*, 24 March 2002)

'Blunkett opens the prison gates' (*Daily Mail*, 22 March 2002)

'[David Blunkett's] decision to tag thousands of criminals and release them early issues a message that is not only uncharacteristically feeble and confused, but an affront to the law abiding' (*Daily Mail*, 22 March 2002)

'Why hound the innocent and let the real vermin free?' (*Daily Mail*, 22 March 2002)

'The country looks to Blunkett to get the bad guys off our streets, not put them back there before they have served their time' (*Sun*, 22 March 2002)

'Tagging can open the cell doors to worst offenders' (*Daily Express*, 22 March 2002)

'Set free to commit crime' (*Evening Standard*, 26 March 2002).

The financial and social costs of an increasing the prison population did not figure in newspaper support for 'penal populism'.

However, criminologists also have a warning for those who believe that the news media's highly selective and emotive coverage blocks out all possibility of reasoned or progressive debate about crime, criminal justice and sentencing. There is increasing recognition that we need to avoid over deterministic and over general readings, recognising, for example, the interpretative creativity of audiences (see for example, Chiricos et al 2000; Heath and Gilbert 1996; Sasson 1995). There is continuous interaction between changing media representations and patterns of criminality, perception of crime risks and criminal justice policy and practice. Demographics, locality, social networks and life experiences connect in complex ways with the reception of news media representations of crime (Sacco, 1995). Chiricos et al (2000: 780) suggest that

> local news effects are most often significant for viewers who live in high crime places, have recent victim experience, or who perceive news accounts of crime as realistic. It seems reasonable to assume for these

people, the news and, in particular, local news reports about crime, will have a resonance that is greater than it is for others.

Neo-Durkheimian analysis notes that through high-profile crime reporting, the news media perform a vital social role of identifying and imposing a moral structure on a disorganised world by highlighting violations and showcasing punishment. Crime reporting provides society with a fascinating and never-ending series of morality tales about conflicts between the forces of good and evil, right and wrong. Equally importantly it also provides society with a gallery of heroes and villains. The conflict over the nature of social order is captured most dramatically in stories about violent predatory crimes committed against persons believed to be vulnerable and blameless. This helps to explain the over representation of particular types of crimes and victims (Best, 1999). Writing in a US context, Katz (1987: 72) develops this theme arguing that to understand what makes crime 'news', 'one must explain the voluntary affliction of disturbing emotional experience of the self, on a mass level, day after day, throughout modern society'. He concludes that crime news provides the raw material 'for a literal working out of the moral perspectives that must be applied to dilemmas of everyday life'. Crime occupies such a central position in newspapers because readers seek opportunities to work through moral positions that they will have taken in a variety of everyday encounters and decisions. To do so they must have crime reports that have enough details to see the incident as potentially within their own experience, that are able to mobilise a response by providing a shock or inviting outrage, and that allow for adjudication and indeed conviction

Katz argues that this also explains why the public does not grow weary of crime stories: 'Laid side by side, stories about violent crime published over a sequence of days may appear quite similar. But they are experienced as new, as "new-s", because the questions they tap re-emerge daily in the readers' social life' (71). Sparks (2001: 209-10) has made a similar point in a UK context: 'Our interest in and attention to the alarming, outrageous, unnerving and disgraceful happenings in crime news and crime stories are more than the tokens of our gullibility or indications of our reactionary and primitive disposition.' High profile news media coverage is important because it prompts public discussion and debate.

Finally, we need to take into account the views of two experienced crime journalists. Campbell (1999: 5) argues that the news media's ability and willingness to run eye catching crime campaigns and investigations has for all its faults focused public attention on social issues 'in a way that countless reports, inquiries or parliamentary debates could never have done'. He notes, for example:

> Issues which were not seen as on the crime beat four decades ago, such as child abuse and police corruption, are now given the coverage that would have been unthinkable then, The Bulger case focused attention on the whole issue of a child's criminal responsibility and the nature of 'evil'. The West case had ramifications for the social services, for missing people and it drew attention to the violence that parents can inflict on their children undetected.

In a similar vein, the *Daily Mail*'s coverage of the Stephen Lawrence case pressurised the government to establish a public inquiry that forced the police to take action against racist violence and hate crime. Rose (2001: 8) points out that news media investigations often take place in the face of considerable opposition from official agencies. Furthermore, he notes that 'if papers are full of sensational and inaccurate reports, to some extent this is because it can be so difficult to acquire information about anything else'.

Part Two

The Research Project: Media Influence in the Shaping of Public Knowledge and Attitudes towards Crime, Criminal Justice and Punishment

Our small-scale research study was funded by the Esmée Fairbairn Trust's Rethinking Crime and Punishment programme. The overall aim of this initiative was to identify ways to improve public knowledge of crime and sentencing, and to foster more balanced public attitudes to non-custodial forms of sentencing. The study aimed to analyse how public knowledge about different types of sentencing is shaped by the media – television and radio in particular. Our research attempted to provide a deeper understanding of how different audiences and publics respond to television and radio narratives of crime and punishment, and how they make judgements about issues of retribution and criminal justice. It situated patterns of response to particular programmes in the context of reactions to stories about crime and punishment in the media more generally. We took into account the seemingly incidental narratives of crime and punishment in mainstream fictional programmes such as soap operas and non-crime television dramas, and attempted to assess their impact on public knowledge and attitudes.

This research was intended to plug a notable gap in the research literature in this field. It should be emphasised that the media research literature does not directly address the questions posed by this research. Audience research into responses to crime and punishment tends to focus, for obvious reasons, on factual news media, and to ignore the various ways in which television and radio dramas might shape attitudes or affect the knowledge and understanding of viewers about sentencing. Moreover the trend in the dominant paradigm of audience studies, 'media effects' research, has been to focus on the behavioural and social effects of watching violent material rather than with broader discourses of punishment. This research on audiences' responses to crime stories in fictional dramas, as well as news and documentary is intended to make a contribution to our understanding of how the media shapes public knowledge and attitudes towards sentencing at a critical moment of policy change.

Questions about awareness, knowledge and understanding and questions about values, beliefs and judgements lay at the heart of the research. Under the rubric of awareness, knowledge and understanding we were concerned to explore whether the fictional or documentary status of a programme affects the way regular viewers exhibit awareness of, or process information about, stories of crime and sentencing. We wanted to understand how regular viewers of crime genres compared, in their awareness, knowledge and understanding of sentencing, with viewers who rarely or never watched such programmes. Do regular viewers of factual TV crime genres feel that their viewing affords them a better understanding and knowledge of the criminal justice system than regular viewers of fictional TV crime dramas? Do regular viewers of crime genres believe that they learn more or less about the criminal justice system from the crime narratives in soap operas and mainstream programming than from crime specific genres? How do questions of realism intervene in judging and inter-preting programmes about crime and punishment?

Under the rubric of values and beliefs, attitudes and judgements we enquired into whether the fictional or documentary status of a programme was significant in shaping values and judgements about sentencing among regular viewers. We asked how regular viewers of crime genres compared, in their judgements about sentencing, with viewers who rarely or never watched such programmes. Do regular viewers of TV crime programmes differ in the puni-tiveness they express towards offenders or in their confidence in the criminal justice system as compared with those who do not watch or rarely watch such programmes? How does the type of crime fiction (and here we have to distin-guish between those series that focus on the crime, or on its detection, or on court procedures and sentencing, or on the experience of punishment as in prison dramas) shape judgements about sentencing? Are viewers able to identi-fy inaccurate information about practices or procedures in TV crime dramas? (For example, that offenders would not be allowed mobile phones in prison or on community service?) Do negative portrayals of legal professionals in fiction-al and factual TV crime programmes reduce confidence in the criminal justice system? Under what circumstances do viewers identify and/or sympathise with offending characters or prisoners? Is empathy with an offender a precondition for adopting positive attitudes towards community sentencing? Which types of offenders and crimes are considered suitable for community forms of sentenc-ing and which not?

In this small-scale, pilot study we attempted to move away from the domi-nant research paradigm in audience studies that is based on the premise that media have discernible, direct, researchable 'effects'. As was noted previously, most of the research conducted within this framework has provided inconclu-sive, contradictory and confused evidence about the nature of the communica-tion process, audience activities and responses, social, cognitive, interpretive and affective. Instead of asking what does the media's coverage of crime, crimi-nal justice and sentencing do to people, we decided to turn the question around and ask what do people 'do' with narratives of crime, criminal justice and sen-tencing? In other words, how do they use and interpret narratives in ways that are meaningful to them as individuals and as members of social groups and categories? What kinds of crime programmes are salient to different audiences?

Our working assumption was that this qualitative approach to understanding how people use and interpret media stories about crime and punishment would have the advantage of highlighting the complexity of audience responses to specific media content, and thus produce more sophisticated and nuanced findings.

Research techniques

Focus groups were used to elicit data in the form of questionnaires and focus group interviews. Ninety-three viewers were interviewed in nine focus groups and given a questionnaire between January and March 2002 in Swansea, South Wales. About three-quarters of the sample were from working class backgrounds, 75 per cent were female and 25 per cent male with a good balance across age groups. The focus groups were self-selecting and drawn from pre-existing social and communication groups. For example the working-class male group was drawn from a local Working Men's club; the middle-class women's group was drawn from a professional social network. This ensured that the groups were already familiar with each other and used to communicating and discussing topical issues. The interaction between regular and non-regular viewers was carefully studied. A questionnaire was used to gather data on the patterns and extent of viewing television crime stories in different genres. A selection of 'cameo scenarios' taken from storylines current in the media were presented to viewers to assess knowledge and attitudes towards crime and punishment.

Members of the focus group were asked to express their views on the nature (form) and extent of punishment (degree of punitiveness) in relation to the crime. Thus, as far as possible, we attempted to base our qualitative data upon actual viewing practices and specific storylines familiar to the viewer. In cases where viewers claimed to have little or no knowledge or experience of crime and punishment narratives, or in need of a memory trigger, the compilation tape was used. The 'cameo scenarios' included storylines from: a criminal justice drama; a fictional programme aimed at fostering more balanced attitudes towards community sentencing; a crime reconstruction show; a radio programme mirrored in the TV soap *Emmerdale*; a crime series; and popular soap dramas.

Findings: consuming crime and avoiding punishment

The viewers we interviewed inhabit quite complex and increasingly individualised media worlds. This is due to the way in which viewers now can select from an increasingly diverse array of media. The rise of multi-channel television has also led to the fragmentation of audiences. Partly as a result of this complexity and diversity in media consumption, it was impossible to uncover any simple, direct causal relations or 'effects' between what our interviewees watched and their knowledge and attitudes to crime and punishment. Rather, a range of social and personal factors, combine with media experiences to shape public knowledge and perceptions of the criminal justice system. In the following section we give a general overview of the kinds of trends and patterns of audience response that our research uncovered before going onto our more detailed finding around specific issues. The findings reported below, though clear from this small-scale pilot survey, are necessarily tentative and will be subject to further validation or falsification in a larger survey. They do provide insights into discernible trend and suggest some important questions and fruitful avenues for future research. Finally, limitations of space here prevent us from giving the kind of detailed and rich empirical evidence that forms the basis of our findings.

Crime stories, in different genres, are seen as a popular and common part of the media experiences of all our interviewees. There is nothing new in the popularity of crime stories. They have always been a part of the social fabric. From classical Greek and Roman times crime dramas have entertained, provoked and provided pleasure to audiences. They have always served a social function, affirming or challenging, policing and pushing the boundaries of social life and moral behaviour. It is often said that crime fiction is the most moral of genres. What is new today is, as we noted previously in this chapter, the ubiquity and pervasive nature of crime stories in the media. It is hard to avoid consuming crime stories in one form or another. There is also an increasing blurring of the boundaries between crime stories in factual and fictional programming. This is not to say that there is confusion among viewers about 'real' crime versus 'fictional' crime. Rather the blurrings are apparent in the ways in which crime stories are told, in their narrative structure and narrational modes, and this is reflected in the way that viewers talk about crime stories.

Crime stories in news and documentary programmes increasingly are told in melodramatic form and are interpreted and discussed by viewers as one might a melodrama or soap opera. The emphasis in melodrama is on the dramatisation of emotions and the intervention of fate or destiny. This narrative structure leaves little room for considering broader political and or policy questions and relegates matters of punishment and sentencing to a time beyond the closure of the narrative. These trends are closely related to processes of tabloidisation discussed above. The kind of melodramatic excess that typifies the reporting of certain crime stories catalyses highly emotive public reactions and fuels popular punitiveness.

Fictional crime stories, in contrast, espouse new forms of (often hyper) realism. For viewers this means entering the everyday professional lives, minds and emotions, not to mention the dead bodies of the characters. The ever more graphic depictions of crimes and of victims of crime, such as the mutilated bodies of victims, do little to put most viewers off. Rather than being seen as a ploy to grab ratings such depictions are seen as part of the heightened realism of crime fictions. Sometimes the realism is judged to be 'gritty' social realism and sometimes pseudo-scientific psychological realism. It may also involve the kind of realism around intimate or professional relationships. Viewers perceive these different kinds of televisual realism as offering more or less accurate and truthful insights into the criminal justice system. They are, for the most part, unable to identify inaccuracy in details or procedures.

As a result of these generic blurrings, knowledge and understanding of crime and punishment among our interviewees, we found, is a unique product of the symbiotic relationship between factual and fictional programming. Information gleaned from both the factual and the fictional appear to be equally influential and are integrated into the broader systems of knowledge, values and beliefs held by individuals. We found little evidence that more regular viewers of factual programmes, as compared with regular viewers of crime fictions, were any more knowledgeable or informed about either the criminal justice system or sentencing. A further consequence of the blurrings of generic boundaries is that news and entertainment genres are seen and discussed as both increasingly realistic and anti-realistic (as in the kinds of melodramatic excess of emotions that sensationalises some crime stories over others). This is a paradoxical feature of the responses of our viewers.

It is clear that the narrative structure of crime stories, whether factual or fictional, rarely provides the 'narrative space' for audiences to address questions about the politics of sentencing or the morality of punishment in a detailed, sustained or sophisticated way. Crime is sexy. Punishment is boring. Most viewers regardless of class or gender demonstrated little knowledge of, or interest in, questions of punishment except in exceptional or sensational cases where judges are deemed over-lenient, for example in the early release of murderers, or in child abuse or motor accident cases. Although a great deal of knowledge about criminal acts, policing and detection is gained from the media, television especially, high levels of ignorance about the criminal justice system in general, and sentencing practices in particular, were evident.

Our interviewees got information about crime and sentencing from a wide variety of media sources, primarily from television, the press, radio, film and best seller paperback fiction. Predictably, education and social class factors are most important shaping which media people consume. It was clear from our research that readers of the tabloids and mid-market daily newspapers such as the *Daily Express* and the *Daily Mail* expressed, much more directly and noticeably, punitive attitudes. We found that those who subscribe to punitive attitudes are more inclined to read the tabloids and mid-market papers and to have their punitive views of the world confirmed and reinforced. This highlights a more general trend among media consumers towards seeking out media that tend to confirm pre-existing values and ideological views. This is just as true of *Guardian* or *Telegraph* readers as it is of readers of the *Daily Mail*. However, when punitive rhetoric was expressed in the focus groups it was noticeably echoing the kind of sound-bite headlines commonly coined by the tabloids and mid-market dailies. This leads us to believe that the tabloids are more influential than television in providing 'scripts' and 'sensational scenarios' from which popular punitiveness may be expressed. The obligations of impartiality, balance and fairness that curtail TV news journalists in their bulletins do not, of course, apply to newspapers.

Viewers are just as likely to acquire and recall useful information about the criminal justice system from dramas, especially soap operas, as from news, current affairs and documentaries. Even though specific facts associated with sentencing are more likely to be acquired via news media, unless the sentence is controversial, it is rarely noted or recalled. This lack of attention or absence of concern about punishment is very significant. The 'structured absence' of any sustained discussion about punishment and sentencing in crime media discourses and in audiences' responses is just as important an effect by its very absence as the effects of what appears obvious or common in the media.

Most dramas end rather than begin with sentencing. This is seen as the job of judges. Judges are considered to be upper class, out of touch with the real world, inconsistent and over lenient. Very few people know what the difference is between a judge and a magistrate. The widespread condemnation of judges suggests that there is a social and communication gap in the criminal justice system that needs to be addressed if public perceptions of over-leniency are to be corrected. This is important because as we noted previously there is evidence that government policy on sentencing is shaped by and responds to popular punitiveness. Yet punitive attitudes are often exacerbated by media coverage of crime which in turn is led by the competitive imperative to sell sensational and dramatic stories for profit. The attractions of lurid crime and detection procedures, however, militate against tackling sentencing issues in more complex ways. So what kinds of crime stories generate more reflective and well-informed responses to sentencing in the media?

Information about sentencing is only turned into useful knowledge (i.e. knowledge that can be transformative of deeply held beliefs) when dramatic weight is given to underlying moral and ethical issues of punishment and crime, and when information about sentencing criteria and decision-making is made available. Prime time soaps and court-room dramas tackle sentencing issues better than other television genres but it is rare that the details or consequences of sentencing are explored in either crime genres (detective and police series especially) or indeed more generally. In general, we found that although television plays at least some part in forming opinions and re-shaping attitudes, media effects tend to be long term and diffuse rather than immediate, easily identifiable or measurable.

Focus group discussions of media stories replicate the way viewers discuss their media experiences in everyday life, underscoring the social and collective nature of crime story interpretation. The focus group itself is a useful forum in which underlying beliefs and values, as well as ambivalence, about the ethics of punishment are explored in their fuller complexity. During the course of focus group discussions participants, even the most vociferously punitive, worked through some of the contradictions in their views and opinions. It was also possible to discern discursive shifts from firm and absolute 'lock em up' to more ambivalent positions in the same participant across the interviews. Deeply entrenched views are hard to dislodge, but when confronted with the difficulties of sentencing from multiple perspectives, and as participants become aware of the gaps in their own knowledge, they began to offer more reasoned and reasonable responses to the complexities and purposes of sentencing.

Viewers' familiarity with and knowledge of retributive and rehabilitative notions of justice was much more evident than notions of restorative justice upon which community forms of sentencing depend. Most viewers had very little understanding or knowledge of the underlying ethical and philosophical principles of restorative justice.

The criminal justice system: knowledge and attitudes
Almost all informants regarded the criminal justice system with considerable contempt and cynicism. It stood accused of being ineffective and 'soft on crime' at a moment when crime was perceived as not only on the increase but 'spiralling out of control'. Focus group discussions indicated that there were considerable gaps in informants' knowledge and understanding of the workings of the criminal justice system. Sentencing and sentences was one of the informants' greatest areas of ignorance. There was a strong tension between the dual demands for general consistency of sentencing, based on a wish for 'objectivity' and for greater certainty about the justice of sentences and for just sentencing to fit the particularities of individual cases. What limited information is avail-

able, whether in fictional or factual genres, appears to give an impression of over-leniency, inconsistency and injustice.

Pervasive personal experience of crime, whether direct or indirect, and fear of crime against oneself and one's property are the most important factors shaping responses to media crime. However, melodramatic, sensationalist and alarmist crime reporting in local, tabloid and mid-market press especially, heighten and exacerbate more general feelings of social insecurity and fear that arise from other social and psychological factors such as poverty, job insecurity and emotional problems arising from being a victim of crime. Yet the fear and insecurity that are generated by crime dramas (and are invariably negated by the narrative closure) are an important part of the pleasure of the genre of crime that excites anxiety only to relive it ultimately and return us to the relative 'safety' and or 'normality' of most of our lives.

Consuming crime

Television crime stories are extremely popular. ninety-six per cent of our sample watched crime programmes weekly. Those in the lower socio-economic groups and the middle-aged category (36-55 years) had the highest percentages of watching crime programmes regularly. Detective series are most regularly watched and preferred. No clear differences in expressing punitive attitudes emerged between viewers who prefer factual and those who prefer fictional crime programmes. Punitive attitudes are more easily correlated with readership of tabloid newspapers rather than with viewing crime. Regular viewers of soaps, especially *Eastenders* with its ongoing crime stories, show a higher awareness of crime and punishment issues, and a more precise knowledge of the criminal justice system than regular viewers of other fictional genres. (This could perhaps be explained by a high profile storyline around domestic abuse on Eastenders and a detailed exploration of the court case and sentencing at the time of the research). *Crimewatch*, a programme that invites viewers to help solve real life crime, has a regular fan base. It is seen to inform viewers about how crimes are committed, what crimes are prevalent and what to watch out for. But also it is blamed for heightening fear of crime. It is also regarded as risible in its indictment of the police: 'they ask us for God's sake!'

Attitudes to sentencing in television crime stories

Most viewers in our sample tended to agree that television and radio usually portray community sentencing (like collecting rubbish or wiping out graffiti) as 'soft' and as 'a joke punishment that doesn't work' (57 per cent). They also tended to agree that television and radio experiences make you think that prison is the only solution to most serious forms of crime' (57 per cent). Viewers tended to agree that they were less likely to express punitive attitudes towards an offender when a programme delved into their background and explained why they ended up committing a crime (44 per cent). Most viewers swayed in their attitudes between moral absolutism and ambivalence. Statements made in focus group discussions and in questionnaires were often contradictory and ambivalent views emerged when the details of particular cases were discussed. Programmes that stimulated moral ambivalence in viewers, as do soap operas quite often, tended to be more successful in challenging extremely punitive attitudes.

Punitive attitudes

Punitive attitudes were commonly expressed by over half of our respondents The punitive rhetoric expressed by informants was articulated in emotive terms and tended to be passionately felt rather than necessarily rationalised or thought-through carefully. The profoundly affective foundations of punitive dispositions (which in some cases seem to relate to early childhood experiences of physical and/or psychological punishment) suggests that in order to tackle extreme forms of punitiveness, viewers' emotions as well as their reason need to be engaged. Punitive attitudes were often articulated through the idioms and vocabularies of tabloid and mid-market newspapers. News headlines and sound bites insinuated themselves into the kind of punitive rhetoric that characterised initial discussions in focus groups but more complex moral and ethical positions were adopted as the complexities of particular individual cases emerged.

Avoiding punishment

Sentencing is one of the greatest areas of ignorance among our informants. What limited information is available, whether in fictional or factual genres, appears to give an impression of over-leniency and inconsistency. This in turn negatively affects attitudes and opinions regarding the criminal justice system and community sentencing especially. There is a clear contradiction between the attitude that the 'punishment should fit the crime' and the desire for circumstances to be taken into account. There is a demand for consistency in sentencing and that the sentence be seen to be 'just' not only for the sake of justice but also for the deterrent effect. Our interviewees tended to show little interest in or knowledge about sentencing practices.

Alternatives to imprisonment

There was a widespread lack of knowledge about alternative sentences. The preferred form was tagging but our informants knew little about how it operates. Details of tagging had been gleaned from news but had only been briefly and 'factually' explained. The indications are that tagging could have more impact and more support if portrayed positively in a popular drama. Viewers are more likely to respond favourably to alternatives when the story or drama focuses at least as much on the crime and the police investigation as on sentencing. However, this may not be seen as making for good drama, nor might encouraging sympathetic identification with offenders by showing why and how characters come to commit crimes.

Lenient attitudes towards punishment were often attributed to 'do-gooders' and 'lefties' (*Guardian* readers according to one group) who were considered to be naïve and who were held in contempt for failing to recognise the important deterrent factor attached to severe punishment. Entrenched punitive attitudes are resistant to change as they are founded on beliefs about the value punishment formed in childhood, deeply held political values and world views. Group discussions, however, did enable informants to work through some of the contradictions in their views and opinions and to shift positions at times. More meaningful knowledge of alternatives to imprisonment is essential if community sentencing is to gain legitimacy.

Interpreting crime stories

Personal experiences of crime, direct or indirect, powerfully shape the way crime media are interpreted and attitudes towards about appropriate forms of punishment. Viewers commute between personal and media experiences of crime. The crime narrative hooks the viewer and connects the two. Direct and indirect experiences of crime also shape more fundamental values and beliefs about crime and punishment. These in turn affect the ways in which media crime stories are judged. The values and beliefs systems that underlie attitudes to punishment are hard to dislodge and generally appear to be unaffected by information provided by media.

The interpretation of crime stories is both an individual and a social activity. Collective processes of interpretation (crime talk) take place in local social networks and are crucial in shaping views on particular crime stories in the news. Our findings suggest that it is through the collective and social interpretations of the moral ambiguities of crime stories that underlying values and beliefs are challenged. While many of our respondents initially expressed deeply punitive tabloid or sound-bite inspired rhetoric, they failed to sustain it. The kinds of deliberation and debate about crime and punishment that took place in focus groups tended to engender less punitive rhetoric as the discussion proceeded.

Crime stories are framed by wider ideological discourses prevalent in the society at a particular moment. The ability to interpret the ideological underpinnings of crime stories in a reflective and sophisticated way depends on educational and cultural competence. Where viewers display large information deficits or a serious lack of knowledge about the criminal justice system they tend to fall back on pre-existing assumptions and prejudices. Interpretations of crime stories are, however, affected by the popular punitive rhetoric of tabloid and mid-level/mid-market dailies. Their serial form enables a sustained ideological trickle effect that foregrounds crime as the central social problem.

Judging crime and punishment
Viewers' judgements of media crime stories indicate significant 'attitude sway' depending on the storyline, sometimes dramatic and sometimes minimal, between moral absolutism and ambivalence. Those with more awareness of the circumstances of specific crimes and offenders (usually as viewers of a fictional genre) were inclined to be less punitive and more positive towards alternative forms of sentencing. When they shared this awareness with those expressing more punitive attitudes, the latter tended to adopt more favourable views

towards alternative sentences. This may be explained in part by the drive towards forging a loose consensus in focus group interviews and to the fact that focus group participation in itself can be functional in shifting and dislodging absolute and entrenched views sometimes – at least for the duration of the interview.

Viewers are more likely to respond favourably to alternatives to prison when the story or drama offers multiple perspectives and identifications. When a drama focuses on the crime and the police investigation (detective or police genres which use crime as spectacle or for the purposes of titillation), rather than on common humanity and shared experiences (as in soaps), viewers are less likely to consider alternatives to prison as satisfactory options. However, more meaningful knowledge of alternatives is required, and this evidently means from the media.

Viewers' knowledge and attitudes appeared to be shaped more by fictional media, often non-crime specific genres such as soaps, together with their personal experience, rather than by factual media. Programmes like *Crimewatch* and the news may have a greater short-term impact, but fictional crime, especially in soaps, is often more salient in people's lives, memories and imaginations.

Conclusions

Our findings may be summarised as follows. First, viewers are just as likely to glean important information and knowledge about the criminal justice system and issues of sentencing from crime fiction, as well as from subplots and storylines in mainstream dramas, as from factual output. Second, viewers may not value the accuracy of the knowledge and information about the criminal justice system that they gain from dramas as much as that gleaned from factual programming but it may be just as effective in shaping attitudes and values. Third, crime fictions are a very important resource for shaping opinions and values about sentencing. Viewers draw upon media narratives as templates and reference points in making judgements about appropriate punishment. As such these narratives function as cultural resources (dramaturgical scripts, social repertoires, and cameo scenarios) to be used in opinion formation, maintenance and transformation about punishment practices. Fourth, knowledge and information gleaned from the media shapes attitudes and values to sentencing in an indirect but critical and constructive way. Few viewers subscribe to moral or ethical absolutes. The context in which the crime was committed, the nature of the crime and the social background of the offender are crucial factors in shaping attitudes to sentencing. Fifth, attitudes and values are more likely to be supportive of non-custodial forms of sentencing both in the media and in actual situations with very specific types of offenders and offences. Sixth, negative attitudes towards non-custodial forms of sentencing are likely to be extremely resistant to change with regards to very specific types of offenders and offences. Seven, viewers who regularly view crime fictions are more likely to feel empathy towards offenders when there is an attempt at representing a depth of insight into character and motivation, and the social circumstances in which the offender lives. Eighth, viewers are more likely to respond favourably to alternatives to prison when the stories focus less on the crime and police investigation (detective or police genres which use crime as spectacle or for the purposes of titillation) and place greater emphasis on shared humanity, and human experiences.

To conclude, the high levels of apathy and ignorance about sentencing among viewers raise serious questions about what we might mean by 'informed citizenship' as well as the relationship between government, criminal justice system, media and the public that merit much more developed investigation than is possible here. In addition, it seems to us that the terms in which crime, criminal justice and punishment are currently framed by the media severely limit the options for progressive public discussion and policy making on these issues.

Acknowledgements
Our thanks to Dr Stephanie Adams and Dr Anthea Symonds who conducted the focus group interviews and provided many rich insights.

References
Altheide, D.L. and Michalowski, R.S. (1999) ' Fear in the news: a discourse of control', *Sociological Quarterly*, 40, pp.475-504.
Baer, J., and Chambliss, W. J. (1997) 'Generating fear: the politics of crime

reporting', *Crime, Law and Social Change*, 27, pp.87-108.

Barak, G. (1994). *Media, process, and the social construction of crime: studies in newsmaking criminology*. New York: Garland Publications.

Barlow, M. (1998) 'Race and the problem of crime in Time and Newsweek cover stories, 1946 to 1995', *Social Justice*, 25, pp. 149-183.

Beckett, K. (1997) *Making Crime Pay: Law and Order in Contemporary American Politics*. New York: Oxford University Press.

Benedict, H. (1992) *Virgin or Vamp: how the press covers sex crimes*. New York and Oxford: Oxford University Press.

Best, J. (1999) *Random violence: how we talk about new crimes and new victims*. Berkeley: University of California Press.

Boyle, R. (1999) 'Spotlighting the police: changing U.K. police-media relations in the 1990s', *International Journal of the Sociology of Law*, 27, pp 229-250.

Burchill, J. (2003) 'What's left for us?', *The Guardian Weekend*, 25 October, p.7.

Cavender, G. (1999) 'The construction of gender in reality crime TV', *Gender and Society*, 13, pp. 643-663.

Campbell, D. (1999) 'Writing Wrongs', *Guardian 2*, 12 April, pp. 4-5.

Chermak, S. M. (1994) *Victims in the News: Crime and the American News Media*. Boulder: Westview Press.

Chiricos, T., Eschholz, S., and Gertz, M. (1997) 'Crime, news and fear of crime: toward an identification of audience effects', *Social Problems*, 44, pp. 342-357.

—, T., Padgett, K., and Gertz, M. (2000) 'Fear, TV news, and the reality of crime', *Criminology*, 38, pp.755-785.

Crandon, G. (1992) *The Police and the Media: Information Management and the Construction of Crime News*. Bradford, West Yorkshire: Horton Publishing.

—, (1997) 'Symbiosis or vassalage? The media and the law enforcers – the case of Avon and Somerset police', *Policing and Society*, 8, pp. 77-92.

Dahlgreen, P. (1998) 'Crime news: the fascination of the mundane', *European Journal of Communications*, 3, pp. 189-206.

Dixon, T. (2000) 'Overrepresentation and under-representation of African Americans and Latinos as lawbreakers on television news', *Journal of Communication*, 50 pp. 131-156.

Dowden, R. (2004) 'The Rwandan genocide: how the press missed the story', *African Affairs*, 103, pp.283-91.

Gans, H. (1979) *Deciding What's News*. New York: Pantheon Books.

Garland, D. (2000) *Culture of Crime Control: Crime and Social Order in Contemporary Society*. Oxford: Oxford University Press.

—, and Sparks, R. (2000) 'Criminology, social theory and the challenge of our times', *British Journal of Criminology*, 40, pp189-204.

Gerbner, G., Gross, L., Morgan, M. and Signorelli, N. (1994) 'Growing up with the TV: the cultivation perspective' in J. Bryard and D. Zillman (eds.) *Media Effects*. Hillsdale, NJ: Erlbaum Books.

Hall, S. et al (1978) *Policing the Crisis: Mugging the State and Law and Order*. London: Hutchinson.

Hamilton, J.T. (1998) *Channelling Violence: The Economic Market for Violent Television Programming*. Princeton NJ: Princeton University Press.

Heath, L., & Gilbert, K. (1996) 'Mass media and fear of crime: opinion on justice in the criminal justice system', *American Behavioral Scientist*, 39:4, pp.379-386.

Hope, T.and Sparks, R. (2000) *Risk, Insecurity and the Politics of Law and Order*. London: Routledge.

Hough, M. (1996). 'People talking about punishment', *Howard Journal of Criminal Justice*, 35, pp. 191-214.

—, and Roberts, J. V. (1999), 'Sentencing Trends in Britain: Public knowledge and public opinion', *Punishment and Society*, 1, pp. 11-26.

Howe, A. (1998). *Sexed Crime in the News*. Leichhardt, N.S.W: Federation Press.

Jermyn, D. (2001) 'Death of the girl next door: celebrity, femininity, and tragedy in the murder of Jill Dando', *Feminist Media Studies*, 1, pp. 343-359.

Katz, J. (1987) 'What makes crime news?', *Media, Culture and Society*, 9, pp.47-75.

Kitt-Hewitt, D. and Osborne, R. (1995) *Crime and the Media: The Postmodern Spectacle*, London: Pluto Press.

Krajicek, D. J. (1998) *Scooped!: Media miss real story on crime while chasing sex, sleaze, and celebrities*. New York: Columbia University Press.

Mawby, R. (1999) 'Visibility, transparency and police-media relations', *Policing and Society*, 9, pp 263-286.

McCormick, C. R. (1995) *Constructing Danger: the Mis/representation of Crime in the News*. Halifax, Nova Scotia: Fernwood Pub.

McLaughlin, E. and Murji, K. (2001) 'Ways of seeing: media reporting of racist violence', in M. May, *Social Problems*, Oxford: Blackwell.

Mitchell, B. (1998) 'Public perceptions of homicide and criminal justice', *British Journal of Criminology*, 38, pp. 453-472.

Myers, K. (2004) 'Who stays in jail or goes free is up to The Sun', *Sunday Telegraph*, 15 February.

Naylor, B. (2001) 'Reporting violence in the British print media: gendered stories', *Howard Journal of Criminal Justice*, 40, 180-194.

Perlmutter David, D. (2000). *Policing the Media: street cops and public perceptions of law enforcement*. Thousand Oaks, Cal. and London: Sage.

Reiner, R. (2000) 'Crime and Control in Britain', *Sociology*, 34, pp. 71-94

Roberts, J.V. et al (2003) *Penal Populism and Public Opinion: Lessons From Five Countries*. Oxford: Oxford University Press.

Romer, D. (1998) 'The treatment of persons of color in local television news: ethnic blame discourse or realistic group conflict?', *Communication Research*, 25, 286-305.

Romer, D. (2002) 'Murderers, rapists and drug addicts', in C.R. Mann and M.S. Zatz, eds, *Images of Color, Images of Crime*, 2nd edn, Los Angeles: Roxbury Publishing.

Rose, D. (2001) 'What's in it for us?' *Criminal Justice Matters* 43, pp. 8-9.

Sacco, V. F. (1995) 'Media constructions of crime', *Annals of the American Academy of Political and Social Science*, 539, pp. 141-154.

Sasson, T. (1995) *Crime Talk: how citizens construct a social problem*. Hawthorne, N.Y.: Aldine de Gruyter.

Scheingold, S.A. (1995) 'Politics, public policy and street crime', *Annals of the American Academy of Political and Social Sciences*, 539, pp155-68.

Schlesinger, P, Tumber, H. and Murdock, G. (1991) 'The media politics of crime and criminal justice', *British Journal of Sociology*, 42, pp397-420.

—, and Tumber, H. (1994) *Reporting Crime: the Media Politics of Criminal Justice*. Oxford: Oxford University Press.

Sparks, R. (1992) *Television and the Drama of Crime: Moral Tales and the Place of Crime in Public Life*. Buckingham: Open University Press.

Surette, R. (1998) *Media, crime, and criminal justice: images and realities*. 2nd edn, Belmont, CA: Wadsworth Pub.

Taylor, I. (1999) *Crime in Context: a Critical Criminology of Market Societies*. Cambridge: Polity Press.

Thompson, K. (1998). *Moral Panics*. London and New York: Routledge.

Young, J. (1999) *The Exclusive Society*. London: Sage.

Chapter Six

Back on the Southern 'Chain Gang Lite'

Vivien Miller

> Every morning we count off through the gate in single file, our voices
> echoing out into the darkness and into the glare of the spotlights on the
> corners of the fence. Once again the squads are reformed and counted as
> we stand at a loose and sleepy attention, greeted by a new day of trucks,
> guns, the hounds barking from the dog pens. At the signal we load up
> into the cage truck, scrambling in quickly for if we are slow the last man
> is certain to be kicked in the ass by the Walking Boss. It is still dark and
> misty, the dawn barely begun. The dawn is gray; as gray as this iron
> world in which we live (Pearce, 1999: 1).

In October 1999, the state of Alabama ended its four-year experiment with the
reinstituted chain gang, not because of moral outrage over a relic of a shameful
past or because of legal disquiet, but because of a massive shortage of correctional officers. With a prisoner-to-guard ratio of 10-to-1 (double the national
average of 4.5-to-1) and a shortfall of 400 guards for a prison population of
25,000, it had become necessary to transfer correctional officers from the chain
gang work crews to the state's nineteen prisons to ensure order and safety
(*Birmingham News (AL)*, 27 and 29 Oct. 1999; 21 and 24 Feb. 2000). The chain
gang had been revived after a forty-year absence on 3 May 1995 under Governor

Fob James' administration, to put inmates to work, to make the prison experience so miserable recidivism would be discouraged, and to demonstrate the toughness of the penal system.[1] Medium-security prisoners were sent out under armed guard to clean up roadways or perform other unskilled work. Limestone Correctional Facility, near Huntsville, housing over 2,000 inmates, sent 320 medium-security inmates chained at the ankles to pick up litter and cut underbrush along the highways for ten hours each day. Originally prisoners were chained in groups of five, reminiscent of slave coffles, ostensibly to prevent escapes (*Birmingham News (AL)*, 26 Oct. 1999). Four months later, in August 1995, 160 shackled inmates at the same prison donned safety glasses and ten-pound sledgehammers in the 80 degree heat, and under the gaze of local, national and international media, began smashing 100 tonnes of limestone boulders into pebbles; this was to be their work detail for ten hours a day, five days a week. As there appeared to be no economic or rehabilitative purpose, some inmates and observers denounced the spectacle as a meaningless waste of taxpayers' money. Proponents argued it demonstrated the state's commitment to getting tough on lawbreakers (*Birmingham News (AL)*, 21 Aug. 1995).

In the mid-1990s several North American states witnessed the return of the chain gang, a form of punishment emblematic of backward, brutal and repressive southern race relations of the late nineteenth and early twentieth centuries. Amid the political hype and media fanfare it became clear that historical understanding of the chain gang or its evolution into the road prison of the mid-twentieth century remains limited. Writing in 1926, University of North Carolina sociologists, Jesse F. Steiner and Roy M. Brown, began their statewide survey of crime and punishment with the observation that 'use of unselected groups of county prisoners for road construction and maintenance has failed to attract the attention it deserves,' and was frequently overlooked in standard texts on penology. They noted further that chain gangs were found in all regions of the United States in the last third of the nineteenth century, and legal provision for convict road work existed in all states except Rhode Island as late as 1923. In his historical overview of American prisons, Blake McKelvey observed that 'successful application of prison labor to road building was an achievement of the west.' Convicts had been used in all types of road construction in Arizona since 1909, Montana since 1912 and Nebraska since 1917 (McKelvey, 1977: 253-

4). Chain gangs however were/are synonymous with the southern region where economic, racial and climatic factors ensured their expansion, while northern and western states preferred large industrial prisons and occasional use of small groups of 'honor prisoners' for road and farm work (Steiner and Brown, 1927: 3–4).

This chapter therefore begins with a historical overview of the chain gang that draws on my research on Florida's road prisons, published historical studies of North Carolina and Georgia, as well as biographical and literary works such as Robert E. Burns' *I am a Fugitive from a Georgia Chain Gang!* (1932), John L. Spivak's *Georgia Nigger* (1933) and Donn Pearce's *Cool Hand Luke* (1966), immortalised on screen by Paul Newman in the 1967 movie of the same name. It goes on to draw comparisons with the revived 'leg-ironed work crews' of the 1990s, giving particular attention to developments in Alabama, Arizona and Florida. While chain gang revival reflects in part current public policy favouring harsher but less expensive prisons, its implementation seems more selective and limited than often realised (Glazer, 1996: 1201). Scholars such as David Garland and John Pratt argue that a new penal culture and new strategies of punitive segregation have emerged over the past three decades. Pratt describes the revival of 'emotive and ostentatious punishments' such as curfews, boot camps, chain gangs, 'three strikes' laws which enjoy public and political support, but represent 'an important departure from what had become the main penal trajectory of modernity,' a formal, bureaucratic management and rationalisation of penal affairs. The re-appearance of the chain gang in the American Deep South is part of a 'decivilizing interruption' to the 'civilizing continuum' grounded in the work of Norbert Elias (Garland, 2000; Pratt, 1999, 2000 and 2003).

The emergence of the southern chain gang
The chain gang, a work squad of predominately African-American men and women chained at the ankles, and together, appeared in the southern states largely after the Civil War, for example in Georgia in 1866 (Colvin, 1997: 220). The post-Civil War and Reconstruction periods saw rapid increases in rates of incarceration. In the context of extremely weak state governments, and dilapidated penitentiaries that were expensive to run, state and county officials strug-

gled to cope with a wave of property and interpersonal violence offences, and severe labour shortages following Confederate defeat and the demise of slavery. They were also unwilling to respond effectively to the problems confronting four million men and women making the transition from slavery to freedom, albeit freedom with severe legal, economic, and political limits. As ninety per-cent of prisoners were black, the 'Negro Problem' became interchangeable with the 'Crime Problem' of the late nineteenth century. The system of leasing con-victs to private employers offered cash-strapped state and local governments a means of profiting from the labour of prisoners, dispensing with expensive pen-itentiaries, and controlling the free black labour supply. Prisoners or 'chain men' worked in the construction of railroads, in cotton agriculture, brickyards, turpentine farms, coal and phosphate mines (Ayers, 1984; Fierce, 1994; Mancini, 1996; Lichtenstein, 1996; Myers, 1998; Curtain, 2000; Miller, 2000; Brown, 2002).

In the early twentieth century, states sought to 'nationalise' their prison sys-tems, so convict labourers moved from private to public ownership, but there were few immediate changes to the actual conditions of their lives and labour. Use of chain gang labour continued as states looked to large-scale penal farm-ing and road construction to employ their prisoners profitably. When Georgia abolished the convict lease in 1908 nearly 5,000 felony and misdemeanour con-victs, ninety-one percent of whom were black, became available for roadwork (Lichtenstein, 1996: 175). By 1910 every southern state legislature had autho-rised use of convicts for public works, to replace the inefficient statute labour system that required male citizens to undertake roadwork every year. In 1919 the state of Florida began dividing its prison population of 1,100 into Grade I for road labour and Grade II for work on the 20,000-acre prison farm. In January 1921, 628 prisoners were located in twenty-four road camps, and 422 prisoners laboured at the prison farm (16th Biennial Report of the Prison Division ... of Florida, 1919-1920: 7-8). In October 1926 North Carolina had 2,400 (1,600 African-American and 800 white) prisoners working on county chain gangs (Steiner and Brown, 1927: 125).[2] An important supporter of the use of convict road labour was the Good Roads Movement which drew support from disgruntled farmers seeking better routes to markets, intellectuals concerned with rural poverty and agrarian decline, businessmen (including tour bus oper-

ators) demanding economic development in the form of highways, unprecedented waves of tourists and autocampers travelling to Florida in the 1920s and
1930s, and growing automobile ownership across the South (Preston, 1991: 5-7,
20 and 122-123).

By the 1920s and 1930s native-born southerners and tourists motoring along
county roads and state highways would often be confronted by lines of dirty,
sweaty, exhausted, bare-chested men, clad in 'stripes' or the trousers of their
'zebra suits,' and wearing twenty pounds of chains, toiling on the roads and in
ditches, and surrounded by shotgun guards. Physical strength was vital for survival and to undertake the back-breaking work; a very muscular masculinity
was on display. Both Spivak (1934) and Burns (1997) described 'keeping the
lick,' the synchronised labour of the Chain Men in Georgia. Burns wrote: 'We
began in mechanical unison and kept at it in rhythmical cadence until sundown
– fifteen and a half hours of steady toil – as regular as the ticking of a clock,' and
'All the pickaxes hit the ground at the same time, all are raised and steadied for
the next blow with uncanny mechanical precision' (Burns, 1997: 143-4). Bodies,
muscles and work tools moved in time to the tempo and speed of an African
American worksong; to work at different speeds would have resulted in death or
injury from fellow convicts randomly wielding pickaxes, shovels and bush axes.

Premised on a racialised view of labour, chain gang road work was deemed
particularly appropriate for African American convicts in a period when
African Americans were freely employed in unskilled positions at low wages
(including railroad and road construction, sewer digging and scavenging, quar-
rying, lumber and mining). The large numbers of African-Americans in southern prisons (the black crime rate was three times that of whites) provided
advocates of racial inferiority with evidence for their views. Further, African
Americans arrested on feeble charges of vagrancy and disorderly conduct constituted a ready supply of labour to build roads for white planters and politicians (Spivak, 1934: 6; Simkins, 1965: 512). But road work also encouraged
juries to mete out convictions with prison sentences to white lawbreakers,
whom they had been reluctant to commit to the convict lease. Thus, as Alex
Lichtenstein has convincingly argued, road labour in the early twentieth century was 'the embodiment of penal humanitarianism, state-sponsored economic
modernization and efficiency, and racial moderation.' It was further promoted

as a healthy alternative to the convict lease and the cellblock, and the Good Roads Movement became 'identified with the movement to take the prisoners out of the cell, the prison factory, and the mine to work him in the fresh air and sunshine' (Lichtenstein, 1996: 160 and 165; Steiner and Brown, 1927: 177). In 1920 the outgoing governor of Florida congratulated himself on ending convict leasing: 'The time was a few years ago when a man was incarcerated and imprisoned and sent to the turpentine farms of the state, he had as brutal a time as if he had been in darkest Africa. That has been changed by taking those men from the turpentine farms and putting them on the state highways' (Quoted in Flynt, 1997: 246).[3]

The federal government aided and abetted this process from 1916-1917 by offering federal grants-in-aid for road improvements if states found matching funds. Before the 1930s southern state governments persuaded the federal government to let them use convict labor as a matching contribution (Lichtenstein, 1996: 191). The early depression years saw resentment toward convict road labourers, charged with taking work from more deserving unemployed whites, alongside demands that convict labour not be used on federally funded projects. During the depression decade, African Americans endured higher rates of unemployment than whites. In some cases, employers let black employees go so as to provide employment for whites, and traditional scorn for certain types of 'nigger work' was temporary suspended. One response was the federally created Civilian Conservation Corps set up to put unemployed white southerners to work on building bridges and roads (Preston, 1991: 159; Bates, 1936: 101-102).

At the same time, southern legislators continued to demand that convicts be employed productively to offset the costs of their confinement (Simkins, 1965: 533-5).[4] They found a powerful ally in Sanford Bates, director of the Federal Bureau of Prisons, who defended working prisoners during the depression, even if free men were unemployed, on the grounds of economic, social and disciplinary necessity. While condemning southern chain gangs as unjustifiable in a civilised community, he nonetheless saw 'enforced and degrading idleness' as equally indefensible. He saw no problems putting able-bodied prisoners to work on road building in both the west and south (Bates, 1936: 92, 101-2 and 109-10). During the 1930s southern prison officials also began to transfer convicts to huge penitentiaries with cellblocks, some built with Works Progress

Administration funds, and long considered by southern wardens to be ware-houses for enforced idleness. Manpower shortages during the Second World War, together with the loss of fifteen million men to the armed forces and the need to create a viable road infrastructure for military traffic, saw a temporary reversal of warehousing. It was also during the 1930s and 1940s that Florida road labourers for example, saw significant changes to their working condi-tions, such as reduced workloads and hours of work, and increased leisure time, including two-hour lunch breaks. The old striped 'zebra suits,' now deemed to present tourists with a negative image of Florida, were replaced with white uni-forms from 1939 (25th Biennial Repot of the Prison Division of Florida, 1937-1938: 23; Florida Board of Commissioners of State Institutions, Minutes, Series 431, Vol. 15 (25 Aug. 1937-3 Oct. 1939): 416 and 468).

Road labour continued into the 1960s, but technological changes in road construction and the professionalisation of engineering, contributed to the degrading and deskilling of convict road work. In the 1910s and 1920s convicts actually built bridges and roads, usually secondary roads or primary highways in Florida, sixteen feet wide, with limerock base materials, gradings of sand and crushed rock, and covered with asphalt. Convict teams were equipped with trucks with hard rubber tyres, mule teams, a wheel tractor, and squads of 'gun-men' armed with picks and shovels. They built parts of U.S. 1 or the 'Dixie Highway' in the 1910s and the Overseas Highway from Homestead to Key West, completed in 1944 but begun in 1935 after a hurricane destroyed the original Flagler railway line. In 1934 there were 1,500 inmates (fifty percent of the prison population) in thirty-one road prisons all over the state (but the majori-ty of road labourers were always free men in any given year) (Kendrick, 1964: 19). By the late 1930s and 1940s convicts were used for grading or preparing roads for machines and the free labourers who built the four-lane arterial high-ways.

In his novel based on his experiences of a Florida road prison in Lake County in the 1940s, Donn Pearce described a hierarchy of labour and skill that accompanied the different tasks of grading, of spreading hot tar and covering it with layers of sand, as performed by the Bull Gang. Fine Graders occupied a position of authority and held privileges such as Eyeballing (or looking around as they worked): 'The rest of us did the heavy work, breaking the ground for the aristocrats in the rear' (Pearce, 1999: 108). From the 1940s to the 1960s, convicts might also clear weeds using 'yo-yos' or weed cutters or be placed on 'trash detail' but work was invariably dull and monotonous. A hated task was clearing away underbrush from the 'shit ditches' or roadside drainage ditches where convicts stood knee- or waist-deep in putrid water wielding a bell-hooked bush-axe with an eighteen-inch double-edged blade. The Walking Bosses organised the work squads, strolled up and down the lines of convicts to regulate their labour, and decided when to break for Smoking Period or Bean Time. Pearce described the guards or Free Men dressed in wrinkled forest green uniforms stained with sweat, and wearing misshapen black cowboy hats stained with hair oil (Pearce, 1999: 7). In his 1962 book, *Florida Trials and Turnpikes*, Baynard Kendrick wrote 'memories, men, mules, materials, machinery, and money that, with blood and tears for a sub-base, make the Florida highways of today' (Kendrick, 1964: 243).

Every evening work squads would climb aboard prison trucks and return to their base camp. Initially convicts were housed in steel-barred 'pie wagons' on wheels with tiers of iron bunks, a zinc pan underneath for the toilet and an open bucket for washing. Spivak likened them to cages 'in which a circus pens its most ferocious beasts' (Spivak, 1934: 4). Florida developed a wooden collapsible 'construction camp' that stayed in one place for up to fourteen months, then was dismantled and moved twenty miles down the road together with mules, trucks, cooking stoves, guards and prisoners, and was much cheaper than a permanent prison. Steiner and Brown point out that portable convict camps differed little from free labour camps, but were 'entirely unsuited as places of detention' hence the reliance on chains, armed guards and dogs for security (Steiner and Brown, 1927: 58). In 1924 the sociologist Frank Tannenbaum drew on official reports, convict testimony and his own field studies to paint a vivid picture of southern bunkhouses, cages and tents with torn and unwashed bedding infested with vermin (from cockroaches and other insects to rats); the meagre rations of substandard and unwholesome food (an unvarying diet of molasses, cornbread, pork fat, and coffee) swarming with flies from the soil pits; the lack of sanitation making the hazards of skin, eye and venereal infections, tuberculosis, and pneumonia unavoidable (Tannenbaum, 1969: 84-102). Most states constructed permanent road prisons in the 1930s and 1940s with marked improvements in conditions, particularly sanitation, although they were still very basic.

Corporal punishment was used to punish insubordination, stealing state properly, attempted escape and getting caught with a weapon, but there were fixed rules governing its use (although these were not always observed). Captains, sergeants or trusties were officially limited in the number of blows they could administer and were not to draw blood; incapacitation was not the object as the convict was expected to be able to return to work within a short period. A heavy leather strap, four inches wide, a quarter of an inch thick, and three feet long hung from the belts of camp sergeants in Mississippi. While not a bullwhip or cat-'o-nine-tails, yet the strong racial overtones were hard to miss, even though it was used on both black and white convicts. Labeled 'da strop,' 'Black Annie,' or 'Black Aunty,' by African-American inmates, in the early twentieth century it was the main means of delivering 'positive punishment' (Taylor, 1999: 60-1 and 123). In contrast to other southern states, corporal punishment was abolished in Florida in June 1923 following a highly publicised incident where a young white male convict from North Dakota died after a punishment beating of over fifty blows administered by a prison guard. From the 1920s and 1930s southern states disciplined prisoners by sending them to the sweatbox for hours or days. A cramped wooden box, rather like an upright coffin, with no room to move or sit down and with holes in the roof, the intense heat of the sun engulfed the occupant. Modern isolation cells appeared in Mississippi and Florida in the 1950s.

Opposition to southern chain gangs increased during the 1930s in part because of government and prison fiscal crises, partly because of popular culture, and partly because of the changing racial composition of southern prison populations. In 1932 Robert E. Burns's *I am a Fugitive from a Georgia Chain Gang!*, a daring, heroic, manly adventure story in which the hero escapes twice from Georgia's brutal penal system, and its adaptation in 1933 as a Hollywood movie, did much to shape public opinion and opposition to southern penal practices. From the 1930s, from Florida to Mississippi to Texas, the numbers of white prisoners began to increase,thus challenging white southern penal sensibilities.

Florida stopped using leg irons and chains on its prisoners in 1945, except for 'incorrigibles,' and thus in effect ended its chain gangs. Most southern states began to abandon chained labour squads in the period during and after the Second World War. Prisoners continued to be assigned to road labour in Florida until the late 1960s and housed in stockades or barracks (there were thirty-five road prisons each on roughly twenty acres of land with an average of fifty-five prisoners). The arrival in July 1967 of fifteen white prisoners to a camp at Berrydale, north Florida, housing thirty-six black prisoners as part of desegregation of the prison system, led to unrest. A riot broke out around 10 p.m. on 16 July when prisoners locked into the barracks smashed prison property and set fire to newspapers and toilet paper. The fire spread rapidly through the wooden ex-Second World War building, and thirty-seven inmates died as guards struggled to find keys (*Panama City Herald*, 5 Apr. 1998). Yet, road prisons did not entirely disappear, but continued to operate as 'honor squads' for low-risk prisoners. On 21 May 1989 the *St. Petersburg Times* reported on the Brooksville Road Prison where up to seventy inmates in groups of five were employed in picking up rubbish along Interstate-75 or clearing drainage ditches in Hillsborough County, in exchange for time off their sentences. There were no chains and no shotgun guards.[5]

The 1990s chain gang: Alabama and Florida

Alabama Prison Commissioner Ron Jones courted controversy when he reintroduced chain gang work duties to Alabama on 3 May 1995. Lawsuits were immediately filed by the American Civil Liberties Union, Southern Christian Leadership Conference, and Southern Law Poverty Center charging that this violated the Eighth Amendment proscription on cruel and unusual punishment. As Alabama became the 'unlikely template for a new kind of justice,' various legislative or law enforcement delegations came to watch the chain gangs in action and to voice support for their reintroduction in other states (*Birmingham News (AL)*, 26 Sep. and 18 Oct. 1995; *St. Petersburg Times*, 25 June 1995). Arizona, Florida, Iowa, Oklahoma, Nevada, Tennessee and Wisconsin soon followed Alabama's example. While most of these states passed chain gang statues, in Alabama and Oklahoma this form of punishment was a condition of imprisonment, inflicted at the discretion of prison officials.[6] In the states that revived chain gangs, inmates performed similar tasks of clearing roads and highways of litter and weeds, tasks similar to standard road squads, except inmates on the chain gangs were literally chained at the ankles. While Alabama initially chained prisoners in groups, most states opted for individual chaining. Another common feature was the use of conspicuous uniforms, such as old-fashioned black and white stripes, white overalls with 'CHAIN GANG' in large black letters, orange or pink jumpsuits, or bright yellow shirts, which critics felt underlined the primary purpose: to humiliate and degrade, and create a public spectacle with deliberate racial bias, as the majority of prisoners were African American (Peloso, 1997: 1482; Bright, 1996: 848; Gorman, 1995: 452).[7]

The reaction among convicts varied but it was, not surprisingly, overwhelmingly negative. Some Alabama prisoners agreed that the chain gang experience made it less likely they would return to prison and more likely that they would stay out of trouble. One conceded that it had taught him a lesson about freedom and self-responsibility. But many said they were filled with anger and hate and would be more likely to use violence to avoid another stint on the chain gang. One former inmate who had spent 52 days on a chain gang at Staton Correctional Facility for a drug conviction declared:

> It's going to the pits. It's not going to be long before there's going to be two or three killings on the chain gang. If the chain gang don't make you humble and break your pride and let you know you're just a man, it'll bring out the hate in you. I've seen it do both. For most of them, it's going to bring out the hate (quoted in *Birmingham News (AL)*, 10 Feb. 1996).

Chain gang revival re-energised an ongoing debate over the system's effectiveness in reducing recidivism and encouraging rehabilitation. During a fact-finding visit to Alabama in September 1995, Mississippi Lieutenant Governor Eddie Briggs defended Mississippi's record on vocational training and rehabilitation efforts in reducing rates of reoffending: 'There is a tremendous demand for physical laborers all over. Anyone willing to work in Mississippi will have a job. Let's face it, there's not many rocket scientists out on the rock pile' (*Birmingham News (AL)*, 26 Sep. 1995). Another Alabama prisoner was quoted as declaring, 'This ain't doing nothing for my drug habit. When I'm on the outside drinking and smoking, all I'm thinking about is the next hit. I'm not thinking about breaking rocks on the chain gang'(Ibid). Seventy years earlier, Steiner and Brown concluded, 'No one expects the prisoners to leave the chain gang improved in character or better prepared for citizenship' (Steiner and Brown, 1927: 174).

Yet, chain gang revival had popular support. It drew on public frustration over 'molly-coddled' prisoners, a cause taken up by politicians across the spectrum, on public resentment at the estimated $30 billion plus (in 1992) annual cost of the prison system, and on public weariness with prisoners' rights and rehabilitation programmes (Peloso, 1997: 1461; Gorman, 1995: 456). In the United States 'getting tough' on criminals reflects a hardening of attitudes and implementation of punitive policies toward welfare recipients, immigrants, and other politically unpopular and marginalised groups over the past thirty years. Determinate sentencing from the 1970s pushed prison numbers upward. In the 1980s the Reagan administration 'invoked an image of crime that linked violent street crime to welfare, to liberal social policies, and to declining respect for traditional moral values,' fuelled by the appearance of crack cocaine in urban areas in the mid-1980s along with illegally-armed young men protecting their markets. Fears of drugs and street violence came to dominate fears of crime, while an aggressive 'war on drugs' complete with a new set of mandatory sentencing penalties, produced an almost limitless supply of arrestable and imprisonable offenders. The neo-liberal dismantling of welfare programmes, differential criminalisation of drug use, further punitive sanctions such as 'three strikes,' as well as class and racial discrimination shaped the dynamics of a prison population of 2.1 million by 2001 (Mauer, 2001: 9-15; Bright, 1996: 846-8; Pratt, 1996).

For Garland, these new strategies of crime control are rooted 'in a new collective experience of crime and insecurity, an experience which is itself structured by the distinctive social, economic and cultural arrangements of late twentieth-century capitalism,' in tandem with new political alignments and arrangements. He identifies a specific shift in the 'collective mentalities and sensibilities' of the professional middle classes that brought about decreasing support for the post-Second World War penal-welfare framework, loss of faith in the ability of penal experts and criminal justice systems to deal with high rates of crime, and increasing support for punitive responses (Garland, 2000).

With rapidly growing suburban and urban middle-class populations over the past four decades, older Sunbelt states such as Florida, and more recently, parts of Alabama and Georgia, have undergone massive demographic, economic, cultural and political transformations at the same time that high crime rates have become normal social facts. The emergence of reactionary attitudes towards criminals and the politicisation of crime and punishment therefore resonates with these Sunbelt transformations. In 1969 Kevin Phillips identified an 'emerging republican majority' in the South; by the 1980s it was preoccupied with issues of crime and disorder, moral breakdown, incivility, and the decline of the family and by the 1990s it had become receptive to new strategies of control. Once the chain gangs were part of a penal system linked to the patronage politics of the southern Democratic Party. Since the 1970s the Republican Party has gained enormous political strength in the South. Thus in Alabama and Florida, the calls for chain gang revival come from Republican politicians.

For Tessa Gorman, Alabama's chain gangs seemed to be 'part of an environment created to appease society's hostility to prisoners, dissatisfaction with criminal justice, and intolerance of further crime' (Gorman, 1995: 455). Yet, the chain gang of the 1990s differed significantly from past models. Instead of permanent heavy iron chains, prisoners now wear lighter, removable stainless steel ankle chains, often with leather cuffs, that weigh three or four pounds. There were clear health and safety regulations and procedures that included prohibiting men from crossing the highways in chains, hourly water breaks, regular health checks, forbidding inmates from 'horsing around,' and monitoring weather conditions. Prisoners breaking rocks were required to wear protective safety glasses and take rest breaks every twenty minutes. The *Economist* of 13 May 1995 called this 'Chain Gang Lite'. However, prisoners were still expected to complete the work assigned; those who refused or attempted escape were punished, and not with a strap.

In February 1996, Prison Commissioner Ron Jones reported 'only minimal problems' such as 'bee stings, spider bites, bruises from flying rock chips and mashed fingers' when weighed 'against the increased cost of savings of working more inmates outside prisons with fewer guards supervising them.' Other hazards included verbal abuse (often racial), being hit by objects thrown from passing cars, or on one occasion even being shot at by a passing motorist (Peloso,

1997: 1486). Prisoners used issues of dignity and rights in voicing their continuing opposition to Jones' policies. One issue that rankled was the lack of sanitary provision for inmates working out on state roads and highways. One complained of being shackled to a pole for refusing to defecate in a field, another of the filthy conditions of the small portable toilets provided, and another of having to dig a hole in a nearby field, adjacent to the roadside and in view of passing motorists (*Birmingham News (AL)*, 15 May 1996).

Writing from Pennsylvania's death row, journalist and activist, Mumia Abu-Jamal accused Alabama of leading 'America Backward'. He denounced the return of the chain gang: 'While the highways of 'Bama are beautified, their treatment of sentient humans are uglified. As an act of state power, corrections are a synonym for "humiliation", a legislative echo of degradation.'[8] In June 1996, U.S. Circuit Judge Nathaniel R. Jones, a federal appeals judge in Cincinnati, reluctantly ordered the return from Michigan of an Alabama fugitive. Thirty-nine-year-old Phillip Chance, an African American convicted for a 1972 robbery-homicide of a white 81-year-old shopkeeper, had spent the past fifteen years in Michigan, where he had married, had children and generally led a law-abiding and respectable life. In announcing his decision, Jones made note of the 1931 Scottsboro case and the revival of the chain gang in 1995 when he announced his regret in 'sending any human being to a jurisdiction and prison system with a wretched history and, even more distressing, a present demeanor violative of international standards on the treatment of all prisoners' (*Birmingham News (AL)*, 13 June 1996).[9] Seventy percent of Alabama's prison population in 1995 was African American. Alabama prison officials downplayed the racial dynamics of the revived chain gangs choosing to emphasise the goal of reducing recidivism. Lichtenstein notes that each group of five chained inmates included three blacks and two whites, 'in exact proportion to their numbers in the state prison system' (Lichtenstein, 1996:176). For African-American legislators and inmates the revival of the chain gang further underlined the racism embedded in state and national criminal justice systems, and the return of 'white man's slavery' was a reminder of centuries of racial hatred and racial abuse (*Birmingham News (AL)*, 20 Feb. 1996). For others, however, the only resemblance between the chain gang and slavery was the chains, and to draw comparisons between those who forfeited their freedom by deliberately committing a crime, and innocent men, women and children whose freedom and dignity was taken from them, offended the memory of slaves (*St. Petersburg Times*, 11 May 1995).

In the late 1990s, African-American males comprised less than seven percent of the total United States' population but nearly half of the total gaol and prison population. One third of all young black men were either in prison or directly under the control of a state or federal correctional system. For Angela Davis, it was

> the peculiarly racialized and gendered history of punishment in the United States that has, in part, facilitated and ideological transformation of the penal system into a Prison Industrial Complex that imprisons, dehumanizes, and exploits ever-increasing numbers of people, the vast majority of whom are poor and black (Davis, 2001: 35-6).

It was therefore no coincidence that rehabilitation had retreated as a penal goal at precisely the same time that increasing numbers of black men were caught up in this expanding complex. Pratt and Garland note that in the same period that faith in the rehabilitative ideal was waning, the authority of penal experts was also eroding as the gulf widened between the public and the bureaucrats who administered prison policy (Pratt, 1998: 509). In an editorial originally published in the *Economist*, it was observed, 'America's racial divisions are impossible to deny. Four decades after legal segregation began to break down, first through the courts and later through federal legislation, old prejudices remain: Americans regard their black compatriots are less intelligent, less hard-working and keener to live off welfare.' It was also noted that most Americans and foreigners continued to 'regard the Deep South in general, and Alabama in particular, as an especially shameful spot on the racial map' (*Birmingham News (AL)*, 26 Oct. 1997).

For Pratt, the 'civilizing process' occurred at a slower pace in the American South, in fact, 'the Deep South indelibly represented the opposite pole of the civilising continuum and its largely unwanted characteristics' as compared to Northern European nations in part because governments were less centralised and bureaucratic, and in part because of the issue of race. As a result, southerners tolerated forms of punishment and suffering, including chain gangs, lynching, use of stigmatic clothing, much longer than other modern societies (Pratt, 2000: 429-30). Yet, in the mid-1990s, of the eight states that reintroduced chain gangs, only three (Alabama, Florida, and Tennessee) were located in the South. So where does that leave Iowa, Oklahoma, Nevada, and Wisconsin on the 'civilizing continuum'? Further, one Deep South state, Georgia, rejected the idea of reviving its chain gangs. While both Elias and Pratt note the importance of localities in modernist and postmodernist penal frameworks, the American South is a rather more complex and variegated place than at first glance. Further, drawing comparisons between the current period of mass incarceration and the Reconstruction period, Lichtenstein argues that punishment in the United States is 'at root an exercise of private power' and thus many Americans had traditionally had little faith in the capacity of the state

> to punish transgressors of community mores with due efficiency or retributive cruelty. They have expressed a deep suspicion of the adequacy of state-based punishment especially in times and places that criminality and the desire for social order have been racialized and harnessed the project of white supremacy.

It was not surprising that such views were associated with the southern region, 'a section persistently bedeviled by high degrees of personal violence and elevated crime rates, anxieties about racial control, and the highest incarceration rates in the country, if not the world' (Lichtenstein, 2001). Those states that currently boast the highest incarceration rates in the United States are California, Texas, New York and Florida, but they are also the most populous states.

Many southern states are caught between the legacy of the Old South, the shortcomings of the New South and the allure of the Sunbelt South, none more so than Alabama, home of the Confederate Constitution and the site of many civil rights battles. Yet, Alabama is no longer reliant on steel and cotton, but boasts high-tech industries in space, automobiles (Governor James Folsom lured Mercedes-Benz to Tuscaloosa in 1993 with state subsidies of $300 million) computer chips, and medicine, and several leading universities. While there is a growing black middle class, at the same time, the state is engaged in ongoing battles with poverty, especially non-white poverty, growing gaps in education and wealth, the effects of low service-sector and manufacturing salaries, and inequitable access to medical care. Part of Alabama's problem lies with a populist government philosophy of minimal public service provision and low taxes, but these problems and philosophy are hardly unique to Alabama or the Deep South (*Birmingham News (AL)*, 26 Oct. 1997). While the state tries to move on from 'the burden of its past, a legacy of loss and defeat' connected to the Confederacy, and a history of resistance to racial change and opposition to social, economic and political equality connected to the Black Freedom Struggle, the return of the chain gang in 1995 seemed to embody a rejection of thirty years of progress, outside investment, and moving on (*Birmingham News (AL)*, 22 June 1997). Some blamed the resulting public relations disaster on Governor James' willingness to play to the 'populist gallery' by promising to be tough on crime without considering the wider implications (*Economist*, 13 May 1995: 58).

Populist politics also surrounded the return of the chain gang to Florida after an absence of fifty years. In June 1995 Governor Lawton Chiles (a Democrat) allowed the law requiring the Department of Corrections to command certain inmates to perform labour in leg irons and in chained work groups on the highways by 1 December, to become law without his signature. The legislation had been pushed through by Senator Charlie Crist, R-St. Petersburg, during the last hours of the May legislative session. In the rhetorical style of a politician courting publicity, Crist was quoted as wanting to see the 'dregs of the system – killers, rapists, armed robbers – sweating in shackles in muddy highway ditches under the shotgun, where everyone can see them and know that Florida has no mercy on criminals' (*Bradenton Herald (FL)*, 29 May 1995). Corrections Secretary Harry Singletary was left with the task of implementation but there immediately opened up a difference of opinion between Crist and Singletary as to what exactly constituted a 'chain gang'. Drawing on boyhood memories of inmate road labourers in Florida to imagine what a chain gang should look like, Crist wanted inmates to be linked together as in Alabama, to make escape more difficult. Singletary argued that Alabama was 'where Florida was 20 years ago,' denounced Crist's plans as a publicity stunt, and announced he planned to shackle inmates individually as in Arizona, to ensure production (noting that under Crist's scheme if one prisoner wanted to go to the toilet, the whole squad of five would have to go with him). Crist's reply

– 'I'm not overly concerned that they are incredibly productive, so long as they are out there working hard and we really do have chain gangs' – seemed to indicate that saving taxpayer's money was not as central to the scheme as many Republican legislators had thought (*St. Petersburg Times*, 21 June 1995). An editorial in the *St. Petersburg Times* (24 June 1995) denounced Crist for failing 'to understand that corrections officials are not required to help him choreograph this issue for political gain'. It concluded: 'Reaching into the past and reviving chain gangs is typical of the Legislature's backward-looking philosophy on crime and punishment.'

Florida's 'Restricted Labor Squad' of twenty-four inmates wearing chains round their ankles shuffled out for duty on the morning of 21 November 1995 to dig a potato field on prison property, followed by two guards in grey jumpsuits and armed with walkie-talkie head-sets, shotguns and 9mm pistols. Florida's chain gangs were to include maximum-security inmates with a history of disciplinary problems. Seven Florida prisons were to field chain gang work squads by 1 December. Prisoners were shackled individually much to the disgust of Senator 'Chain Gang Charlie' Crist who dismissed the squad as a 'pretend chain gang'. He also expressed disgust at officials' decision to allocate less than two hundred inmates (out of a total prison population of 63,000) to leg-ironed work squads, even though the legislature had appropriated no money to pay for chain gang implementation (*St. Petersburg Times*, 12 Oct. and 22 Nov. 1995). In a direct challenge to Florida's corrections officials and others who denounced the chain gang as an 'inhumane spectacle' which was expensive to administer and increased inmate hostility, Crist attempted in 1996 and 1997 to make his original law more rigorous. He wanted the revived Florida chain gang to be a strong and powerful symbol in the fight against crime, to ensure prisoners felt 'the pain of hard labor and public shame.' A legislative appropriation of $1.2 million was secured in 1996 but there was little change to official policy. Crist's 'chain-gang train' came off the rails in April 1997 when the House Corrections Committee opposed forcing chain gangs of violent offenders to work along state highways on grounds of cost, public safety, and the absence of any serious work or rehabilitation for prisoners (*St. Petersburg Times*, 8 Aug. 1996, 19 Feb. and 1 May 1997).[10]

Throughout their existence chain gangs were sites of often violent and bloody confrontations between inmates, and inmates and guards, and of daring attempts at escape. Inevitably, the revival of the chain gangs brought incidences of violent confrontation and escape. In January 1996, two male inmates in Alabama (both convicted burglars) were reported as having used pruning shears to cut their chains while working along Interstate-65 east of Prattville. Both were recaptured separately several hours later (*Birmingham News (AL)*, 18 Jan. 1996). A more serious incident occurred in June 1997 when two men, one serving a life sentence for rape, robbery and burglary, and the other serving a fifteen-year sentence for burglary, escaped from a thirty-seven-man work crew at the Limestone Correctional Facility cemetery, while under the watch of one guard (in line with regulations on ratios of guards to inmates on work details). The convicted burglar was recaptured in the early hours of the following morning, but the lifer, chased by police, went on a seven-hour 'crime spree' of robbery, assault, and hostage-taking across the neighbouring states of Alabama, Tennessee and Georgia. He was captured after one of his hostages, a Georgia local councilman, secured one of the inmate's weapons and shot him three times (*Birmingham News (AL)*, 27 June 1997).

In Alabama in May 1996 an officer shot and killed 21-year-old Abraham Israel McCord, serving a three-year sentence under the Youthful Offender Statute, who was attacking another inmate with a bush axe. The incident occurred while two chain gang squads totaling seventy men were working along Interstate-65 south of Montgomery. The prisoners had been unshackled in preparation for the bus ride back to Staton Correctional Facility when the altercation started. One correctional officer fired a warning shot with a shotgun, but as the attack persisted, another officer drew his service revolver and shot McCord. The actions of the officers were denounced by lawyers from the Southern Poverty Law Center in Montgomery who were representing Alabama prisoners in a federal lawsuit alleging that chain gang labour violated the Eighth Amendment proscription on cruel and unusual punishment. In the brief, it was alleged that chain gang use 'creates a substantial and constant risk of violence among the chain-gang members and poses a serious and constant threat to their health and safety. Numerous arguments and fights have taken place on the chain gangs. Inmates have used rocks, tools and even their leg irons as weapons during fights' (*Birmingham News (AL)*, 16 May 1996).[11] The circum-

stances of McCord's death also provided evidence that the chain gang reproduced destructive forms of masculinity where class, race, gender, and sectional
antagonisms between prisoners were magnified.

Women prisoners and the chain gang

Of the 20,000 Alabama state prisoners in 1996-97, less than 800 were female and
all were held at the Tutweiler State Prison for Women. Prison Commissioner
Ron Jones' decision to extend chain gangs to women prisoners with disciplinary
records, to clear bushes, weeds and drainage ditches, and to work on garden
crops on prison grounds while under armed guard was a step too far for
Governor James who declared, 'There will be no woman on any chain gang in
the state of Alabama today, tomorrow or anytime under my watch.' Jones'
announcement on 26 April had been prompted by a lawsuit filed by male convicts alleging discriminatory and unfair treatment. A day later he was demoted
by Governor James to his former post as prison warden of Elmore Correctional
Facility. Governor James appeared to be the consummate chivalrous southern
gentleman. His actions drew support from those who applauded his chivalry
and sense of civility, including Mrs. Frances Wideman of the conservative, anti-
Equal Rights Amendment, Eagle Forum (which advocates special or preferen-
tial treatment for women), who decried female chain gangs and increasing
female crime rates as the inevitable and sorry results of the misguided push for
sexual equality. James' actions were met with disgust from those who regarded
giving women special treatment because of their perceived weaknesses as patro-
nising, paternalistic and unforgivingly patriarchal, including the National
Organization for Women (NOW) which denounced chain gangs for both male
and female prisoners (*Birmingham News (AL)*, 26, 27 and 28 Apr. 1996).

An editorial of the *Birmingham News* (30 Apr. 1996) rejected emotional arguments against female chain gangs and called for more imaginative use of prison
man – and womanpower. It observed:

> the overall thrust of the feminist movement for the past three decades
> has been that women are capable of doing almost any job a man is capa-
> ble of doing. Here's another threshold to cross. Chain gangs: You've
> come a long way, baby. Obviously there are physical differences,
> strength, differences, that might dictate a difference in labor to be per-

formed. But why a female check kiter could not perform highway litter duty just as adroitly as a male check kiter escapes us.

This view seemed to resonate with the results of a poll of 420 Alabamians taken by the *Mobile Register* and the University of South Alabama which found fifty-eight percent in favor of women prisoners being placed in leg irons and assigned to chain gang duties on the same terms as men (*Birmingham News (AL)*, 30 Apr. and 6 May 1996; 14 Apr.1997).[12]

Meanwhile, in Maricopa County, Arizona, where chivalry was truly dead, Sheriff Joe Arpaio boasted of running the only all-female chain gang in the United States, thus augmenting 'his self-declared image of being the toughest sheriff in America'. Human rights groups expressed concern over conditions where the 8,000 inmates in the county gaol, most serving sentences of up to twelve months or awaiting bail, worked six days a week, received two meals a day, had no 'luxuries' such as cigarettes or coffee, enjoyed little recreation provision, paid ten dollars to see a nurse and used special postcards with the sheriff's picture to write to families. Many lived in a tent city or 'canvas incarceration compound' set up in 1993 to relieve overcrowding. Convicts were clad in black and white striped uniforms and pink underwear. A chain gang squad of fifteen women was employed as of 1996 to bury Phoenix's indigents, pick up rubbish or undertake weeding in public areas. All women (and men) volunteered for thirty days of chain gang duty to escape the alternative of 23-hours of lockdown in the county jail. Arpaio also set up a gaol high school in 1998. Critics decried any deterrent effect but Arpaio's tough policies drew popular and electoral support, ensuring his election in 1992, and subsequent re-elections. The sheriff rejected national and international criticisms and defended his 'equal opportunity incarceration'. In a Radio Amsterdam interview in October 2003, he declared:

> Sure it's hot here in Arizona. I don't think it's right to have inmates enjoying a nicely air-conditioned jail while our troops in the Middle East during wartime live in tents sometimes in temperatures exceeding 100 degrees (Fahrenheit). If inmates complain about the inconveniences in my jail system, I tell them 'Don't come back' (Amsterdam Forum, 2003; see also CNN, 2003 and Elsner, 2003).

The limits of chain gang 'Lite'

The removal of Ron Jones as Alabama Prison Commissioner and the appointment of Joseph S. Hopper (who had served as prison boss during Fob James' first gubernatorial term in the early 1980s) heralded some important moderations to Alabama's chain gangs.

> A square-jawed, board-shouldered man with slow, deliberate speech and the confident demeanor of a boxer, Hopper has stopped chaining inmates together, no longer forces them to shatter rocks, and has settled a federal court complaint that had challenged five-man shackled crews as being cruel and unusual punishment.

Likening Alabama's chain gangs to a 'Sunday School outing' compared to his experiences of Texas prisons, Hopper was hardly a soft touch. Limestone inmates were reassigned from rockbreaking to clearing stumps from prison land. Hopper declared: 'That's productive and, at the same time, it's a lot harder work than was being performed on the rock pile.' He also announced plans to make prisoners pay an 'inspection fee' on incoming packages (to pay for the costs of checking for contraband) and a three-dollar tariff for non-emergency medical care (to reduce frivolous sick calls and the annual $23 million prison medical costs). Emphasising his aim of making chain gang labour more productive, Hopper's support for individual shackles centered on easier use of equipment, less damage to crops, less risk of injury to other inmates, and maintaining inmate productivity (*Birmingham News (AL)*, 7 July 1996).

In June 1996, it was announced that state convicts would be shackled individually at the ankles, rather than in five-man gangs. The Southern Poverty Law Center welcomed this move, and a key issue in a federal lawsuit was settled. This was hailed as 'a victory for common sense' in a *Birmingham News* editorial (21 June 1996). The editorial continued:

> Alabamians have made clear they want prisons to be tough on criminals, but the corrections system also needs to be imaginative, as well. Prison officials should continue to look for new, more effective ways to get work out of inmates. There's got to be more that inmates in their individual chains can do than pick up trash.

Prison authorities also agreed to provide soap, water, toilet paper and one portable toilet with heavyweight canvas privacy screens for each highway crew of forty prisoners.

The revival of the chain gang drew attention to other controversial practices unique to Alabama prisons in the 1990s, namely the use of 'hitching posts' to punish disruptive prisoners or those who refused to work (but it was also used improperly for prisoners who refused to walk or had been caught masturbating in front of female correctional officers). Usually located near the back gates of the prisons, hitching posts were a longstanding feature of the state's prisons, prisoners were shackled to an iron bar for hours in the baking sun, sometimes over a period of days. According to the lawsuit filed by the Southern Poverty Legal Center (which also challenged the resumption of chain gangs), provision for water and toilet breaks was laid down in the prison rules but frequently ignored. Inmates complained of the humiliation of having to wear soiled clothes while shackled to the hitching post. Others complained of being stretched as bars were placed way above their heads. In August 1998, chaining convicts to iron bars was deemed to be cruel and unusual punishment and in violation of contemporary standards of decency. U.S. District Judge Myron Thompson likened it to the pillory (but where convicts sat down to endure punishment). Within a month (September 1998) the Alabama state prison system had removed 'hitching posts' from seven prisons, and aimed to install video cameras to monitor use of those remaining, although some were abandoned altogether. However, a year after Thompson's ruling, Governor Don Siegelman signaled his desire to bring back the practice of 'handcuffing malingering inmates to outdoor metal posts' because, according to state prison commissioner Mike Haley, 'the restraints encourage prisoners to work as hard as the taxpayers who provide their upkeep' (*Birmingham News (AL)*, 8 and 11 Oct. 1996; 9 Mar. 1997; and 12 Aug. 1998).

By early 2000, Alabama's prison management was in danger of imploding (and its prisons of exploding). In addition to the serious shortage of prison officers, the number of inmates was increasing by approximately 100 per month; nearly 2,000 inmates were waiting for spaces in state prisons and being held in county jails in violation of a 1998 court-ordered agreement limiting their county confinement to thirty days. All this was at a cost of $8 million. City and county jail inspections had been halted because the Department of Corrections had neither the money nor the staff to undertake this biannual duty, and a new prison in Bibb county was half full because there was no money to equip or staff it (*Birmingham News (AL)*, 21 and 24 Feb. 2000). In a damning editorial in the *Birmingham News (21* Feb. 2000), it was noted that:

> Crowded prisons and understaffed, overworked corrections officers make for a dangerous situation. Not only are prison guards' and inmates' safety compromised, but the public's safety is at greater risk as well from riots and breakouts ... If Alabama doesn't do more to make sure corrections officials have the manpower and tools to keep prisons safe, we're going to get burned.

There was no clearer demonstration that an under-funded and understaffed prison system was incompatible with popular and political demands for mass incarceration, where mandatory sentences, 'three strikes' and chain gangs have enormous financial and human costs.

The chain gang experiences of Alabama and Florida illustrate that this form of emotive and ostentatious punishment had limited, even token, application. Approximately 4,000 Alabama prisoners were assigned to chain gang duties when this form of punishment was revived. In Florida on 30 January 1998 a total of 179 individually chained prisoners were assigned to 'restricted labor squads' at seven correctional institutions to work under armed supervision on institutional property. In comparison, there were 3,000 inmates assigned to Florida's Community Work Squads, which assisted the Department of Transportation with road, hurricane and storm work, and to Interagency Community Service Work Squads, which cleared litter, worked on roadways, construction, and grounds or building maintenance for state agencies, cities and municipalities, and non-profit organisations (Corrections in Florida, 1998). In contrast, from the 1920s to the 1940s, the state of Florida assigned over fifty percent of its prison population to road prisons, smaller units for medium- and low-security prisoners, that offered a very different inmate experience from the large cellblock prisons common to northern and western states, and the large penal farms of the South. So was the 1990s experiment just symbolic tokenism to appease public opinion and a few vocal politicians?

That Senator Crist's pronouncements were more rhetorical than real for the Department of Corrections was underlined in their limited commitment to reviving the chain gang. In Florida, where the chain gang issue led to a very public tussle between penal experts and politicians, a central problem was cost. The economic benefits of reinstituting chain gangs were always questionable because of expensive start-up costs associated with equipment and personnel. In Florida, the start-up costs for a chain gang to work on institutional property but outside a secure perimeter fence was given as $152,717, and $100,000 per year thereafter, as three staff (one per ten inmates) were required. The start-up and annual costs of a chain gang working inside a secure perimeter fence was $40,000 largely because fewer staff were required (one per twenty-five inmates) (Corrections in Florida, 1998). And to what extent could chain gang labour within the secure perimeter fence function as an exercise in humiliation and degradation as the chains, stripes and guards were hardly on public view? However, the prisoners in chains and stripes whether on public display or not undoubtedly felt they were deprived of rights, and undeserving of respect or dignity. The Alabama experience showed that states cannot do prisons on the cheap and while taxpayers are increasingly unhappy at the spiralling costs of mass incarceration (Bright (1996:846) noted that in 1995 California spent more on its prison system than its universities) chain gangs are hardly cost-effective. There is, however, evidence that chain gang fervour peaked in the late 1990s as legislatures in Colorado, Georgia, Illinois, Indiana, and Kansas considered but rejected chain gang bills (Peloso, 1997: 1459).

Notes

1. Fob James was elected as a Democrat governor in 1978 and in 1994 as a Republican when he declared his support for chain gangs, creationism in schools and states' rights.
2. North Carolina operated a dual county-state system of imprisonment from 1860s to 1933 where some state prisoners were leased to railroads or worked in prison industries, state public works projects or prison farms. Some were retained by the counties to work on local public works projects. From the 1890s the numbers of able-bodied inmates sent to the state prison declined as county prison numbers grew. In 1925 the 2,500 in road camps was almost double the number of 1,400 prisoners in the state prison. The county system was abolished in 1933 and the Stae Highway Commission took control of all convicts serving more than 30 days. (Hawkins, 1992: 327 and 335)
3. The leasing of state prisoners ended in 1918-1919, but county prisoners were leased unitl 1923 when exposure of the death of Martin Tabert at the hands of a whipping boss and subsequent cover-up prompted legislators to abolish leasing, corporal punishment of prisoners, and hanging (replaced by electrocution) (Miller, 2003)

4. 78 per cent of southern convicts were employed in 1929 as compared to the national average of 58 per cent (Simkins, 1965: 512)
5. Brooksville was one of six road prisons in Florida in 1989, employing nearly 400 prisoners, all male, usually with drug or burglary convictions. It was reported as a good programme for taxpayers but offered little opportunity for rehabilitation. The higher rates of reoffending were noted as compared to prisoners who took part in PRIDE or Florida's Rehabilitative Industries and Diversified Industries Inc.
6. The Arizona and Florida legislatures adopted statutes that mandated statewide implementation of chain gangs by 1 December 1995, but one sheriff in Arizona introduced chain gangs in May 1995. The Iowa legislature passed a statute in 1995 but it was not fully implemented until 1997. Alabama prison commissioner Ron Jones began ordering the use of chain gangs in May 1995, and an Oklahoma sheriff began a voluntary chain gang programme in May 1996. Most chain gang 'graduates' received reduced sentences (Peloso, 1997: 1468-1481).
7. In Alabama bright pink uniforms were used to punish prisoners caught masturbating in front of correction officers. Some were doubly punished by being placed on the chain gang in bright pink overalls (Alabama chain gang uniforms were normally white) (*Birmingham News* (AL), 20 October 1995).
8. Ex-Black Panther, Mumia Abu-Jamal was convicted after a flawed trial in 1982 for killing a Philadelphia policeman. He has been on death row for over twenty years. See Mumia Abu-Jamal, 'The return of the chain gangs', 1995, http://flag.blackened.net/revolt/ws95/chain46.html
9. In 1931 nine black men were arrested near Scottsboro, Alabama, charged and convicted on the false allegations of rape by two white women. Eight were sentenced to death, although none was executed after national and international campaigns. (Carter, 1979; Goodman, 1994).
10. Crist went on to greater things. He was elected education commissioner in November 2000, and then state Attorney General in November 2002.
11. The mother of the inmate shot to death (Abraham Israel McCord) later sued the state prison commissioner and Department of Corrections for failing to properly restrain her son. Her suit alleged that if McCord had been properly handcuffed and restrained with leg irons, the attack would not have occurred (*Birminhgham News (AL)*, 16 Feb. 1997). Prison officials have an Eighth Amendment duty to protect an inmate if there is a strong likelihood he will be assaulted or is being assaulted (Glazer, 1996: 1220)
12. A federal magistrate later found Alabama's policy of excluding women prisoners from chain gangs and leg irons did not violate the equal protection clause of the Fourteenth Amendment. Governor Fob James also drew criticism in January 1999 for commuting the death sentence of a conbicted child murderer, Judith Ann Neelley, who had been on the state's death row since 1983 (*Birmingham News (AL)*, 16 January 1999)

References

Amsterdam Forum, Radio Netherlands, 3 October 2003, 'Back on the Chain Gang', transcript at http://www.vnw.nl/amsterdamforum/html/031030chain.html

Ayers, Edward L. (1984) *Vengeance and Justice: Crime and Punishment in the 19th Century American South*, New York: Oxford University Press.

Bates, Sanford, (1936) *Prisons and Beyond*, New York: The Macmillan Company,.

Bright, Stephen B. (1996): 'The Electric Chair and the Chain Gang: Choices and Challenges for America's Future,' *Notre Dame Law Review* 71, 845-860.

Brown, Gary, (2002) *Texas Gulag: The Chain Gang Years 1875-1925*, Blue Ridge Summit: Republic of Texas Press.

Burns, Robert E. (1997) *I am a Fugitive from a Georgia Chain Gang!* Athens and
    London: University of Georgia Press.
Carter, Dan T. (1979) *A Tragedy of the American South*, revised edn., Baton Rouge:
    Louisiana State University Press.
CNN.com, 29 October 2003, 'Sheriff runs female chain gang' at
    http://www.cnn.com/2003/US/Southwest/10/29/chain.gang.reut
Colvin, Mark, (1997) *Penitentiaries, Reformatories, and Chain Gangs: Social Theory and
    the History of Punishment in Nineteenth-Century America*, New York: St. Martin's
    Press.
Corrections in Florida: 1998 Opinion Survey, 'Inmate Work and Unstructured
    Time,' on http://www.dc.state.fl.us/pub/survey/work.html
Curtain, Mary Ellen, (2000) *Black Prisoners and Their World, Alabama, 1865-1900*,
    Charlottesville and London: University Press of Virginia.
Davis, Angela Y. (2001) 'Race, Gender, and Prison History: From the Convict Lease
    System to the Supermax Prison,' in Don Sabo, Terry A. Krupers, Willie London,
    eds., *Prison Masculinities*, Philadelphia: Temple University Press, pp. 35-45.
Downes, David, (2001) 'The *macho* penal economy: mass incarceration in the
    United States – a European Perspective', *Punishment and Society* 3/1: 61-80.
Elsner, Alan, (2003) 'Sheriff revels in female chain gang's misery',
    http://www.smh.com.au/articles/2003/10/31/1067566085163.html
Fierce, Milfred C., (1994) *Slavery Revisited: Blacks and the Southern Convict Lease
    System, 1865-1933.*
Florida. 16th Biennial Report of the Prison Division of the Department of
    Agriculture of the State of Florida, 1919-1920. (Florida State Library,
    Tallahassee, Florida)
Florida. 25th Biennial Report of the Prison Division of the Department of
    Agriculture of the State of Florida, 1937-1938. (Florida State Library,
    Tallahassee, Florida)
Florida Board of Commissioners of State Institutions, Minutes, Series 431, Vol. 15
    (Aug 25, 1937-Octo 3, 1939). (Florida State Archives, Tallahassee, Florida)
Flynt, Wayne, (1977) *Cracker Messiah: Governor Sidney J. Catts of Florida*, Baton
    Rouge: Louisiana State University Press.
Freeman, Robert, (2000) 'The Public Image of Corrections: Myth Vs. Reality or
    Correctional Staff: Bone Breakers or Corrections Professionals,' *Correctional
    Compass (FL)*, (October): 3-4.
Garland, David, ed., (2001) *Mass Imprisonment: Social Causes and Consequences*,
    London: Sage Publications.
—, (2000) 'The Culture of High Crime Societies,' *British Journal of Criminology* 40:
    347-375.

—, (1997) *Punishment in Modern Society*, Oxford: Clarendon Press.

Glazer, Yale, (1996) 'The Chains May Be Heavy, But They Are Not Cruel and Unusual: Examining the Constitutionality of the Reintroduced Chain Gang,' *Hofstra Law Review*, 24: 1195-1224.

Goodman, James, (1994) *Stories of Scottsboro*, New York: Vintage Books.

Gorman, Tessa M., (1995) 'Back on the Chain Gang: Why the Eighth Amendment and the History of Slavery Proscribe the Resurgence of Chain Gangs,' *California Law Review* 85: 441-478.

Hawkins, Darnell F. (1992) 'State Versus County: Prison Policy and Conflicts of Interest in North Carolina,' pp. 326-363 in Eric H. Monkkonen, ed., *Crime & Justice in American History: Historical Articles on the Origins and Evolution of American Criminal Justice*, Vol. 6: *Prisons and Jails*, Part 1, Munich, London: K. G. Saur.

Kendrick, Baynard, (1964) *Florida Trails to Turnpikes, 1914-1964*, Gainesville, FL: University of Florida Press.

Lichtenstein, Alex, (2001) 'The private and the public in penal history: A commentary on Zimring and Tonry' in David Garland, ed., *Mass Imprisonment: Social Causes and Consequences*, London: Sage, 171-8.

—, (1996) *Twice the Work of Free Labor: The Political Economy of Convict Labor in the New South*, London and New York: Verso.

McKelvey, Blake, (1977) *American Prisons: A History of Good Intentions*, Montclair: Patterson Smith.

Mancini, Matthew J. (1996) *One Dies, Get Another: Convict Leasing in the American South, 1866-1923*, Columbia: University of South Carolina Press.

Mauer, Marc, (2001) 'The causes and consequences of prison growth in the United States,' *Punishment & Society*, 3: 9-20.

—, (2001) 'Crime, Politics, and Community Since the 1990s,' in Don Sabo, Terry A. Krupers, Willie London, eds., *Prison Masculinities*, Philadelphia: Temple University Press, pp. 46-53.

Miller, Vivien, (2003) 'The Icelandic Man Cometh: North Dakota State Attorney Gudmunder Grimson and a Reassessment of the Martin Tabert Case', *Florida Historical Quarterly* 81/3: 279-315.

—, (2000) *Crime, Sexual Violence and Clemency: Florida's Pardon Board and Penal System in the Progressive Era*, Gainesville: University Press of Florida.

Myers, Martha A. (1998) *Race, Labor & Punishment in the New South*, Columbus: Ohio State University Press.

Oshinsky, David, (1996) *'Worse Than Slavery': Parchman Farm and the Ordeal of Jim Crow Justice* New York, The Free Press.

Pearce, Donn, *Cool Hand Luke*, (1999) London: Prion Books.
Peloso, Wendy Imatani, (1997) 'Les Miserables: Chain Gangs and the Cruel and
   Unusual Punishment Clause,' *Southern California Law Review*, 70: 1459-1511.
Pratt, John, (2003) 'The decline and renaissance of shame in modern penal
   systems,' in Barry S. Godfrey, Clive Emsley, Graeme Dunstall, eds., *Comparative
   Histories of Crime*, Cullompton and Portland: Willan Publishing, pp. 178-194.
—, (2000) 'Emotive and ostentatious punishment,' *Punishment & Society*, 2: 417-439.
—, (1999) 'The Return of the Wheelbarrow Men; Or, the Arrival of Postmodern
   Penality?' *British Journal of Criminology*, 40: 127-145.
—, (1998) 'Towards the "Decivilizing" of Punishment?' *Social and Legal Studies*, 7:
   487-515.
—, (1996) 'Reflections on recent rends towards the punishment of persistence,'
   Crime, Law & Social Change, 25: 243-264.
Preston, Howard Lawrence, (1991) *Dirt Roads to Dixie: Accessibility and
   Modernization in the South, 1885-1935*, Knoxville: University of Tennessee Press.
Rosenblatt, Elihu ed., (1996) *Criminal Justice: Confronting the Prison Crisis*, Boston:
   Southend Press.
Rotman, Edgardo, (1998) 'The Failure of Reform: United States, 1865-1965', in
   Norval Morris and David J. Rothman, eds., *The Oxford History of the Prison: The
   Practice of Punishment in Western Society*, New York and Oxford: Oxford
   University Press, pp. 151-177.
Sabo, Don, Terry A. Krupers, Willie London, eds., (2001) *Prison Masculinities*,
   Philadelphia: Temple University Press, pp. 3-18.
Simkins, Francis Butler, (1965) *A History of the South*, 3rd. edn,. New York: Alfred A.
   Knopf.
Simon, Jonathan, (2001) 'Fear and loathing in later modernity: Reflections on the
   critical sources of mass imprisonment in the United States', *Punishment &
   Society* 3/1: 21-33.
—, (2000) 'From Big House to the warehouse,' *Punishment & Society*, 2/2: 213-234.
Spivak, John L. (1934) *On the Chain Gang*, 2nd edn. New York: International
   Pamphlets.
Steiner, Jesse F. and Roy M. Brown, (1927) *The North Carolina Chain Gang: A Study
   of County Convict Road Work*, Chapel Hill: University of North Carolina Press.
Tannenbaum, Frank, (1969) *Darker Phases of the South*, New York: Negro
   Universities Press.
Taylor, William Banks, (1999) *Down on Parchman Farm: The Great Prison in the
   Mississippi Delta*, Columbus, OH: Ohio State University Press.
Terrill, Tom E. and Jerrold Hirsch, eds., (1978) *Such As Us: Southern Voices of the
   Thirties*, Chapel Hill: University of North Carolina Press.

Chapter Seven

Electronic Monitoring in France: Present Situation and Perspectives

René Lévy

In October 2000 France joined the ever-growing group of European countries that have added some electronic monitoring (or EM) procedures to their list of penal sanctions and measures (for an overview of the rapidly changing European situation, see Mayer, Haverkamp, Lévy, 2003; CEP, 2003; Whitfield, 2001). As of 1 May 2004 2,312 EM measures had been meted out since its introduction, and 615 were being served. The reticence of the left-wing government had led to a relatively hesitant start. However, once the right returned to power, and spurred by the sharp upturn in the prison population since 2001, from 2002 electronic monitoring became a penal policy priority. This accounts for the ambitious goal of 3,000 EM in stock set for 2007.

The present chapter presents a tentative assessment of the implementation of EM in France, and gives an idea of its prospects. Following a reminder of how the French scheme came into existence and of its salient features we discuss its main achievements, and in conclusion, recent reforms affecting the measure and the perspectives they offer.

Birth and design of French-style EM

The history of penology, at least since Tocqueville and de Beaumont, is to a large extent the history of the international circulation of ideas and innovations as to how to deal with criminals, and of the reception they met. This history remains to be written where EM is concerned. We know it began in the USA (Ball, Huff, Lilly, 1988, 34 ff.; Renzema, 1992 ; Mainprize, 1996), and it is easy to see the phases through which different countries imported the scheme. Much more difficult to determine is what intellectual channels and which individuals or pressure groups furthered it, who served as intermediaries for the manufacturers of the equipment, what opposition it met and why it did or did not succeed in catching on.

We know, for instance, that in Great Britain a pressure group, the Offender Tag Association (OTA), created in 1982 by a journalist and prison visitor, campaigned for EM whereas the organisation representing probation officers, the NAPO, was staunchly opposed to it, to the point of encouraging the government of the time (which had no need to be pushed) to resort to the private sector (Nellis, 1991, 168-171; Nellis, 2001). In France on the other hand, things are not as clear and the list of people consulted by the two parliamentary representatives who successively proposed the adoption of EM gives no hint as to how the idea progressed. The beginnings of electronic monitoring were full of hesitations. Whereas it was first suggested in 1989, it was only legalised at the end of 1997, and another three years passed before the first devices were ready for use. A distinction may be made, then, between the gestation phase, marked by some parliamentary initiatives, not immediately successful, and an experimental phase.

The first proposals

EM made its first appearance in an official text in France in 1989, in socialist deputy Gilbert Bonnemaison's report on 'The modernisation of the public correctional services', where it was called house arrest under electronic monitoring (ADSE in French) (Bonnemaison, 1989; on the creation of this report, see Froment, 1998, 281-286). The measure was linked to a *numerus clausus* for confinement, aimed at limiting prison overcrowding. The idea was to select those inmates susceptible of being placed on EM so as to leave room for new arrivals, be they in pre- or post-trial detention (as a probationary measure in the latter case). The report also considered the possibility of using EM to replace short prison sentences. Inspired by what was done in Florida and by projects then under study in Great Britain, the report argued that EM was 'an effective sanction, whereas it is too often thought that prison is the only real punishment' (p. 28).[1] At the same time, it enabled offenders to maintain family ties, to keep their job or get training. Finally, the report urged that its cost would be considerably lower than the cost of confinement.[2]

The Bonnemaison report briefly outlined what was to become the French scheme, but it received no immediate follow-up. The issue was raised again in 1995-96 in another parliamentary report, prepared by a right-wing senator Guy-Pierre Cabanel, this time under the title 'For improved prevention of recidivism' (Cabanel, 1996). The Cabanel report reviewed the experiments under way in other countries (Great Britain, the Netherlands, Sweden) and came to the conclusion that EM was an effective, financially advantageous tool for preventing recidivism, and a way of combating prison overcrowding. The scheme proposed aimed essentially at using EM to replace short prison terms and for probationary purposes at the end of longer prison sentences. It also expressed serious reservations about the use of EM in the pre-trial phase. In accordance with his report, the senator attempted to have a bill voted introducing EM. He finally succeeded with the Act of 19 December 1997 (Act no. 97-1159), which set up EM as a mitigating measure for a prison term of less than one year or when less than one year remained to be served (Kuhn, Madigner, 1998, 676; Pradel, 1998; Couvrat, 1998).

A new phase began with the Act of 15 June 2000 on the presumption of innocence and the rights of victims (Act no. 2000-516), another parliamentary initiative which authorised the enforcement of pre-trial detention by the use of EM. The Act of 9 September 2002 further extended the pre-sentencing use of EM, which could now be proposed for any indicted individual irrespective of recourse to pre-trial detention (Pitoun, Enderlin-Morieult, 2003). More recently, another reform, discussed below, added EM to the list of sentences susceptible of being meted out by courts but which represented a break with the previous philosophy.[3] Theoretically, then, EM is now applicable to adult and juvenile offenders at all points in the penal procedure.

A slow start and a reversal of the correctional situation

Almost three years went by between the 1997 Act coming into force and the implementation of EM. Why this unusual hiatus? Although some writers would disagree, I believe the reason for the lag is that the corrections administration (AP in French) was unprepared and reluctant to apply EM. Indeed, in the French political system, it is a considerable feat for a member of parliament to succeed in forcing the government's hand by obtaining the adoption of a bill that s/he has introduced. Most of the time projected legislation is formulated within the ministries, where it has generally been subjected to lengthy preparation involving working parties, studies and the consultation of specialists. In the case of EM it was only well after the bill was voted that the corrections administration had to have a series of studies done by a firm specialised in technological counselling so as to find out what Justice Department executives thought, assess experiments in other countries and design several feasible scripts for the French scheme. In short, between September 1998 and April 1999, the administration had to collect the basic information required for achieving EM.[4]

In point of fact, the relative inertia of the AP authorities (the *Direction de l'Administration Pénitentiaire*, or DAP) should probably be sought in the evolution of the prison situation. As shown in the graph below, between the point when Senator Cabanel began his fight to introduce EM and the point when he succeeded in getting the bill adopted, a reversal had occurred in the demographic situation in prisons. From the early 1980s to 1996, the prison population had risen steadily, although not at a constant pace (see graph 1). But a reversal occurred in 1996 and the downward trend continued until the second semester of 2001. At the same time there was a tremendous increase in non-custodial sentences, with about 100,000 people in stock in 1994 and 141,000 in 2002. In other words, and irrespective of the causes of these changes, in our opinion the DAP, not very favourable to EM to begin with, was clearly in no hurry to look into an additional community-based measure since the inflationary pressure on prison populations was declining. Conversely, and we will have more to say about this further on, the new interest in EM and the ambitious objectives now set for it by the DAP coincide perfectly with the 2001 upswing that produced a staggering rise in the prison population.

Graph 1: Prison Population in France (as of 1 January 1980–2004)

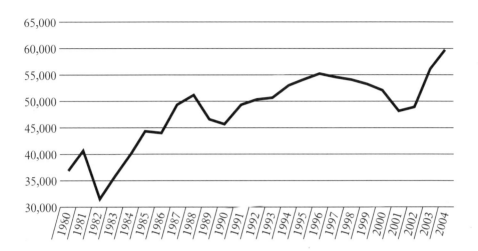

Implementation of EM

A broad outline of the initial scheme

Initially, the French system was predominantly a probationary measure, or backdoor scheme,[5] implemented by the judge in charge of sentence-enforcement (JSE) backed by the Corrections Department Integration and Probation Office (SPIP) and the particular custodial facilities (for a detailed juridical analysis, see Herzog-Evans, 2002, 309-323 and Pitoun, Enderlin-Morieult, 2003. For the controversies raised by the measure, see Kaluszynski, Froment, 2003). Technically speaking it relies on what are known as first-generation devices, capable of determining, at long distance, a specific person's presence in a specific place, usually the person's home, during pre-defined hours. It may be applied to both adults and juveniles, though in practice, so far, it has only been applied to adults. The public prosecutor or the person involved may request the measure, but the final decision is up to the judge.

   Sentenced offenders, whose consent – as well as that of the people sharing their home – is required, are first subjected to a social and technical enquiry aimed to make sure they are fit to benefit from the measure and that the assigned place is suitable. It is not necessary that they have a job.

Eligibility for EM applies in two distinctly different situations:

- It may be a substitute means for the enforcement of an unsuspended custodial sentence not exceeding one year (or of several sentences totaling no more than one year);[6]
- It may be used for early release from prison when less than one year remains to be served; in this case EM may also be used as a probationary measure preceding the granting of parole.

Furthermore, in its initial form, the French scheme was exclusively in the hands of public institutions. This point is about to be modified, and in all probability from 2005 the private sector will play a greater role (see below).

In practice

EM is located at the crossroads of two trends affecting the criminal justice system in developed countries everywhere: firstly, the tendency to resort increasingly to all sorts of long-distance surveillance; and secondly, a loss of confidence in traditional intermediate sentences, considered too lenient and insufficiently intimidating or compelling, so that more coercive community-based sentences (not necessarily implying highly technical measures) are judged preferable. As opposed to the English-speaking and northern European countries (the Netherlands and Scandinavia), France was not affected by this evolution for a long time, since no major change in the range of probationary tools had occurred since the introduction of the community service order (*travail d'intérêt général*) some twenty-odd years ago (Ministère de la Justice, 1994). The simultaneous intrusion of new technology and of greater coercion represents a major change, then, which may lead to the redefinition of the various agents (judges, prison guards, probation workers) involved.

Moreover, just when EM was being set up, the functions of the two main actors involved were being extensively reformed. For one thing, the SPIP were a relatively recent creation, the outcome of a merger, in 1999, between the departments working with sentenced offenders outside of prison, within the community, and other departments working in a custodial context and dealing with prisoners.[7] This reform set up a single category of social workers within the corrections administration, entailing a redefinition of their functions and thus producing tensions that had not yet been dissolved when EM was implemented. Secondly, the function of the JSE had just been modified in depth by the Act of 15 June 2000 which 'jurisdictionalised' sentence enforcement, meaning that the procedures involved more defence (the lawyer of the convicted offender was given a greater role) and were more formal, creating some upheaval in the (more cumbersome) procedures and methods of the judges involved.

The novelty of EM plus this peculiar context explain why the DAP was convinced of the need to implement the scheme gradually, so as to try it out, test the equipment and programs offered by different manufacturers, give the different categories of personnel affected by the new measure time to familiarise themselves with it and evaluate the reactions of individuals assigned to EM. There was also the need to leave local actors sufficient leeway in the implementation of the measure so that innovations susceptible of subsequent generalisation might come to light. It was in this perspective, and following examination of a number of possibilities, that four pilot sites were chosen for implementation of the new scheme for about one year (from October 2000 to October 2001), within basically the same legal and organisational framework (For an analysis of the various scripts visualised, see Lévy, Pitoun, 2004; for implementation on the four pilot sites, see Kensey, Pitoun, Lévy, Tournier, 2003).

The criteria for choosing experimental EM sites seem to have been largely empirical. Initially, the DAP wanted the sites selected to be extremely overcrowded, to be run by someone capable of piloting the operation and to have a JSE who was interested.[8] Finally, it seems that the risk of union protest against the measure, along with good relations between the prison director and the SPIP director, or between the court authorities and the corrections officials, were also considered. In the last analysis:

> each pilot site chose the computer programs and devices it viewed as most appropriate, locally, for monitoring. It also decided how to allocate responsibilities among its staff members, in accordance with local constraints, and defined its procedures for organising the work, especially the following jobs: placing and removing the bracelets, installing and recovering receivers, responding to alarms and checks.[9]

Graph 2: Monthly number of persons under EM

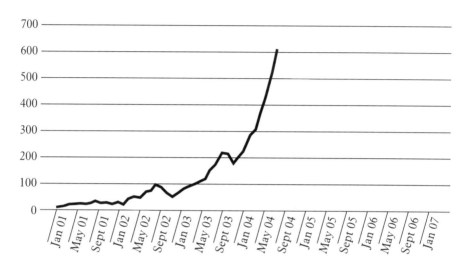

Since the original scheme was small-scale, the number of tagged individuals has risen slowly. It is increasing little by little with the gradual extension of the measure to the entire country since late 2001. However, as will be seen below, it is still far below Justice Department expectations.

Although at the time of writing (June 2004) implementation is not yet complete, we are already able to describe use of EM accurately, using data from two sources: first, the monthly DAP statistics and secondly, a survey of about one fourth of all such measures pronounced since the outset.[10] On the basis of these findings, we are in a position to determine how utilisation of the measure has changed, under what conditions it is used and the targets to which it is applied.

Relative increase in use of EM

As shown by graph 2, the absolute number of EM under way (in stock) has risen sharply since January 2003, with an apparent acceleration in the growth in recent months. Since we are still in the phase of extending implementation of EM across the country, however, the decisive factor here is the increasing num-

Graph 3: Average monthly number of measures per site (stock)

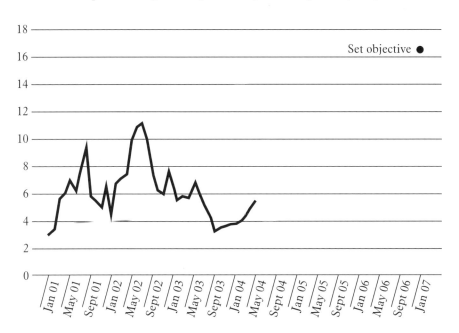

ber of courts implementing the measure. Graph 3 shows clearly that if we disregard monthly variations in the number of sites, by calculating the average monthly stock per site, the increase in the number of EM is much slower, since it did not resume until late in 2003, and the objective of 3,000 measures in stock by 2007 (shown by the mark in the upper right corner of the graph) still seems very far away. As of 1 May 2004 an average of 5.5 measures were being served per site, the goal being to reach 16.6. Since 112 out of 181 courts now resort to EM, the present theoretical stock of EM should be 993.

Main features of EM[11]

Circumstances under which EM is used

As mentioned above, the version of EM in use before 9 March 2004 (with the exception of its practically non-existent use in replacement of pre-trial surveillance) could be used either as an alternative to prison or as a means of early release. Since the latter might be of two sorts, this made for 3 situations in all. In practice, there is a tremendous disproportion in use of the three possibilities: use as an alternative to one or several unsuspended prison terms totalling less than one year represents 87 per cent of cases; early release for a less than one year remainder of a longer prison sentence represents 12.3 per cent of cases; and use for early release on probation only 0.7 per cent.

EM is massively employed as a substitute for confinement, then, but the existence of other, similar alternatives makes it impossible to determine what proportion of these sentenced offenders would actually have been placed in detention otherwise. Our observations and the occasional conversations I have had with judges and DAP officials seem to indicate that EM is often used for sentenced individuals who reside too far from a semi-liberty centre for this to be a feasible measure, thus avoiding unsuspended imprisonment for at least some of these. It is also quite possible, however, that EM is simply used in replacement of other alternative measures, with which it is legally interchangeable.

Schedule and assigned place

In almost all cases (99 per cent) the place assigned was the tagged person's home. Hence, the existence of a fixed place of residence turns out to be an unwritten requisite for EM, since other living places such as an institutional home, or even the person's workplace, are legally allowed.

In three quarters of cases, this assignment to the home only applied to working days (Monday to Friday) and in one sixth of cases it also applied on weekends. In nearly 10 per cent of cases the schedule was more complicated.

Requirements

Theoretically, a great variety of requirements may be imposed since, in addition to those inherent in the measure, the judge may impose any requirement mentioned in articles 132-44 to 132-46 of the Code of Criminal Proceedings, which is to say those applying to probation. These include checks obliging the person to respond to a series of summonses and to inform the authorities of any change in his or her situation, as well as obligations or prohibitions pertaining to the person's place of residence, professional or other activities, the people and places frequented, and financial obligations. Finally, the person may be offered social or material assistance.

In practice, the obligation to work is applied to nearly three quarters of tagged individuals (73.6 per cent), and in the great majority of cases (60 per cent of the tagged) it is the only obligation. This is less an externally imposed requirement than an acknowledgement of the facts, since over 60 per cent of these people held a stable or casual job. No other obligation or prohibition or combination thereof (and there was a great variety of combinations) affected more than 10 per cent of these people.

Once the requirements were set they remained unchanged in 61 per cent of cases: in 31 per cent of cases there were one to two changes; the rest had three or more changes (the most being 13!). But as we might expect, the number of modifications is correlated with the duration of the measure: the proportion of tagged individuals demanding three changes was 50 per cent higher beyond three months, and doubled beyond four months, in comparison with the average (this amounted to, respectively, 12, 16 and 8 percent). This of course reflects a degree of reactivity to changes occurring in the life of the person under EM.

Implementation period

The average duration of EM is 75 days, or two and a half months (but the median is only 64 days), with a minimum of two days and a maximum of 257 (8.5 months): 85 per cent of EM lasted less than four months.

For those sentenced offenders for whom EM was an alternative to detention – the majority of cases (504 out of 580), as seen above – this duration depended on the quantum of the initial unsuspended custodial sentence. In Table 1 we crossed the quantum of detention with duration of EM, expressed as three-month periods. Obviously, the duration of EM tends to rise with the quantum, as it logically should. However, the table also shows that the duration of EM usually does not correspond to the sentence it replaced, except for the shortest sentences. While everyone sentenced to three months of imprisonment or less effectively served about that much time on EM, this is only true for a minority of those sentenced to between three and six months (85 per cent of whom spent three months or less on EM). In the group with a six to nine months prison sentence only 3 per cent actually served approximately that time on EM, whereas 50 per cent served three months or less on EM. The situation is similar for those with a nine to twelve-month sentence; nine out of ten of these spent less than six months on EM.

Consequently, conversion of their sentence into EM was definitely beneficial in terms of duration for these sentenced offenders, although we are unable to say how many of these people actually avoided imprisonment thanks to it.

Table 1: Length of initial prison sentence and duration of EM measure, in months (EM as alternative to imprisonment only)

Length of EM	0 to <3m	3 to <6m	6 to <9m	9 to <12m	Total
0 to 3m	100	85.8	50	40.0	71.7
3 to 6m	0	14.2	46.9	52.5	26.6
6 to 9m	0	0	3.1	7.5	1.7
Total	100	100	100	100	100

Incidents and cancellations

The great majority of EM measures were terminated normally. According to the DAP monthly statistics, the failure rate for EM, measured by the cancellation rate for the measure, was 5.4 per cent (126 out of 2,312). Cancellation was mostly due to non-respect of the imposed obligations (64.3 per cent of cases, 81 out of 126). Committing another offence came next, but was far behind, with 19.8 per cent of cases (25 out of 126), followed by absconding (11 per cent, 14 cases) and misconduct (4 per cent, 5 cases). There was also 1 case (0.8 per cent) in which the person requested termination.[12]

But as may be seen, cancellation, an extreme measure, is rarely used. Indeed, our study shows that most EM (61.4 per cent) are eventless; one or two incidents occur in 28.5 per cent of cases and more than two in 10.1 per cent. Over half of cancellations of the measure were due to repeated incidents.

Checks and supervision

Our findings do not indicate the kind of surveillance done by social workers. We do have one indicator, however, which is the number of visits to the person's home independently of any incident. This is not the only indicator, of course, since these people may be called into the office for talks, or have regular talks with their supervisor over the phone. But aside from the fact that we have no information on these other forms of interaction, we may consider that home visits are the strongest way for the SPIP to show its interest in tagged individuals. About 35 per cent of these people never received a visit, 38 per cent were visited once and about 27 per cent received two visits or more (see Table 2).

Table 2: Number of home visits by supervisor

Home visits	Cases	%
0	202	34.8
1	219	37.8
2+	159	27.4
Total	580	100

On the whole, and predictably, the number of visits is closely correlated with the duration of the measure. The longer it lasts, the greater the chances of being visited at home. Irrespective of the duration, the proportion of those who received no visit was quite high: a large third for one to three months, still a large fourth for three to four months, and even 20 per cent for placements exceeding four months.

What conclusion may be drawn? It all depends on what our reference criteria are. Compared to the situation in other countries, the degree of supervision by the SPIP may seem rather poor. But we have heard people testify that given the extremely heavy caseload of French probation officers, it is quite exceptional for them to go to the homes of the paroled prisoners they are monitoring.[13] Seen from this angle, then, people on EM receive exceptional attention.

The beneficiaries: their socio-demographic characteristics

We have relatively detailed information on the people given an electronic bracelet, but it is not necessarily easy to compare them with other groups 'in the hands of the law', for lack of accurate data on the latter. Two points of comparison were chosen for Table 3, below: first, some very succinct information on individuals receiving non-custodial measures; secondly, an analysis of the characteristics of individuals in detention.[14]

Technically, offenders sentenced to EM are in the latter category, but in practice they are in the first group.[15] As shown below, their sex, nationality and age distribution is nonetheless closer to that of people with non-custodial sentences than to those incarcerated. They also are more frequently living with a partner than the latter, more frequently have dependent children and are better educated. A majority are employed. These broad findings lead us to the conclusion that EM beneficiaries were selected from among those sentenced offenders whose better social integration had prompted a more optimistic prognosis.

Table 3: Characteristics of groups subjected to EM or to a custodial sentence or non-custodial sentence

Characteristics	EM (n = 580)	Non-custodial sentence[16]	Custodial sentence[17]
Women	7.2 %	10%	5% *
Foreigners	8.1 %	7%	24%
Average age	33.0*	32.5	29.0
Married/Partner	44 %	"	25%
Dependant children	50.5 %	"	33%
Elementary school/illiterate	18.6 %	"	48%
Employed (stable/temporary)	63.6 %	"	31%

* The youngest was 16 (the only minor among the first 580 people under EM); the oldest was 80

The Offences

EM is intended to cover a relatively broad range of offences, but classification of these by order of frequency reflects neither the entire series of sentences for moderately serious offenses nor the series of those sent to prison.

–in comparison with all sentences for moderately serious offenses, thefts are over-represented in EM, along with violence, drug-related offenses and frauds, whereas drunken driving is considerably under-represented;

–in comparison with prison inmates (but most of whom have not yet been sentenced definitively), an over-representation of drunken driving, drug-related offenses and frauds is found for EM, whereas cases of violence, sexual violence and other highway offenses are approximately equivalent in the two groups.

Table 4 : Type of offence amongst EM and amongst all convictions and amongst prison inmates

Offence	EM	% EM	% of convictions 2001[18]	% of inmates 2002[19]
Theft/Receiving	146	25.2	18.6	30.2
Violence*	120	20.7	13	20.2
Drunken driving	86	14.8	24.4	5.9
Drugs	80	13.8	5.1	12.6
Sexual violence	38	6.6	1.9	5.5
Embezzlement	31	5.3	3.2	2.9
Other driving offences	22	3.8	5.1	3
Other	57	9.8	28.7	19.5
Total	580	100	100	100

* Including violent theft.

Within the group placed on EM, there is a clear-cut difference connected with age and offences committed. When these two variables are crossed, a definite divide between people under 30 among whom drug-related offences, violence and thefts are over-represented, and those over 35 among whom driving offences with or without drinking, sexual violence and fraud are over-represented. Furthermore, a look at their penal situation shows that in the over-35 group, highway offences are only found among those for whom EM is an alternative to confinement.

In other words, a broad typology of EM shows three types:

    –One group, the youngest (under age 30), characterised by drug-related offences, violence and thefts, irrespective of their penal situation;
    –A group of sentenced prisoners avoiding prison thanks to EM, over age 35, characterised by offences connected with driving, sexual violence and malicious offences;[20]
    –A group of inmates given early release, with the same characteristics as group 2, with the exception of highway offences.

Table 5: Offence by age for EM convicts

	<20	20–<25	25–<30	30–<35	35–<40	40–<45	45–<50	50+	NSP	Total
Drunken Driving	14.29	4.41	10.94	**19.35**	**21.21**	**19.15**	**23.40**	**24.07**	0.00	14.83
Other driving off.	0.00	3.68	3.91	2.15	**7.58**	**6.38**	4.26	0.00	0.00	3.79
Sexual violence	0.00	0.74	1.56	7.53	7.58	**10.64**	**12.77**	**22.22**	0.00	6.55
Other	0.00	6.62	7.03	5.38	**12.12**	**17.02**	**21.28**	**14.81**	0.00	9.83
Embezzlement	0.00	0.74	1.56	3.23	**7.58**	**8.51**	8.51	**20.37**	50.00	5.34
Drugs	0.00	**18.38**	**21.88**	15.05	7.58	8.51	6.38	1.85	0.00	13.79
Violence	**57.14**	**30.88**	**22.66**	20.43	16.67	8.51	17.02	5.56	0.00	20.69
Theft/Receiving	**28.57**	**34.56**	**30.47**	26.88	19.70	21.28	6.38	11.11	50.00	25.17
Total	100	100	100	100	100	100	100	100	100	100
Number	7	136	128	93	66	47	47	54	2	580

Recent reforms and prospects

I have described the birth and present utilisation of EM. However, the present scheme is about to be profoundly reworked, both organisationally and in its philosophy, and there is no way of foreseeing what consequences this will have for future use of the measure. These changes affect the link between the public and the private sectors in the implementation of EM, the place of this measure in the overall range of sentences and last, the decision-making process. These three aspects are briefly discussed below.

Toward greater privatisation

Whereas at its inception the scheme only conceded a limited role to the private sector, confined to renting equipment to the administration and supplying maintenance for it, the September 2002 *Loi d'orientation et de programmation de la justice*, used by the right, then back in power, to set its priorities for the judiciary, mentioned 'the outsourcing of part of the management of the alarms'. This intention was cemented by a ruling, in March 2004, defining the requisites for the habilitation of natural persons or legal entities given responsibility, by contract, for implementing the 'technical arrangement enabling the long-distance surveillance of individuals subjected' to EM.[21] The path is clear, henceforth, for demanding bids, along the following lines :

–The different operations involved in the implementation of EM would be allocated between private operators and the corrections administration, depending on whether or not they are viewed as involving the sovereignty of the State. Civil servants would continue to be in charge of placing the bracelets and checking the alarms, whereas private companies would install receiver sets and do the long distance surveillance.

–Each private operator, then, would be in charge not only of supplying the equipment and providing upkeep, as is now the case, but would also do the actual surveillance and define the nature of alarms: a technical alarm would send a technician to the tagged person's home, whereas a 'real' alarm would be transmitted to the competent custodial institution, whose corrections workers would then proceed with a check.[22]

–France would be divided into three zones, each with its own market[23] and its own surveillance centre.

This new arrangement is expected to become operational sometime in 2005, gradually, as the present local contracts expire.

Extension of EM to the court trial phase

As we have seen, EM was initially visualised exclusively as a backdoor scheme. Attempts to extend it to the pre-sentencing phase soon saw the light, but so far have been largely unsuccessful. The Act of 9 March 2004 went a step further by authorising the sentencing court to pronounce an EM sentence directly, in lieu of an unsuspended prison sentence of one year or less. Technically, EM is still a post-sentencing measure, but here it is prescribed immediately, without awaiting the intervention of the judge in charge of sentence enforcement. EM is thus applicable, now, to all phases in the penal process. It is difficult to predict the effect of this new provision, which goes against the prevailing consensus, since experts all agree that 'the risk of net-widening ... tends to rise when the mode of sentence-serving is decided earlier in the penal process' (Kuhn, Madignier, 1998: 675). It should be noted, however, that the right-wing representative Jean-Luc Warsmann, rapporteur for the bill, hearty supporter of EM and of any measure likely to reduce recourse to imprisonment, does not believe that this scheme will be developed very much.[24] Time will tell whether this reform, clearly dictated by the inflated prison population, will live up to the expectations of its promoters.

The growing role of the corrections administration

While, as seen above, the cards are about to be reshuffled between the public and private sectors with respect to the organisation of EM, other changes will modify roles within the public sector itself. Until now the SPIP was simply in charge of enforcing the JSE decisions on EM. It did the prior social investigation, followed by the implementation and surveillance of tagged individuals, jointly, with the custodial establishment involved. Moreover, starting with the 1997 Act, the judicial character of the decision was strongly emphasised with the compulsory presence of the person's lawyer at the hearing, an unusual demand for non-custodial sentencing and one which was not extended to the rest of this category until the Act of 15 June 2000.

The reform of 9 March 2004 breaks partially with this logic, not because it denies the need for the tagged person's enlightened consent, but in that it increases the role of the SPIP and correlatively pushes the judge further into the background, at least in some situations.

In case of a prison sentence of one year or less, to be converted into EM, nothing changes. But for early prison-leaving, the initiative is henceforth in the hands of the SPIP, as in the case of the British Home Detention Curfew. Indeed, its mission will be to select all those inmates eligible for non-custodial sentences and to recommend them to the JSE. The main innovation resides in the fact that, provided there is no opposition from public prosecutor's office, a lack of response from the JSE within three weeks automatically entails acceptance and enables the SPIP to set up the desired measure. In other words, the formal intervention of the judge will only be required when the various actors in the process disagree, whereas if they manage to agree on criteria for each measure,[25] this form would make early release from prison practically automatic. The government has high hopes for these arrangements, which it views as a way of slowing down the rapid increase in prison populations. But here again, in the last analysis this will all depend on the good will of the different actors in the penal system, and on their ability to cooperate.

Summary

In the present chapter we have described the way EM came into existence in France and how it has been enforced so far, followed by the changes it is about to undergo. Introduced quite recently, EM has already been reformed repeatedly. Its future organisation as well as its use as a terminal prison-leaving arrangement tends to bring it closer to the British model. As such, it follows the same trend as the entire non-custodial sentencing system toward making the corrections administration more independent of the judge in charge of sentence enforcement, as opposed to the earlier tendency to accentuate the role of the court in this procedure.

There is no way of foreseeing the extent to which the new arrangements will stimulate greater use of EM, and if so, whether it will be implemented in the initial area of application (EM as a sentence or to mitigate a sentence with no previous detention) – with the attendant risk of net-widening – or whether it will be used for early release from confinement. Be that as it may, the increase in EM, were it to occur, may well run into two bottlenecks: first, the difficulties encountered in enforcing sentences since a sentenced offender who is not already in detention frequently waits seven to twelve months before serving the sentence; and secondly, the work load of the SPIP, which will have a hard time coping with their new attributions barring a considerable increment in the resources at their disposal.

(This chapter was translated by Helen Arnold)

Notes

1. This echoes criticism commonly heard in the United States, that measures outside of prison are only a 'slap on the wrist' for offenders (Tonry, 1990, 184).
2. The Bonnemaison Report did not conceal the disadvantages of EM, namely the risk of greater social control through net-widening as well as social discrimination and of being an offence to the person's dignity, but refuted them (pp.29-30)
3. Act no. 2004-204 dated 9 March 2004, on the adjustment of the justice system to new trends in criminality, stipulates that EM may also be pronounced by the judge *judging the facts of the case* (as opposed to the judge in charge of sentence enforcement), as a means of serving a sentence of imprisonment for no more than one year, or it may be proposed for an indicted individual by the Public Prosecutor under the framework of the French version of plea-bargaining, simultaneously introduced in this bill.
4. Perrin, Kouliche, 1999. Kaluszynski, Froment, 2003 disagree, arguing that the DAP favoured EM for some time, but came up against a lack of political will, and that the intervention of Senator Cabanel enabled it to get around that obstacle. This argument does not seem compatible with this administration's blatant unpreparedness.
5. EM has practically never been used as a pre-sentencing measure.
6. In which case the judge has other alternatives. The sentence may be converted into semi-liberty, placement in the community or parole, or even be suspended or split into several parts.
7. The 186 socio-educational services attached to the facilities and the 183 committees for probation and assistance to released prisoners (CPAL) were then replaced by 100 SPIP, so that the probationary measures would not entail a break, in prisoner follow-up
8. DAP Note, 14 February 2000.
9. DAP, *Note de présentation générale*, dated 15 May 2001, 5-6. In all cases, the participation of private enterprise was confined to supplying and maintaining equipment, training and assisting personel. Initially, two suppliers were chosen: the firms ON Guard Plus France and Elmotech. The latter gradually obtained most of the local contracts.
10. This survey is part of a research project conducted by the CESDIP and the DAP (Kensey, Pitoun and Lévy, Tournier 2003). It covers 580 EM measures served between October 2000 and July 2003.
11. Unless otherwise specified, the figures given here are all taken from our survey (n=580).
12. Although relatively low, the figure for another offence is deceptive, as in an undetermined number of cases the offence had been committed prior to tagging, but a final sentence had not been pronounced. When it is, it may cause cancellation either because it shows the measure to be inappropriate in that particular case, or because the sentence makes the person ineligible for EM.

13. They average over one hundred cases per worker (as of 31 December 2000, there were about 1,350 integration and probation agents, plus 230 senior officials for a stock of 140,622 individuals under supervision as of 1 July the same year (see *Administration pénientiaire*, 2002, 241, 290). This figure conceals considerable local disparities. In 2001, a social worker attached to the SPIP for the city of Lille was in charge of about 130 tagged individuals (*Direction régionale des services pénitentiaires de Lille, maison d'arrêt de Loos, Note de synthese relative au dispositif PSE, 3 mai 2001*). According to Ottenhof and Favard (2001, 10), the number of cases was between 150 and 200 on the three sites they studied; another study in 1999 shows 70, 90, and over 140 placements per agent in three other offices (Chauvenet, Gorgeon, Mouhanna, Orlic, 1999), 76, 115, 157. In Paris, according to Patureau (2000, 100), 25 workers (some part time) are in charge of 5,000 cases; i.e. 200 each.

14. In this case, people entering prison (admissions), that is, flow data, whereas the other figures are given in terms of stock, but this difference does not affect the comparison of socio-demographic profiles. Secondly, the reference year is not the same in the three cases, an unimportant fact here as the indicators are stable.

15. Offenders sentenced to EM are legally part of the prison population (they are subject to the same formalities registering them in a correctional facility, known as 'inscription on the prison rolls' and to the same punishment if they escape). They are counted as prison inmates in the correctional statistics.

16. Files opened in 1989 Guillonneau, 2000).

17. National Prison Record (Fichier National des Détenus or FND), 2000.

18. Number of convictions for moderately serious offences (*délits*; total: 22, 549), (*Ministere de la Justice*, 2003), p. 149.

19. Admissions in prison for 2002; the total number of admissions was 76, 836 following conviction and 58, 705 for pre-trial detention (i.e. not definitively convicted); 296 admissions were for various other situations.

20. This is probably where the largest group of women is to be found d, as nearly 90 percent of women are not in detention and nearly three-quarters were sentenced for theft, violence or drug-related offences.

21. This intention is written into the report appended to the *Loi d'orientation et de programmation pour la justice* (*LOPJ*), 9 September 2002 (*Journal officiel*, 10 September 2002, number 211, 14934 ff); its enforcement is prescribed by the Décret number 2004-243, 17 March 2004, article 24 (*Journal officiel*, 20 March 2004, 5396-97.

22. Such checks would be done long distance; the ruling also authorises procedures for voice or fingerprint identification, making such verifications possible.

23. Twelve surveillance centres are operating currently. This is obviously excessive, but it is no doubt partly due to the gradual extension of EM across the county, so that each new section was given its own surveillance centre.

24. See his statement at the conference 'Trial and punishment without imprisonment: the alternatives to detention', Paris, Ecole nationale de la magistrature 93-5 May 2004). Warsmann feels the implementation of this measure is awkward at the sentencing phase because of the need for a feasibility study beforehand. It is probably that the SPIP are relatively poorly equipped to conduct such investigations within the short delays imparted by trials.

25. The non-custodial arrangements involved semi-liberty, placement outside of prison and EM. They affect people for whom 'three months remain to be served in prison, following one of several custodial sentences totalling two years or more but not exceeding five years'. (New articles 723-20 50 723-28 0f the Code of Criminal Proceedings).

References

Administration Pénitentiaire (2002) *Rapport annuel d'activité 2000*, Paris, Ministère de la justice.

Ball, R.A., Huff, C.R. and Lilly, J.R. (1988) *House arrest and correctional policy. Doing time at home*, Newbury Park etc., Sage.

Bonnemaison, G. (1989) *La modernisation du service public pénitentiaire. Rapport au Premier Ministre et au Garde des Sceaux*, Ministre de la Justice.

Cabanel, G.-P. (1996) *Pour une meilleure prévention de la récidive. Rapport au premier Ministre*, Paris, La Documentation française.

CEP (2003) *Electronic Monitoring in Europe. Report of the CEP workshop (Egmond aan Zee, NL, 8-10 may 2003)*, CEP.

Chauvenet, A., Gorgeon, C., Mouhanna, C., and Orlic, F. (1999) *Contraintes et possibles: les pratiques d'exécution des mesures en milieu ouvert*, Paris, Acadie/CSO-CNRS/CEMS-EHESS.

Couvrat, P. (1998) 'Une première approche de la loi du 19 décembre 1997 relative au placement sous surveillance électronique', *Revue de science criminelle*, 2, pp. 374-378

Froment, J.-C. (1998) *La république des surveillants de prison (1958-1998)*, Paris, LGDJ.

Guillonneau, M. (2000) 'Sanctions et mesures en milieu ouvert', *Cahiers de démographie pénitentiaire*, 8, 4 pp.

Herzog-Evans, M. (2002) *Droit de l'application des peines*, Paris, Dalloz.

Kaluszynski, M. and Froment, J.-C. (2003) *Sécurité et nouvelles technologies. Evaluation comparée dans cinq pays européens (Belgique, Espagne, France, Grande-Bretagne, Suisse) des processus de recours au placement sous surveillance électronique*, Grenoble, CERAT-IEP.

Kensey, A., Pitoun, A., Lévy, R., and Tournier, P.V. (2003) *Sous surveillance électronique . La mise en place du 'bracelet électronique' en France (octobre 2000-mai 2002)*, Paris, Ministère de la Justice, Direction de l'administration pénitentiaire.

Kuhn, A., and Madignier, B. (1998) 'Surveillance électronique: la France dans une perspective internationale', *Revue de science criminelle*, 4, pp. 671-686

Lévy, R., and Pitoun, A. (2004) 'L'expérimentation du placement sous surveillance électronique en France et ses enseignements (2001-2004)', *Déviance et Société*, 28, 4, pp. 411-37.

Mainprize, S. (1996) 'Elective affinities in the engineering of social control: the evolution of electronic monitoring', 18 in *Electronic Journal of Sociology*, 2, 2, 1899: http://www.sociology.org.content/vol1002.002/mainprize.html

Mayer, M., Haverkamp, R. and Lévy, R., eds. (2003) *Will Electronic Monitoring Have a Future in Europe?*, Freiburg im Breisgau, edition iuscrim.

Ministère de la Justice, (1994) *Le Travail d'Intérêt Général a dix ans, le résultat en vaut la peine*, Paris, Ministère de la Justice.

Ministère de la Justice, (2003) *Annuaire statistique de la justice*, Paris, La documentation française.

Nellis, M. (1991) 'The electronic monitoring of offenders in England and Wales', *British Journal of Criminology*, 31, 2, pp. 165-185

—, (2001) 'Interview with Tom Stacey, founder of the Offender's Tag Association', *Prison Service Journal*, 135, pp. 76-80

Ottenhof, R., and Favard, A.M., (2001) *L'exécution par l'administration pénitentiaire des mesures de milieu ouvert*, Nantes, Université de Nantes, faculté de droit et des Sciences politiques, Unité de recherche Droit et changement social.

Patureau, R. (2000) 'La probation, prisonnière sous contrôle', *Panoramiques*, 45, pp. 99-105

Perrin, J., and Kouliche, E. (1999) *Expertise des solutions techniques envisageables pour la mise en application du placement sous surveillance électronique, modalité d'exécution des peines privatives de liberté. Rapport phase 3.*

Pitoun, A., and Enderlin-Morieult, C.-S. (2003) 'Placement sous surveillance électronique', *Encyclopédie juridique Dalloz, Répertoire de droit pénal et de procédure pénale.*

Pradel, J. (1998) 'La "prison à domicile" sous surveillance électronique, nouvelle modalité d'exécution de la peine privative de liberté. Premier aperçu de la loi du 19 décembre 1997', *Revue pénitentiaire et de droit pénal*, 1-2, pp. 15-26

Renzema, M. (1992) 'Home confinement programs: development, implementation, and impact', in Byrne J.M., Lurigio A.J., Petersilia J., eds, *Smart sentencing. The emergence of intermediate sanctions*, Newbury Park, etc., Sage, pp. 41-53.

Tonry, M. (1990) 'Stated and latent functions of ISP', *Crime & Delinquency*, 36, 1, pp.174-191

Whitfield, D. (2001) *The Magic Bracelet. Technology and Offender Supervision*, Winchester (UK), Waterside Press.

Chapter Eight

Restorative Prisons: A Contradiction in Terms?

Ivo Aertsen

Underlying Issues

There are many tensions when we explore new avenues in integrating a victim dimension or a restorative perspective to the administration of the prison sentence. First, the punitive societal climate at present does not invite the rethinking of crime and punishment in a nuanced way. New forms of punishment are launched, building on the same, traditional and abstract conception of crime. The focus is on how to react, much less on how the problem of delinquency can be re-defined. Second, developing a restorative dimension in prisons presupposes an understanding of restorative justice as a broad, theoretical and operational framework. From this point of departure, restorative justice cannot be reduced to a diversionary approach, neither can it be seen as just a sentencing strategy. Restorative justice as a broad option contains 'a set of principles which may orientate the general practice of any agency or group in relation to crime' (Marshall, 1999). Third, does the restorative justice idiom represent more than a political or ideological discourse? How strong is its innovative potential in practice, and does it effectively meet the specific needs of victims, offenders and others involved? In recent years in particular, these questions have become more relevant, since a proactive interest in restorative justice can clearly be observed at policy level within several European countries and within international institutions such as the Council of Europe and the European Union (Home Office, 2003; Aertsen and Peters, 2003). This brings us to a fourth tension, which relates to the discussion of whether restorative justice should be approached from an instrumentalist point of view or rather from its participatory and democratic values on their own. A demonstration of the first orientation is the strong focus in some countries on the effect of restorative justice programmes on reoffending. This crime reduction concern is less prominent when the emphasis is more on procedural restorative justice. The latter is more inspired by an emancipatory philosophy, where citizens and their surroundings participate actively in an ongoing interaction with criminal justice agencies. A fifth problematic topic relates to the assumption of prison's central role in the criminal justice system: the prison as the eternal reference point in sentencing policies and practices, the prison as a persistent system, and one that fundamentally should be neither questioned nor changed.

These challenges form the undercurrent to this paper. We will return to some of them more explicitly in what follows. Is it possible, against the background of the above-mentioned tensions, to conceptualise something as restorative detention? An initiative of this sort was undertaken in Belgium in the late 1990s. In what follows it is our aim to present and to discuss the Belgian nationwide model of re-orienting prisons in a restorative direction. We start by drawing the context, which should help to understand the emergence of the programme of 'restorative detention'.

Part One The Belgian context

The victim's position

Victims in Belgium have gained a relatively strong position within the criminal justice process. In order to get financial compensation the injured party has been present, for a long time, in the inquisitorial process in the shape of the *partie civile*. During the 1990s, under the influence of several political and societal events and evolutions, the victim's position was strengthened. Indeed Belgium has been identified as the European country where the greatest efforts have been undertaken to improve the legal position of the victim (Brienen and Hoegen, 2000). This evolution reached a provisional conclusion in 1998 with the Franchimont law which considerably enlarged victims' rights within the criminal procedure.[1] More far-reaching proposals were put forward in 2003, such as those of the Holsters Commission whereby, in respect of both the sentencing process and the execution of the prison sentence, the victim was given an even more important role (Commission, 2003).

Victim-offender mediation

Academic work and research have been influential in the domain of restorative justice in Belgium. Action research and evaluative research have accompanied the setting up of several types of restorative justice programmes. Restorative justice in its strict sense – as method – is most developed in Belgium in the form of victim-offender mediation, as is also the case in many European countries (European Forum, 2000; Lauwaert and Aertsen, 2002; Miers, 2004). In Belgium, the initial impetus came from small-scale initiatives in the field of juvenile delinquency in the second half of the 1980s. During the following decade, however, mediation in adult criminal law grew faster than for minors. At present, restorative justice is on its way to becoming general both for adults and minors in all judicial districts of the country. Mediation programmes are available at all stages of the criminal justice procedure: at the police level; as an alternative to prosecution; in parallel with prosecution; and after sentence. At present, only one type of victim-offender mediation programme is regulated by law: the so-called penal mediation, which is organised from within the public prosecutor's office.[2] In the other mediation programmes, the role of NGO's and inter-agency partnerships is more important. In the field of juvenile law a pilot project on family group conferences, based on the New Zealand model, started in 2000 in the Flemish part of the country (Vanfraechem, 2003). It is important to stress that all types of victim-offender mediation in Belgium are offered by professionals and not by volunteers.

The 'mediation for redress' programme is of particular interest here. This type of mediation is orientated towards more serious types of crime, for which a dismissal by the public prosecutor is out of question. The outcome of mediation might influence the sentence. Through its intensive co-operation with the judiciary, the programme aims at an ongoing reflection on criminal justice processes and decision-making (Aertsen, 2004).

Part Two Restorative justice and prisons

Evolutions in the administration of the prison sentence

The orientation towards victims and towards how an offender might make amends during the period of the prison sentence has received much support in Belgium. It is, perhaps, a logical consequence of the increased attention on the victim at the stage of the criminal investigation and sentencing process. The Dutroux affair, which hit the headlines in the summer of 1996, catalysed victim-focused policies, but, in reality, this development started some years before. Since 1996, two ministers of justice have stressed in policy papers the interests of the victim during the period of the prison sentence and have opted for an integration of principles of restorative justice as far as is possible (De Clerck, 1996; Verwilghen, 2000). A preliminary draft of a 'Prison System and Execution of Detention Act' proposed, as main objectives for the period of the prison sentence, a limitation of the harm resulting from detention on the one hand, and reintegration of the offender and restoration to the victim on the other (Dupont, 1998). This line of thinking was confirmed more recently by the Holsters Commission.

A legal manifestation of increased victim care can also be found in the new legislation of 1998 on conditional release.[3] This new legal framework put into practice a more victim-sensitive regulation. As a part of the decision making procedure, for example, one of the possible contraindications to be investigated before granting parole concerns the attitude of the detainee towards the victim. Moreover, some categories of victims can communicate to the Parole Commission any concerns about parole conditions that might be imposed in the victims' interest. Some categories of victims also have the right to be heard by the Commission. Finally, victims can be informed about the conditional release and the conditions imposed in their interest. Unavoidably, the very significant presence of the victim in the context of conditional release influences, in practice, the interpretation of 'restorative detention'.

The national programme on restorative detention: History[4]
Initially part of a larger research programme,[5] 'restorative detention' became an independent research project in January 1998. It was an action research ordered by the Ministry of Justice from the universities of Leuven and Liège. Central to the research was the question of how punishment in general and prison in particular can contribute to a more just and more balanced adminis- tration of criminal justice for the offender, the victim and society. The objective of the action research was to give imprisonment a more victim focused and restorative justice orientation. The action research project was set up in six Belgian prisons where researchers started concrete restorative justice initia- tives, taking into account the specific context of each penal institution. Action, aimed at the phased or cyclical implementation of change in certain well- defined areas, was accompanied by research on the process and the outcome of the actions. Research was, however, not only instrumental in the immediate evaluation and steering of the activities and in the question of generalisation, but was also intended to contribute to the process of formulating a theory.

After nearly three years of experiment, and based on several evaluative reports, the minister of justice decided to implement the project in all Belgian prisons. The main strategy for this was the recruitment, in October 2000, of a restorative justice adviser for each prison and two national co-ordinators. The background and objectives of the national programme and the tasks of the advisers were set out in a ministerial circular of 4 October 2000.

Restorative justice advisers
In the ministerial circular the national programme is situated clearly in the context of 'restorative justice', which, also in a prison environment, aims at 'restoring the relation between the victim, the offender and the community'. The mission of the restorative justice advisers is to support a culture of respect within the prison and to help in the development of a coherent prison policy on restorative detention. The activities of the advisers are not orientated directly towards individual inmates and victims, but rather towards prison staff and prison structures. Restorative justice advisers work towards developing atti- tudes, skills, programmes and organisational changes to be administered by the prison staff and others.

Restorative justice advisers operate at the level of the prison management directly under the authority of the prison governor. The advisers all have a university degree, usually in criminology, sociology, psychology or education. They are employed on a full time basis and their tasks are focused exclusively on the development of restorative justice.

The following objectives can be discerned for the restorative justice advisers. The first two are defined in order to introduce or to support a culture of respect within the prison:

– Developing consultation structures between the various departments of the prison;
– Raising the awareness of prison staff with regard to restorative justice.

The next three objectives are orientated towards making direct and/or indirect communication between the prisoners and the victims possible:

– Setting up consultation structures between internal and external services;
– Raising the awareness of the prisoners regarding victims' issues and restorative justice;
– Raising the awareness of victims and the community regarding detention and restorative justice.

One might argue that some of these objectives, in particular those concerned with internal and external consultation, are not new and not specific to restorative justice. However, putting these objectives in a new perspective might help to surmount existing obstacles and can stimulate the active involvement of groups such as prison officers or external social services.

Restorative actions

In order to influence the prison context effectively the restorative detention programme has to address as many aspects of the 'prison community' as possible (Robert and Peters, 2003). Establishing a restorative justice prison culture implies not only the active involvement of some key figures, but the support of all prison staff and an effective orientation involving very different aspects of the prison organisation. Hence, a restorative justice prison structure constitutes a basis for a culture of respect.

Initiatives towards prison personnel are, as a consequence, of the utmost importance. Their contribution can be decisive for the success or failure of a restorative detention programme. Secondly, factors of an administrative or organisational nature in the prison have to be taken into account and action taken in these areas. Furthermore, activities involving prisoners, individually or in groups, have to be designed so that they bring the victim into focus to stimulate reflection and responsibility. Finally, a restorative detention programme has to be linked to the outside world and concrete action must be taken in this respect.

Concrete action in the context of restorative detention can be divided in six categories:

a) Preparatory action. The list here might include: developing a strategic communication plan for staff within a given prison involving all concerned groups; adapting and re-structuring the prisoners' files in order to collect and include more information on the possibilities for making reparation (sometimes the most essential data are lacking in the prison dossier, for example on the identity of the victims and on the judicial decisions in respect to compensation).

b) Sensitisation. For example: starting a discussion group among inmates on the subject of 'restorative justice'; making the local community outside the prison aware of prison issues.

c) Informative action. Examples: modifying the intake brochure for detainees in order to include victim related topics; organising information sessions for prison officers on victim experiences.

d) Training. More systematic training programmes designed to integrate a victim perspective in daily work can be organised, for example, for probation officers or psychological staff within the prison; victim awareness programmes are offered to inmates.

e) Networking. Examples are: establishing a temporary or permanent consultation group with local victim support workers; taking part in a local steering committee on mediation and restorative justice developments outside the prison.

f) Actions orientated towards direct or indirect reparation. For example: starting, in co-operation with municipal social services, a programme on the settlement of debts; elaborating a programme of face-to-face group meetings between victims and offenders; establishing various types of community service inside and outside the prison.

These are all actions at the level of the local prison. Obviously, developing restorative detention also requires an active policy support from the central prison administration within the Ministry of Justice, and even support and co-operation by judicial authorities who are responsible for or intervene during the execution of the sentence.

Shared responsibilities

From the objectives and types of activities mentioned so far, it becomes clear that realising a restorative detention programme is not solely the responsibility of the restorative justice adviser. Nevertheless, there is an obvious risk that hiring specific personnel with the status of 'restorative justice expert' implies the release of other staff from their responsibilities and necessary contributions to the programme. As a consequence, in first instance, the restorative justice advisers ought not to take upon themselves all possible tasks concerning restorative detention. Rather they should try to motivate and to support other staff members and other services, both inside and outside the prison, to take initiatives in this direction.

An example of this can be found in the work that was done in establishing a so-called 'redress fund'. This project relates to the poor financial situation of many prisoners and their incapacity to reimburse the victim. Inspired by the results of a 'settlement fund' that was already in existence with juvenile delinquents, the initiative was taken from within the restorative detention programme to elaborate a similar model in a prison context. An external NGO – Suggnomè – was found that was willing to host the fund and its administration, and a charity – Welzijnszorg – agreed to act as sponsor. The procedure for the fund is as follows. When an insolvent prisoner wishes to do something for his victim, he can apply for a financial intervention through the redress fund. The fund, after the examination of the case by a special committee, can accept the application on the condition that the inmate performs a number of hours of community orientated work. He can, for example, do some practical or administrative work for an external social-profit organisation. In turn, the prisoner receives from the redress fund an amount of money – up to a maximum of 1250 euros – which he will hand over to his victim. The main focus of the redress fund is, however, not financial compensation (which sometimes is rather symbolic). The focus is primarily on developing responsibility. Making appeal to the redress fund, however, always implies a form of direct or indirect communication between the prisoner and the victim. This is done through the intervention of an external victim-offender mediation service. Thus the victim is also actively involved in the decision-making process. Moreover, the voluntary work is not offered out of an existing database. The prisoner himself must reflect on what might be meaningful work for him with reference to his victim and he has to search actively for an institution to which he can offer his services. Finally, the prison has to shape the conditions to make this community work possible. In some cases, an exit permission can be granted.

Other examples of multi-agency work in the field of restorative detention are a victim-awareness programme for prisoners, initiated in several prisons by the Flemish Victim Support organisation, and experimental victim-offender mediation programmes in three Dutch speaking prisons and in all French speaking ones (Buntinx et al., 2001; Buonatesta, 2004). These programmes are financed by respectively the Flemish and French Communities.

Resources

Conceptualising and implementing activities in the context of restorative detention require initiative, a lot of creativity and good co-operation both inside and outside the prison walls. The highly demanding task of the restorative justice advisers is facilitated by the daily support of the two national co-ordinators, and by mutual support amongst colleagues. Practice demonstrates that there is a real risk that the restorative justice advisers become isolated both within the prison and in their relations with the outside world. In some prisons, there is often a tendency to call on the adviser to deal with many other tasks or needs for which there are insufficient personnel available. Therefore, it has been found crucial that restorative justice advisers constitute a well-focused and tight group.

In order to support the restorative justice advisers, as well as other persons and services involved in the restorative detention programme, some additional tools have been offered on the initiative of the Ministry of Justice. A *Vademecum* or practical guide has been composed – available in Dutch and French – by the universities of Leuven and Liège, on the effective implementation of restorative justice in prisons (Aertsen et al., 2003). After a general section on restorative justice and restorative detention and its critical factors and ethical issues, the *Vademecum* concentrates on practical implementation matters. A methodological framework to set up concrete actions is presented, according to the phases of (1) analysis and diagnosis, (2) the formulation of objectives, (3) the practical implementation and (4) evaluation. In each phase, it is suggested, special attention needs to be given to the issues of participation, communication and resistance. This structure has been applied in the *Vademecum*, on the one hand, to the global programme of restorative detention in Belgian prisons, and, on the other hand, to 23 concrete examples of actions.

A second instrument has been the compilation of an annotated bibliography on restorative justice and restorative detention, by the university of Leuven (Vanspauwen et al., 2003). This bibliography contains abstracts of some 250 articles, books and papers, of both national and foreign origin.

These kinds of scientific services to the programme of restorative detention place universities and academics in a permanent relationship with developments in practice. For a discipline such as criminology, this interaction – albeit not always easy to realise – has been found extremely beneficial from both the perspective of applied research and the development of theory in the domain of crime and criminal justice.

Part Three Challenges

Restorative detention: (not) self-evident

Orientating a prison in a restorative justice direction might seem a paradox. At least two problematic features accompany such a project. First, some would see an apparent contradiction between restorative justice principles and the essentials of a prison sentence. A custodial setting seems to ignore the very principles of restoration, since incarceration finds its basis in exclusion rather than inclusion, in stigmatisation rather than reintegration. Moreover, security prevails in daily prison life and prison policies. The phenomenon of 'prisonisation' inhibits confrontation with the self and with feelings of guilt. The prison context does not invite the individual incarcerated to assume responsibility or to pay attention to his victim's needs. But, secondly and alternatively, the use of restorative justice can be seen as a new way of legitimating the prison sentence. The prison sentence becomes less problematic, since it can be planned according to the interest of the victim or victims' needs in general.

The idea of restorative detention can be defended from a logical point of view. Integrating restorative justice principles in the administration of the prison sentence (and non-custodial sentences as well) is a consistent option if one is interested in rethinking and reorienting criminal justice as a whole. It can be argued that the restorative dimension must be an inherent part of the subsequent stages of the criminal justice process. This approach opts for restoration not just as an alternative measure for minor offences but as a core element and basic rationale for criminal law independent of the nature or seriousness of the crime. The main objective is first to strive for reparation and pacification as much as possible. Reorienting the administration of criminal justice in a consistent way should also help in avoiding – at least at a conceptual level – a dualisation of penal policies. This dualisation refers to an evolution in penal practices in which community sanctions are deemed as appropriate for minor offences by diverting the offenders away from the penal system at an early stage, whereas the more serious cases should be dealt with in an ever more punitive way within the system. In a country like Belgium, for example, the total number of incoming prisoners on an annual basis (the flux) is not increasing, but the daily prison population rate (the stock) is, mainly as a consequence of an extension of the length of prison sentences for more serious (violent) crime (Snacken, 2001).

Put in a more pragmatic way: if one agrees that restoration should be a main objective of criminal justice, then there is no reason why it should not be included in the administration of the prison sentence. Seen from the perspective of both the victim and the offender, limiting restorative approaches to just one phase of the process (for example to prosecution or conditional release) might even provoke counter-productive effects: how to motivate an offender to take genuine responsibility during the period of his prison sentence, especially if he has learnt to behave and to think in a very defensive or minimalising way before? What sense does it make to motivate and to involve an offender in a mediation process with his victim at the pre-sentence level, if, afterwards, he is sent to prison where he is socialised quickly into a culture of indifference and denial?

It can be argued, finally, that developing restorative detention is a logical consequence of society's duty to create responsible criminal justice agencies (Shapland, 2000). Such a system deals with the needs of victims and others involved not as an additional burden, but as an integral part of its mission.

The victim perspective

The strong offender orientated tradition and culture in which one tries to develop restorative justice remains a critical factor. The task perceptions of probation staff and prison personnel are not victim orientated. Often a conflict of interests is experienced through the implication that working with the offender and with the victim is incompatible. Sometimes the principle of confidentiality is brought forward: probation officers or psychological prison staff are afraid of loosing the personal relationship with 'their client', and – through more victim attention – of being directed to a more controlling role towards the offender. In the restorative detention programme this fundamental problem was dealt with by offering ways of developing new methodological frameworks for psychosocial staff in prisons. One of these was the approach of 'multilateral partiality', based on contextual therapy and going back to the theoretical work of Boszormenyi-Nagy (Boszormenyi-Nagy and Krasner, 1986).

Victim oriented work in prisons risks being narrowed and biased by the strong focus on conditional release and the advisory function of some prison staff. Victim advocates argue that this strong emphasis on conditional release stimulates opportunistic attitudes with prisoners and limits the possibilities for staff to motivate inmates to assume real responsibility.

After all, it must be said that many actions by the restorative justice advisers set out from an offender perspective. The victims' needs or expectations are sometimes presupposed without being thoroughly investigated or discussed. The work of the restorative justice advisers often seems to be determined, to a certain degree, by the institutional context in which they function. Therefore, their location under the prison administration has been criticised. Some have commented that a more neutral operational basis would be more appropriate. The restorative justice advisers could be based, for example, in a mediation service, or in a public or private service within the Flemish and French communities who also have legal competencies in Belgian prisons. The counter-argument is that the impact of the advisers would decrease considerably if they were located outside the prison.

Community involvement

According to the ministerial circular on restorative detention, the community is the third actor or party in restorative justice: the disturbed relation between the victim, the offender and the community must be repaired. As this is often the case in restorative justice discourse, the community is the most vague and abstract element in the whole story. The community is often represented in a 'symbolic' way, without any clarification of the meaning and scope of the symbolic reparation or of those involved.

In the *Vademecum* on restorative detention that was discussed earlier, a more concrete operational definition of 'reparation to the community' is given. It suggests as a criterion that each action towards the community should be conceived in such a way that the effect on the community can be clearly assessed. This is, for example, the case when members of the local community are invited by prisoners to visit the prison and to have discussions with them and with prison staff, or when a prisoner is doing some practical work for an NGO active in foreign aid.

Structural limitations

Four limitations at a structural level, essentially connected to the prison context, must be pointed out. The first is the difficulty that prisoners have in establishing or maintaining external relations with their families, friends or other supportive persons. External influences and emotional support in personal life can be crucial in helping to develop an attitude of sensitivity towards the victim. Many prisoners need to have their self-respect enhanced before respect for others can start to be encouraged. Therefore a restorative justice programme must try to strengthen external bonds. In this regard, a research report in the Netherlands distinguishes three phases in the structure of restorative detention: (1) self-redress and the opening of constructive perspectives for the offender's own future; (2) relational redress for victims of crime and community orientated activities; (3) preparation for reintegration in society (Blad, 2004).

A second limitation concerns the restricted availability of prison labour and the problem of financial debts of many prisoners. Financial reparation to the victim is unrealistic for quite many prisoners. Special provisions can be set up to cope with this situation, such as the redress fund. More fundamental, but more difficult to realise, is the creation of work and income for prisoners. This problem, not yet studied or dealt with by the Belgian restorative justice advisers, deserves priority. Probably only with the support of government can prison labour be made more attractive and rewarding for local employers and industry.

Prison schedules themselves can hinder the implementation of some restorative actions or the individual work of a prisoner. The manifold transfers of prisoners to other penal institutions or the short period of a prison sentence are examples of this. A fourth limitation relates to preventive detention when the suspect is held during the criminal investigation. Practically speaking, actions towards the victim can be limited or forbidden by the investigating judge. Moreover, because of the principle of presumption of innocence, it can be questioned whether initiative in a restorative sense can be expected on the part of the suspect. For this group, it is common sense to assume that involvement in restorative actions can only be considered on a completely voluntary basis. For convicted prisoners however, there is a 'legitimate expectation' that they commit themselves to a form of reparation.

The need for an integrated criminal policy

It is clear that restorative detention cannot be considered as an isolated programme. It cannot be separated from the foregoing and subsequent stages of the criminal justice process. Restorative detention requires the active involvement and support of many actors, both in the prisons themselves and in other sections of the criminal justice system. Civil society needs to be involved. Actions have to be undertaken towards groups in society and towards the media in order to create credibility and community support. Finally, restorative detention, as other programmes in criminal justice, should always be guided by ongoing evaluation and research.

Restorative detention as a programme can only function effectively if it is part of an integrated criminal policy. This is far beyond the capacities and responsibility of a local prison governor or even a national prison administration. This integrated criminal policy, it must be admitted, is not yet present in countries. It requires a sound vision, a political will and a consistent and co-ordinated action plan. Unfortunately, it is often the case that restorative justice is quite easily hijacked or co-opted by the political world. To give but two examples from Belgium: one of the former ministers of justice has referred to restorative justice to defend the idea of electronic monitoring; and programmes have been defined as 'restorative practices' by the Flemish Parliament without any reference to the victims.

Another factor that has been insufficiently studied, at least in Belgian prison history and developments, is the role of trade unions. One illustration of the position of the prison officers' union and its possible impact on a programme as restorative detention was witnessed in 2003. Officers went on strike in several prisons in protest over prison overcrowding and understaffing. In the process of negotiations with the Ministry of Justice, the union claimed that training activities in the context of the restorative detention programme in some prisons should be reduced.

Restorative justice advisers have to work actively on these institutional, community and political levels. This requires some autonomy and freedom of action, which is only possible for civil servants when they affiliate with influential agencies and groups in society.

Part Four Restorative detention: a new perspective for the persistent prison?

Restorative detention can offer a meaningful perspective for the prison. The programme can contribute effectively towards meeting the needs of individual victims and offenders. Victim-offender mediation and other forms of communication show clear evidence of this. This way, redress for victims and social reintegration can be assisted. The programme can support the humanisation of the prison sentence and the valorisation of prison staff. By bringing the community inside the prison, and prisoners inside the community, public perception of crime and delinquency can be modified in a positive way. However, restorative detention should not offer a new legitimation for the extensive use of the prison sentence. Restorative detention can offer a meaningful perspective to the *persistent* prison, in the sense that the programme through the active involvement of victims and community members has a specific potential to question the prison institution in a continuous way. Restorative justice is about participation, responsibility and effective social control, and (thus) about promoting informal processes under the protection of the rule of law.

We conclude that developing restorative justice in prisons – possibly because of its ambiguous character – only can gain impact and credibility if it is part of a more general, integrated project of criminal policy. One of the key elements of such a policy, from a restorative justice point of view, is the consistent reduction of the use of the prison sentence. Although currently the political climate in many countries might be moving in the opposite direction, other countries in the recent past have shown an ability to reduce their prison populations. Restorative justice can provide a logical and positive content to the restricted period of the prison sentence, and should, at the same time, make the prison less persistent.

References

Aertsen, I. (2004), 'Victim-offender mediation with serious offences' in Council of Europe, *Promising Practices in Criminal Justice*, Strasbourg: Council of Europe Publishing (forthcoming).

Aertsen, I., Daeninck, Ph., Hodiaumont, F., Kellens, G., Malempré, H., Parmentier, S., Peters, T., Van Camp, T. en Van Win, T. (2003) *Herstelrecht en gevangenis. Vademecum voor een herstelgerichte detentie*, Brussels, Ministry of Justice.

Aertsen, I. and Peters, T. (2003) 'Des politiques européennes en matière de justice restauratrice', *Journal International de Victimologie/International Journal of Victimology*, 2, October 2003 (no pagination, 13 pages) (http://www.jidv.com/VICTIMOLOGIE_Sommaire_JIDV_2003,2(1).htm).

Biermans, N. and d'Hoop, M.-N. (2001) *Development of Belgian prisons into a restorative perspective* (unpublished paper), Positioning Restorative Justice - Fifth International Conference by the International Network for Research on Restorative Justice for Juveniles, Leuven, 16-19 September 2001 .

Blad, J. (2004) 'Inleiding tot een herstelgericht detentieregime', *Tijdschrift voor herstelrecht*, Vol. 4, no. 2, 7-23.

Boszormenyi-Nagy, L. and Krasner, B.R. (1986) *Between give and take: A clinical guide to contextual therapy*, New York: Brunner/Mazel.

Brienen, M.E.I. and Hoegen, E.H. (2000) *Victims of Crime in 22 European Criminal Justice Systems. The implementation of Recommendation (85)11 of the Council of Europe on the Position of the Victim in the Framework of Criminal Law and Procedure*, Nijmegen: WLP.

Buntinx, K., Dufraing, D. and Raets, G. (Eds.) (2001) *De uitbouw van een herstelgericht aanbod aan gedetineerden vanuit de Vlaamse Gemeenschap. Einrapport november 2001* (unpublished report), Leuven: Suggnomè.

Buonatesta, A. (2004) 'La médiation entre auteurs et victimes dans le cadre de l'exécution de la peine', *Revue de Droit Pénal et de Criminologie*, Vol 84, février, 242-257.

Commission Tribunaux de l'application des peines, statut juridique externe des détenus et fixation de la peine (2003), *Rapport final*, Brussels: Ministry of Justice.

De Clerck, S. (1996) *Oriëntatienota Strafbeleid en Gevangenisbeleid*, Brussels: Ministry of Justice, 1996.

Dupont, L. (1998) *Op weg naar een beginselenwet gevangeniswezen*, Leuven: Leuven University Press.

European Forum for Victim-Offender Mediation and Restorative Justice (Ed.) (2000) *Victim-Offender Mediation in Europe. Making Restorative Justice Work*, Leuven: Leuven University Press.

Home Office (2003) *Restorative Justice: the Government's strategy. A consultation document on the Government's strategy on restorative justice*, London: Home Office Communication Directorate.

Lauwaert, K. and Aertsen, I. (2002) 'Restorative Justice: Activities and Expectations at European Level', *ERA-Forum – Scripta iuris europaei*, no. 1, 27-32.

Marshall, T. (1999) *Restorative Justice. An overview*, London: Home Office.

Miers, D. (2004) *A comparative review of restorative justice and victim-offender mediation in Europe*, Leuven: European Forum for Victim-Offender Mediation and Restorative Justice.

Peters, T. et al. (1999) 'Fondements d'une politique judiciaire cohérente axée sur la réparation et sur la victime' in B. Van Doninck, L. Van Daele and A. Naji (Eds.), *Le droit sur le droit chemin?*, Antwerp: Maklu, 113-160.

Robert, L. and Peters, T. (2003) 'How restorative justice is able to transcend the prison walls: a discussion of the 'restorative detention' project' in E.G.M. Weitekamp and H.-J. Kerner (Eds.), *Restorative Justice in Context. International practice and directions*, Cullompton: Willan Publishing, 95-122.

Shapland, J. (2000) 'Victims and Criminal Justice: Creating Responsible Criminal

Justice Agencies' in A. Crawford and J. Goodey (Eds.), *Integrating a Victim Perspective within Criminal Justice*, Aldershot: Ashgate, 147-164.

Snacken, S. (2001) 'Belgium' in D. Van Zyl Smit and F. Dünkel (Eds.), *Imprisonment Today and Tomorrow: International Perspectives on Prisoners' Rights and Prison Conditions*, The Hague: Kluwer Law International, 32-81.

Vanacker, J. (Ed.) (2002) *Herstel en detentie. Hommage aan Prof. Dr. Tony Peters*, Brussels: Politeia.

Vanfraechem, I. (2003) 'Implementing family group conferences in Belgium' in L. Walgrave (Ed.), *Repositioning Restorative Justice*, Cullompton: Willan Publishing, 313-327.

Van Poucke, A. and Daelemans, A. (2002) *Restorative Justice and redress in prison: Some key questions from the field* (unpublished paper), Second conference of the European Forum for Victim-Offender Mediation and Restorative Justice, Oostende, 10-12 October, 2002.

Vanspauwen, K., Robert, L., Aertsen, I. and Parmentier, S. (2003) *Herstelrecht en herstelgerichte strafuitvoering. Een selectieve en geannoteerde bibliografie – Restorative justice and restorative detention. A selected and annotated bibliography*, Leuven: K.U.Leuven, Research Group Penology and Victimology.

Verwilghen, M. (2000) *Federaal Veiligheids- en Detentieplan*, Brussels: Ministry of Justice.

Chapter Nine

Rethinking Crime and Punishment

Rob Allen

The Rise of Prison

What do the following activities have in common?
- Collecting and selling lost golf balls
- Failing to send your children to school
- Stealing birds' eggs
- Cutting down or refusing to cut down a hedge
- Running on to a football pitch
- Growing cannabis
- Enhancing the test results of primary school children
- Shouting abuse at someone with a sun tan

The answer is that over the last three years, people in the UK have found themselves sentenced to prison for engaging in them. The people involved may not be typical of those who go to prison. But the very fact that the severest penalty available in our jurisdiction has been used for such a range of misbehaviour suggests the increasingly central role which prison has come to play in our society. This centrality is shown by the way in which prison is being used for many offences and offenders that could be dealt with in other ways, and indeed would formerly have been dealt with in other ways. There has, for example, been a four-fold increase in prison sentences for motorists over the last 10 years: almost 14,000 men and 2,750 women were sentenced to prison for shoplifting in 2002 – the equivalent of more than 40 people each day. In addition prison is sometimes used for those convicted of minor crimes but who are seeking swift access to drug treatment. Prison is also increasingly used for those who breach community sentences. Over 9,000 offenders were received into prison following a breach in 2002; four times as many as in 1992. The statistics also show significant numbers of people received into prison with no previous convictions – 17 percent of young male offenders, 14 percent of adult male offenders and 32 percent of adult females.

It was to counter this increasing reliance on imprisonment that in 2001 the Esmée Fairbairn Foundation set up Rethinking Crime and Punishment (RCP) – a strategic grant-making initiative designed to raise the level of debate about prison and alternatives. (www.rethinking.org.uk). RCP has made 60 grants to improve public understanding, increase community involvement and inject fresh thinking into the debate about how to respond to crime. RCP has undertaken research particularly on public attitudes and set up a major independent inquiry into alternatives to prison due to report in September 2004.

RCP's key focus on public attitudes has been based on an analysis of why the prison population has grown. Research conducted for RCP (reported in Chapter Five) found that the 80 percent rise in the size of the prison population since 1992 has been caused by the courts becoming much more severe in their sentencing. It suggests that a more punitive climate of opinion about crime engendered by the media and politicians has put pressure on sentencers that leads to community punishment being used instead of fines and prison instead of community punishment. As Home Office minister Paul Goggins told the Parliamentary Committee on Human Rights in March 2004:

> the increase in severity in sentencing bears no relation whatsoever to an increase in criminality or seriousness of offending. It is simply an increase in the seriousness of penalties that are meted out, and we have to tackle that because there is no evidence to say that it is reducing re-offending rates.

What's wrong with prison?

There are several reasons why greater use of imprisonment is not a desirable direction in which policy and practice should be moving. First, at a practical level it causes major problems for the prison service in accommodating the people concerned in a decent and dignified way. The Lord Chief Justice has called overcrowding the Aids or cancer of the prison system. It leads to an inevitable diminution of the regimes and activities available in prisons. The Director General of the Prison Service has called the rise in numbers 'insane' and called for an end to our 'love affair with custody'.

It would be in theory possible to build enough prison places to cope with the demand although no country has succeeded in doing so. But at a fiscal level prison is expensive. Prison costs the taxpayer an average of £35,000 per prisoner per year. A new prison costs an average of £60 million. Capital costs of a new primary school and secondary school is estimated to be £2.5 million and £8 million respectively.

At a moral level, rising numbers can also represent injustice by in Lord Bingham's words: 'the imprisonment of those for whom that penalty is not strictly necessary'. In societies that do not use the death penalty, imprisonment is the most punitive and coercive sanction the state imposes on its citizens. In democracies which value freedom and humanity, there is a strong case for using non-coercive, less formal and more positive approaches wherever possible and appropriate. The present Lord Chief Justice is in no doubt that: 'Today too few community sentences are imposed and too many and too long prison sentences are imposed. The consequences are doubly destructive of the needs of society.'

Prison has an important role to play in protecting the community against the most dangerous offenders and in punishing the most serious crimes. But research and experience have shown the many disadvantages of over using imprisonment. Imprisonment can harm the chances people have to make amends and fulfil their potential as citizens. By definition prison limits the opportunities people have to contribute to civil society and democratic life. In theory, prison could provide its captive audience with decent education, training and employment opportunities. With one or two notable exceptions in the form of resettlement prisons, such opportunities are not provided on anything like the scale required. Most prisoners therefore leave prison no better equipped to fit into society than when they entered it. Some leave a good deal worse off. We know from research and statistics that there is no clear relationship between the use of imprisonment and the rate of crime in the UK or internationally. Properly designed community measures or early interventions are a more cost-effective route to prevention than imprisonment.

It is in this context that RCP has been considering the question of the role punishment should play in modern Britain. Drawing on the work it has funded, this chapter looks at three questions: Are there particular groups of offenders for whom alternatives should be a priority? If prison is to be used less what do we replace it with? And will the public accept a different approach?

Priorities for Alternatives

RCP's work has suggested that there are four types of offenders for whom prison seems to have particularly damaging consequences. These are children in conflict with the law, women, especially those with dependent children, drug addicts and people with mental health problems.

Children

Despite widespread consensus that children should be locked up only as a last resort, under-18s in the UK are detained in prisons and other secure units at the rate of more than one every two hours. Exploring how best to deal with young offenders has been an important priority for Rethinking Crime and Punishment, 15 of whose projects relate specifically to the problem of youth crime. The emerging findings from these fall into to four areas: prevention, education, making decisions and locking up children.

Prevention

Perhaps the most important finding is that much more should be done to prevent children becoming violent or persistent offenders in the first place. There is a broad political and professional agreement that more constructive early intervention in the lives of youngsters most at risk could produce enormous dividends. The consortium of children's charities working together in a project called SHAPE – Reshaping Children's Lives and the Youth Crime Debate have argued convincingly that dealing with the causes of child neglect and abuse will help to address the causes of youth crime. The view of the consortium, comprising the National Children's Bureau, NSPCC, Children's Society, NCH, Barnardo's and Nacro is supported by the Children's Rights Alliance report *Rethinking Child Imprisonment* which concluded that if you select at random any inmate of a Young Offender Institution 'you will almost certainly find a heartbreaking history of personal misery, professional neglect and lost opportunities'. Official studies have found that two-fifths of girls and a quarter of boys in prison report violence in the home, with over half having had a history of care or involvement with social services.

Work funded by RCP has not only identified the problems but has also proposed solutions. A consultation with young people undertaken by the YMCA found a great deal of support for the introduction of parenting education for mothers and fathers of young offenders 'to induce a sense of responsibility'. The Inquiry into Youth Crime undertaken by NCH in Scotland argued for a new Home Care service, and greater use and availability of family support and advice centres. RCP's work on restorative justice has highlighted the role which family group conferencing can play in strengthening the way children are brought up. While more projects on the ground will undoubtedly make a difference there are important implications for policy too. An international seminar held by Children Law UK heard that delinquency in Finland is tackled on the basis that 'good social development policy is the best criminal policy'.

What is not always appreciated is that there is a huge amount of popular support for a preventive approach. In a Mori poll for RCP at the end of last year, when asked what two or three things would do most to reduce crime in Britain, six out of ten people chose the option of better parenting. When we asked in 2001 how the public would spend a notional £10 million on dealing with crime, the most popular option was to set up teams in 30 cities to work with children at risk. This suggests that the public would back an expansion of government initiatives such as Sure Start that aim to support children most at risk of crime and other social problems.

Education
The second key findings relate to the important role which education should play in dealing with offending. Research by Ecotech has found that nearly three

quarters of people think schools and colleges have an important role in preventing young people from offending and re-offending, with teachers seen as more important in this regard than police, courts or custody. The RCP Mori survey found that 45 percent chose better school discipline and 41 percent more constructive activities for young people as the best ways of dealing with crime. For the young people consulted by the YMCA, tackling bullying and truancy was a key approach to prevention. Interestingly too, school suspension and exclusion for bullies was not seen as an effective means of punishment as it gives offenders a 'holiday' from school. More, not less, schooling should be used as a punishment instead of suspension and exclusion. These findings about what the public thinks are highly consistent with recommendations made by the Audit Commission in their review of the reformed youth justice system *Youth Justice 2004*. This found that children in trouble need to be kept in education and schools much more directly involved in preventing offending.

Making decisions about children in conflict with the law
RCP is also able to shed light on what is the best forum for making decisions about those young people who do get into trouble. In Scotland, children who commit crimes do not generally go to court but are dealt with by a Children's Hearing, along with those who suffer neglect or abuse or fail to attend school. NCH's comprehensive inquiry into the Scottish system of Children's Hearings recognised current social anxiety about youth crime but found great strengths in the relatively informal, child centred approach in which a panel of lay members decide when compulsory measures of care or supervision are needed. The NCH Inquiry concluded that there should not be a return to court-based approaches and punishments for errant young people and their parents. They did suggest that the operation of the hearings could be improved if mainstream health, education and social services provided an earlier and more robust response to children at risk. They also felt that more could be done to increase the diversity of panel members, and recommended better evaluation and dissemination of the results of interventions and greater involvement of young people themselves in various ways – as mentors to other youngsters, in the training of panel members and in the actual process of the panel meetings.

The Inquiry also felt that the hearings should place a greater emphasis on personal responsibility and accountability on the part of the young offender but did not believe that an increasingly punitive response would be right or effective. Rather the Inquiry recommended an extension of community mediation and the enforcement of children's rights to receive full time education and the health services they need. It also suggested that a greater role for the police would make hearings more effective and credible in responding to the more persistent offenders.

On the other hand, the young people consulted by the YMCA did feel that harsher punishments should be given to young offenders and their parents. However, they argued that part of the offenders' rehabilitation should involve meeting their victims, or participation in a victim awareness scheme. This growing interest in restorative justice was strongly supported by an inquiry into RJ conducted by legal reform group JUSTICE. They found the introduction of RJ in England and Wales to be 'largely successful' and suggested there is further scope for RJ to develop as an alternative to prosecution and custody for all age groups. The possibilities of RJ are discussed in detail below.

NCH had reservations about making the repair of the harm done the sole or primary aim of youth justice because this might detract from meeting the needs of the offender, but it seems likely that RJ in one form or other will grow in significance in Europe. Starting a victim offender-mediation process is one of the options open to the Juvenile prosecutor in Spain, one of several continental youth justice systems explored by Children Law UK. Their work confirmed that in almost all European countries the age of criminal responsibility is higher than in the UK jurisdictions, in some cases as high as 15. Further study of how such countries deal with serious and persistent offenders under that age seems well worth pursuing.

There are many (including the UN Committee on the Rights of the Child) who consider that the criminal courts engage too soon and too severely in the lives of young offenders in England and Wales. In the current climate there is little chance of the age of criminal responsibility being raised. There is however renewed interest in restoring a link between the criminal court and the family proceedings court. Dame Elizabeth Butler-Sloss, writing in *YJB News* 'would like to see the youth court given the jurisdiction to require the relevant local authority to investigate the family in accordance with the Children Act and in serious cases... make a care application in the Family Court'. The Children Bill currently in Parliament offers the opportunity to introduce such a change. In the meantime, children who offend are subject to what Dame Elizabeth calls 'our punitive approach'.

Locking Up Children
A further set of findings from RCP projects relate to the use of prison custody for children. Most reached the view that too many children are being locked up, in the wrong kind of establishments, for longer than necessary and not always as a last resort. At their international seminar, Children Law UK heard that the UK detains youngsters at a higher rate than other European countries. Although Government Minister Hilary Benn told them: 'We do not want to lock up children – let us be absolutely clear about that.' He went on to say that 'custody is clearly appropriate for the most serious and dangerous young offenders and may be necessary in the case of many persistent offenders'. The NCH Inquiry was highly critical of the financial and human cost of the increased detention of young people in England and Wales in the last ten years, describing it as 'a criminal waste of money and an appalling waste of young lives'. The Children's Rights Alliance argued for a system which 'strictly limits the deprivation of liberty to those who need to be locked up in order to stop them damaging others' and that decisions to detain should be subject to frequent reviews. They also wanted a radical reduction in the numbers of locked places for children and responsibility for those that remain to be moved to welfare based department of state such as DfES or DH – not the Home Office or Prison Service.

SHAPE's proposal that we need to support and expand community penalties that reduce re-offending was perhaps the one which received most support from RCP projects. Whatever the legal framework or type of decision-making forum in place, intensive community based programmes offering 25 or more hours a week supervision contact are needed to turn round the lives of the most troublesome young offenders. More than nine in ten members of the public told an RCP Mori poll that there should be more use of such intensive punishment with only three per cent disagreeing. But our work has revealed that there is still more to do to in building magistrate and community support for community alternatives to prison, particularly for the more serious and persistent offenders. Hilary Benn told Children Law UK that we need better public understanding of what sentences involve, evidence that they work to reduce re-offending and a better 'connection' between the individuals and communities who have suffered from the crime and the way that criminal justice process responds to offenders. This last theme was echoed in research into the reputation of community sentences undertaken by Henley Management College. This found that both sentencers and the wider community would like information about prison alternatives' performance on three dimensions: performance with victims, with communities, and with offenders. Applying a business metaphor they describe this as a 'triple bottom line'.

What then should we conclude are the priorities for youth crime policy? First of all we need much greater emphasis on prevention initiatives with children at risk. RCP hosted a seminar in March 2004 looking at the scope for what the Americans call justice reinvestment – transferring resources away from the negative spend of incarceration to the more positive development of social programmes. Second, we need to make decisions about young offenders in a forum that prioritises problem solving over punishment and makes appropriate use of measures that make amends to victims. Finally, we need to develop alternatives to prison which are sufficiently intensive to meet the needs of often highly damaged young people but which also seek genuinely to involve ordinary members of the community in contributing practical solutions to one of the society's most intractable problems.

Women

One of the most troubling aspects of criminal justice in the last ten years is that the number of women in prison has tripled. Often detained many miles from home and family, imprisonment on remand or under sentence can represent a harsher punishment for the 4,500 women prisoners than for the 70,000 men. Yet women represent some of the least dangerous and most vulnerable offenders to come before the courts. RCP has funded the Fawcett Society's Commission on Women and the Criminal Justice, which has published an important report on women and offending. This concluded, inter alia, that

• The National Probation service should develop gender specific community programmes that meet women's needs
• Local support and rehabilitation centres should be established; the centres in Glasgow and in Worcester offer models worthy of replication
• Sentencers should take account of the impact that sentences have on women and their families.

Many of the women remanded or sentenced to prison are involved in one way or another with illegal drugs. At Styal women's prison, an estimated 75 percent of the total number of receptions have drug problems (House of Commons Written Answers, 8 April 2003, Col 218W). Some are charged with, or convicted of possession, intent to supply or trafficking. Others have committed theft from shops, fraud or other acts of dishonesty to finance a drug habit. Many will be caught up in a network of exploitative and violent relationships, with their drug use often associated with that of boyfriends and other significant men. An RCP funded campaign, 'Using Women; Women Drugs and Prison', has sought to raise public awareness of the links between drugs and prison and to promote more constructive solutions to the underlying problems.

The research paints a sorry picture of the characteristics of women drug users in prison. More than seven out of ten of all women in prison said that they have been physically assaulted at some point in their lives and two thirds had been sexually assaulted or had unwanted sexual experiences. Women subject to this kind of abuse were more likely than others to be drug dependent or heavy drinkers. Three quarters had no qualifications and a fifth had been assessed as having special educational needs. Two thirds had visited their GP for mental health problems and half reported at least one act of self-harm.

With such a catalogue of physical, emotional and social problems to contend with, it might be tempting to see a spell in prison as some sort of respite, an opportunity to come off drugs and start to make plans for a fresh start. It is not unknown for women and men to ask the courts to send them to prison for these reasons. The joint report by the criminal justice inspectorates into the 2002 Street Crime Initiative quotes anecdotal comments that offenders who were serious in their desire to free themselves of drugs stood the best chance of success if they were sentenced to imprisonment.

It is true that while in prison, some women can start to undergo the process of detoxification and treatment that is essential to coming off drugs. But prison based programmes at best can only provide a start. All too often, release from prison can mean a return to the familiar but destructive lifestyle that went before.

This is certainly not an argument for longer prison sentences. While it may be true that in prison women take fewer drugs than on the outside, it would be a mistake to think that prisons are entirely drug-free environments. Indeed, almost half of the women in the Home Office study reported that they had used an illegal substance while in custody – 27 percent heroin, 21 percent cannabis and 17 percent tranquillisers – albeit less frequently than in the year prior to imprisonment. More worrying is the fact that the prevalence of drug use among women in prison rose significantly between 1997 and 2001 with a particular increase in the use of heroin and crack cocaine. Home Office researchers suggest that this may in part be a consequence of mandatory drug testing in prison which can encourage switching to harder drugs which are detectable in urine tests for shorter periods than cannabis.

If prison can make drug use worse rather than better, it can also exacerbate the underlying problems of mental ill health suffered by many of the women who offend. The Prison Ombudsman is currently inquiring into the recent suicides of six women in Styal prison. Given the concentrations of distress in all women's prisons, suicide and self-harm are an everyday risk throughout the country.

Imprisonment can also damage the relationships which women have with their children. Almost half have children under the age of 16 and a third have children under five. Most of these children are unable to remain in the family home during their mother's incarceration. While some are looked after by family members, others go to foster parents or even residential care, where the outcomes are often poor.

There is one significant and growing group of women in prison whose drug related problems require an altogether different approach. These are the foreign national women charged with, or convicted of, trying to import drugs, mainly cocaine into the country. At the end of June 2003, one in five women in prison in England and Wales did not hold a British passport. Almost half of them (425) were Jamaican, almost all of who were in prison for drug offences. 90

percent were first time offenders, mostly single parents in their mid thirties with three or more dependent children.

So-called drug couriers, or 'mules', are almost always minor links in the international drugs trade and are largely hired by organised criminal gangs. Yet on conviction they face some of the longest prison sentences handed down by the courts. Almost three quarters of women foreign nationals in prison are serving sentences of more than four years compared to a third of UK national women, two thirds of foreign national men and half of UK national men. Almost all are deported at the end of their sentence. The maximum sentence for supply, intent to supply or importation of Class A drugs such as cocaine is life imprisonment. A prison sentence of at least ten years is recommended in sentencing guidelines for importing 500 grams.

The rationale behind such long sentences is deterrence – that other would be couriers will be discouraged by the prospect of a long period of imprisonment thousands of miles from home and family. Consideration of the length of sentence is generally related to the quality and quantity of drugs involved. Little account is taken of personal mitigation relating to the individual circumstances and culpability of the offender or the impact of the sentence on any dependants. Such an impact is substantial. Over a thousand children from outside the UK are kept apart from their mother because of her imprisonment. In Jamaica, where there is no effective child welfare system, children are left to fend for themselves and are vulnerable to abuse, rape and recruitment into crime.

The impact on the UK prison service is significant too. It currently costs £25 million a year to keep foreign national women drug couriers in prison. With the prison population at record levels, there is a strong argument for developing a new approach for this particular group.

The Rethinking Crime and Punishment briefing paper 'A bitter pill to swallow' has suggested a series of new policy proposals. These include that the sentencing advisory panel review the sentencing guidelines in England and Wales so that drug couriers do not normally receive long custodial sentences and are considered for community sentences. These new guidelines should allow courts to take account of the individual circumstances of the offender in particular the effect of sentencing on the welfare of children dependent on the offender. A repatriation agreement needs to be negotiated with the Jamaican government which would enable offenders sentenced to community penalties to serve these in their country of origin .New guidelines should allow courts to impose a community penalty where the offender agrees to undertake this in their country of origin and a place on a suitable programme is available.

Drug Addicts

The problems of dealing with women with addictions highlighted above reflect broader links between drugs and crime, many of which result from the policies of criminal prohibition in place nationally and internationally. There are up to half a million problem drug users in England and Wales. Many of these people spend time in prison. In RCP's view a serious attempt to expand alternatives to imprisonment needs to recognise the central role of drug misuse and look to develop the infrastructure of treatment and other services which can reduce dependency.

There has been increasing recognition by Government of the links between the misuse of Class A drugs and crime. A whole raft of reforms, including the establishment of the National Treatment Agency in 2001 and the introduction of sentences such as Drug Treatment and Testing Orders are intended to lead to more effective solutions to problem drug use. The Government's Updated Drug Strategy, published in December 2002, sets out the action to be taken to tackle the harm caused by drugs, including increasing the annual spending on treatment services to £537 million by 2005. Using the criminal justice system, including prisons, as a gateway into drug treatment is a key component of the Government's drug strategy.

Against this background, work undertaken for RCP has shown that while attempts to tackle the links between drugs and crime are welcome, there are limits to the extent to which it is appropriate to use the criminal justice system in general, and prisons in particular, as a gateway to drug treatment, and that investing in early interventions and community drug treatment could prevent some problem drug users from entering the criminal justice system at all. Despite the fact that there has been increased investment in community drug services and that every £1 invested in drug treatment saves £3 in reduced criminal justice costs, many problem drug users are still unable to access appropriate treatment without delay.

Although there have been significant improvements in waiting times, current delays may still deter problem drug users from accessing treatment. Presenting for drug treatment is often a major step for someone to take and if treatment is not immediately available, motivation may well be lost. While national average waiting times have improved, in some parts of the country people still face very lengthy waits. In Croydon, for example, waiting times for specialist prescribing is 16 weeks and in Blackpool waits for residential rehabilitation stood at 15 weeks in September 2003.

In much of the country it appears that drug treatment is more readily available in prisons than outside. According to 'Streets Ahead', the review of the street crime initiative: 'In HMP Liverpool, where community residential detoxification waiting times were reported as lengthy, the local authority had requested permission to send community patients to the local prison for faster treatment provision.'

When they appear for sentence, courts now have the option of making a drug treatment and testing order (DTTO). The DTTO enables courts to review progress while offenders undergo a programme of treatment. Results from research into the three pilot DTTO areas published recently appear disappointing, with almost four out of five offenders (male and female) who were made subject to the orders reconvicted within two years. Only a third of offenders completed their orders successfully, but those who did were significantly more likely to stay out of trouble than those whose orders were revoked. The lesson from the evaluation is not that treatment does not work but rather there is a need for a major expansion of the range and type of treatments available so that offenders can gain immediate access to the most suitable programme. There is a strong body of international research showing the benefits of treatment, particularly residential treatment, both in helping people to give up drugs and reduce drug-related crime. Contrary to what was the prevailing orthodoxy, research has shown that drug users within the criminal justice system who are coerced into treatment achieve the same outcomes as those who enter on a voluntary basis.

Almost nine out of ten of the drug-dependent women in prison said to Home Office researchers that they would have liked some help with their drug problem in the year before imprisonment. Some did in fact receive help, mostly maintenance medication, counselling or needle exchange. Yet while a third said they would have liked residential treatment only nine per cent actually underwent such treatment. There is an acute shortage of residential treatment facilities in parts of the country. The total number of residential rehabilitation beds in England is fewer than 1800. Given that prison capacity has increased by 12,000 since 1997, the scale of investment in residential treatment looks wholly inadequate.

While the Government's commitment to increasing treatment provision will be undoubtedly welcome to courts, residential and hospital-based programmes account for only a small proportion of treatment options currently available. Of treatment episodes in the six months to March 2001, only about seven percent involved in-patient or residential treatment. The vast majority involved community based drug services of one form or another. While these may provide the right kind of treatment for most addicts, for those offenders who are facing a de facto residential placement in prison, a health service or the court should at least consider voluntary sector residential option.

Removing problem drug users from their home community as part of their drug treatment can prove beneficial if accompanied by intensive and ongoing support. Residential drug treatment, when followed up by ongoing support, can provide some of the benefits of prison-based treatment by temporarily enabling people to leave behind the environment in which they were problem drug users, without the negative impacts that imprisonment can present.

People with mental health problems

There is widespread agreement that prison is not a suitable place for people suffering from adverse mental health. Lord Fellowes, shortly after becoming the chairman of the Prison Reform Trust told the House of Lords in March 2002 that an aspect that he had found especially shocking and moving in his visits to prisons was 'the number of sufferers from mental illness who are, by any humane standard, quite wrongly held in prison'. It does not take an expert to see how the gloomy conditions in large Victorian gaols, with their limited space for activities can worsen the health of mentally disordered offenders. Nor is it hard to imagine how overcrowding, and the day-to-day placement decisions currently needed to manage the population add to already high levels of stress.

The scale of the problem is substantial. Research by the Office of National Statistics in 1997 found that 14 percent of women, ten percent of men on remand and seven percent of sentenced men had a functional psychosis such as schizophrenia or manic depression in the year leading up to their imprisonment. The percentage of young men with these serious mental health conditions was ten percent. The proportion of prisoners with neurotic symptoms, such as depression and phobias were far higher than in the general population. Nine out of ten young offenders were estimated to suffer from mental health problems – broadly defined to include drug misuse and conduct or personality disorders. This suggests that today about 5,000 adult men, 600 girls and women and 1,000 young men may be in prison today with the most serious illnesses with a majority of the rest suffering a range of other mental health problems. While there is no central record of re-offending among prisoners with mental health problems, we do know that six percent of restricted patients under the Mental Health Act discharged in 1999 were reconvicted with only one percent convicted of a grave offence.

The assumption of responsibility for prison health care by the NHS and investment in mental health nursing have led to welcome improvements in many prisons. There is a strong case for a more fundamental rethink of the way in which the police, courts, prisons, health and social services deal with mentally disordered offenders. If, as a society, we want to respond to those who are sick with care and treatment rather than punishment, proper consideration needs to be given to how that should best be done and how the necessary resources should be found and deployed. Such a rethink should address questions such as:

- Do all of those with mental health problems who currently go to prison need to be detained at all? Are there some such as those remanded for medical reports who could be properly dealt with in the community? Are new diversion, remand or sentencing options necessary?
- What infrastructure of health and social care services is needed to cope with those who currently go to prison? How many more places are needed in medium secure units, and how should greater numbers of places in supported hostels or other forms of accommodation be made available?

• What mechanisms are needed for diverting cases from police and magistrates' courts into the health and social care settings? Could the default accommodation for offenders in need be a secure mental health bed rather than a prison cell?

• What training and resources are needed if the police, courts, probation and prison services are to play their roles effectively? What should be the role of the voluntary sector?

It may seem odd to recommend yet another review so close on the heels of the Halliday Review of Sentencing, the Auld Review of Courts and the Carter review of the Correctional Services, but none of these had very much to say about responding to mentally disordered offenders. The Chief Inspector of Prisons recently suggested that a new generation of small units should be created. This is certainly a suggestion worth proper consideration.

Replacing Prison

Whatever the factors that lie behind criminality, every society needs a system for holding offenders to account. One of the questions RCP wanted to address was about how as a society we should do that. Is punishment through imprisonment the only way? Or are there other paradigms which have fewer financial, social and moral costs which cause less in the way of 'collateral damage' and do more to build offenders' stake in conformity, rather than take away what little many of them often have. RCP funded a number of pieces of work looking at how this might be done, The findings of the largest project, Lord Coulsfield's independent inquiry into alternatives are not available at the time of writing. But the conclusions of other funded work, particularly that which has looked at Restorative Justice and community penalties, offer some important pointers.

In terms of reducing crime and rehabilitation offenders, it is clear that the measures needed to steer many of the most chronic and persistent offenders away from crime lie well beyond the reach of sentencing. What is needed is a new emphasis on problem solving justice. Rather than seeking to bring about changes in an offenders behaviour by punishment, such an approach would involve diverting offenders into the kind of health, educational and social programmes which can help them to turn their lives around. Alongside these the justice system must hold offenders to account for criminal behaviour, but there is much to be said for a system which enables people to make constructive amends for wrongdoing rather than one which simply punishes them.

Restorative Justice

Restorative justice (RJ) has a major role to play as an alternative to prosecution and as a sentencing option for adults. An inquiry into RJ conducted by legal reform group JUSTICE, is positive about the potential of RJ. When people are asked what values should drive sentencing, apologising and paying back rank highly. Yet the day-to-day work of police, prosecutors, courts, probation and prison services all too often loses sight of what should be guiding principles for responding to crime.

There are already restorative elements in the criminal justice system today. Magistrates' courts are required to consider whether to make a compensation order in each case they hear, although Home Office figures suggest orders are made in fewer than 15 percent of cases (and only seven percent in the Crown Courts). Offenders carry out more than 8 million hours of unpaid work in the community each year. The rationale for the community punishment order, formerly community service, is that offenders should give something back to society to make amends for their offending. And courts can defer sentence to enable offenders to make reparation to the victim.

In the youth justice system, there are more opportunities for face-to-face contact at various stages in the criminal justice process. Restorative cautioning developed by the Thames Valley police is widely used when children first offend and are given a reprimand or final warning. Rather than simply getting a telling off, youngsters are required to hear directly about the harm they have done through their crime and are given a chance to make some restoration. A similar idea lies behind the Youth Offender Panels that deal with offenders subject to Referral Orders. Here not only are victims invited to meet the offender, but trained members of the local community play a key role in decision-making. The decision-making in the panel takes the form of the agreement of a contract rather than, as in a court, the imposition of the sentence. In addition to enabling face-to-face contact, panels display the other key elements of RJ: community involvement in the form of the panel members and a participative process. The absence of legal representation allows participants to speak for themselves and reaching agreement requires more interactive communication than is usual in a court setting.

The sentences available in the youth court also include several RJ options. The reparation order requires offenders to make good to the victim or to the wider community. In practice, it tends to be the latter although opinions vary as to whether the kind of reparation to be undertaken should be specified by the court or can be left to the Youth Offending Team. Other community based penalties such as the action plan or supervision order can include elements of RJ. So too can the Intensive Supervision and Surveillance Programmes (ISSP) which currently deal with over a thousand serious and persistent young offenders as an alternative to custody and will be available to all youth courts later this year. Early indications suggest that where RJ is used, youngsters are more likely to complete the programme and stay out of further trouble.

In the adult system, there are fewer opportunities available for RJ although the Criminal Justice Act 2003 contains some important innovations. As well as reparation becoming one of the statutory purposes of sentencing, the new conditional caution will enable restorative cautioning to be used with adults as it has been with juveniles. Overall, it is none the less hard to disagree with David Garland's contention that RJ currently operates 'on the margins of criminal justice, offsetting the central tendencies without much changing the overall balance of the system'. The Home Office are currently consulting on a strategy which would build RJ more systematically into the existing work of the probation and prison services, and into new initiatives such as intermittent custody centres (where weekend imprisonment will be available), and community justice centres, which will bring a local, problem solving approach to low level crime and disorder at neighbourhood level.

One reason for the current interest in RJ is the growing body of evidence, largely from abroad, that it can meet victims' needs more effectively than conventional criminal justice, reduce the rate of recidivism among offenders, and boost public confidence in the response to crime. The research does not show that RJ invariably works. Indeed, it is becoming clear that it is more likely to reduce re-offending in certain kinds of cases. The evaluation of the RISE project in Canberra, currently being replicated in an experiment in London, found the greatest impact in cases of violence. The effect on juvenile property offenders was much less pronounced. In cases of drunk driving, offenders involved in restorative conferences were slightly more likely to re-offend than those dealt with in court. This suggests that RJ works best when an offender, confronted by the reality of the harm they have caused, is able to appreciate the wrong they have done, feel a sense of shame and express genuine remorse. This can be the start of a process of conscience building, which can bring about positive changes in both attitude and behaviour. Magistrates and others working with young offenders are all too familiar with the way bad behaviour can be justified through what the sociologist David Matza called techniques of neutralisation – 'It wasn't my fault', 'They were insured', 'They deserved it' – are examples of barriers to taking proper responsibility for one's actions. RJ can remove those barriers. Where the harm is less palpable – as in cases of shop theft or drunken driving – being held accountable is likely to produce less of an impact or may even be counterproductive – because it can increase a sense of unfairness or alienation.

The body of research is generally much more positive about the effects of RJ on victims. The theory is that by being given a voice that is denied to them in conventional criminal justice, a chance to put questions to the offender and to express the hurt and loss they feel, victims are at best able to achieve what is called 'closure'. This enables victims to put the crime behind them and psychologically move on.

Given the promising results it is little wonder that RJ has become a fast growing movement across the world. Whether it is victim-offender mediation, restorative conferencing, family group conferencing or circle sentencing, RJ techniques are much more widespread in Australia, New Zealand and parts of Europe and North America than in the UK. RJ operates in various ways, in some jurisdictions taking place as a diversion from criminal proceedings, in others running alongside but separate from such proceedings and in one or two, particularly New Zealand, highly integrated in the justice system.

In R v Collins (*Times Law Report*, 14 April 2003), the Court of Appeal reduced a sentence for unlawful wounding and robbery from seven years to five. One reason was that the appellant had taken part in an RJ conference 'at which not only the robbery victim and members of her family attended, but also members of his own family... The programme was by no means a soft option.' The

Court of Appeal concluded that RJ 'which was designed to ensure effective sentencing for the better protection of the public, appeared to be going at least some way to achieving its purpose and should be encouraged.'

If RJ were to be more deeply embedded in criminal justice, an agreement could be reached in a meeting to be put forward to a sentencing court for ratification, as happens in New Zealand and parts of Canada. In most cases courts do ratify the agreement. The court's role is an important one, providing an impartial backstop to ensure what is proposed is not unreasonably harsh or unduly lenient given the requirements of proportionality and the wider public interest.

Improving Community Sentences

Alongside investigations into RJ, RCP has funded a range of work looking at the effectiveness of community penalties. Interim findings suggest the need to address three elements. First, alternatives to prison need to form part of a comprehensive community response to offenders that seeks to resolve the variety of health, education, employment and accommodation problems, which are linked directly or indirectly with their offending or antisocial behaviour. Helping offenders to address these difficulties necessarily involves the efforts and resources of both statutory and voluntary agencies at local level. While the specific programmes and services to be commissioned by the new National Offender Management Service (Noms) at regional level will have an important part to play, effective rehabilitation requires a lot more. Providers of education, work opportunities, drug treatment and housing need to be prepared to work with damaged people whose behaviour and attitudes can be highly challenging. Incentivising this work, financially or otherwise will be a high priority. One way of achieving this is to require representatives of key agencies to participate in local arrangements for offender work. RCP has been impressed by the way in which the 155 Youth Offending Teams bring together local agencies to work with offenders under 18. A similar local structure could be set up for older offenders, starting initially with the young adult age group (18-21).

Second, alternatives need to strengthen their links with the community. There is scope for creating formal links between local provisions for offenders, in particular prisons and local authorities in whose area they are located. This will help to ensure that offenders are included in consideration of the needs of local communities when services are being planned and commissioned by local government.

There is also a case for extending the role of community panels, which draw up contracts of intervention with first time young offenders. There is no reason why similar panels should not operate in respect of first time and minor offenders of all age groups. The contracts drawn up by youth offender panels have the twin aims of enabling the offender to make amends for his crime and assisting the young person to stay out of trouble. Making amends to the community should play a more central role in sanctions for all age groups.

There is also an opportunity to create mechanisms through which local communities, through the local authority or other body, can decide on the nature of the work to be undertaken by offenders subject to community orders and where appropriate in prison. There are models both in the UK (the Restorative Prisons project in North East England) and abroad (the Reparative Probation Boards in the US state of Vermont) which have a great deal to offer.

Sentencers' involvement in alternatives

In order to ensure alternatives are used as such and to avoid net widening, there is a need to involve sentencers more closely in their design, implementation and management. More careful attention needs to be paid to the targeting of alternatives both in legislation – through criteria for custody – and in everyday practice. Presentence reports, prepared by probation officers are crucial in ensuring information about the offender's circumstances and the range of suitable options for meeting them are put before sentencers. More consistent and targeted sentencing will depend on the new Sentencing Guidelines Council, supported by the Sentencing Advisory Panel.

Sentencer involvement in community sentences is relatively low. Research has suggested that a quarter of magistrates and judges and seven percent of district judges had visited a community service placement in the previous two years. Research conducted for RCP by the Henley Management College found that magistrates were keen to be more fully involved in the work of community penalties. The RCP funded research, 'The Decision to Imprison', found that for the most part sentencers expressed their satisfaction with the range and content of community sentences available to them. However, many also had concerns that under funding and understaffing of probation have repercussions for the supervision of offenders on community sentences. The demands and expectations which community sentences place on offenders need to meet in practice. The Home Affairs Select Committee in 1998 was alarmed at the non-adherence to standards in respect of enforcement but since then there has been a marked improvement. Offenders are nowadays required to comply with the demands of their sentences much more strictly than in the past. This is not necessarily the public perception however, although more than four in five magistrates rated the probation service as effective in enforcing community sentences. The latest standards require offenders to be taken back to court or breached after no more than two absences. The most recent audit of performance found that breach action was taken in 70 percent of cases where it should have been.

In their review of the youth justice system, the National Audit Office were concerned about the relatively high rate of non-completion of the ISSP programme. They recommended that the YJB examine whether existing standards governing attendance on the programme are being interpreted consistently and whether other sanctions short of custody are available to the courts for dealing with non-compliance. There is sense in the new national offender management service conducting a similar exercise in respect of non-compliance by adult offenders.

Will the public accept a different approach?

The position on public attitudes can be summed up by the former Lord Chief Justice who told the *Spectator*: 'Everybody thinks our system is becoming soft and wimpish. In point of fact it's one of the most punitive systems in the world'. The review of the correctional services conducted by Patrick Carter concluded that tougher sentencing has brought it 'closer in line with public opinion' and is concerned that the public continue to believe that sentencing is too lenient. What this ignores is the fact that asked a simple question, a majority will always tell pollsters that sentencing is too soft, whatever the objective sentencing levels are. This is largely because the public systematically underestimate the severity of sentencing. When respondents are properly informed about sentencing levels, and given detailed information about cases, a different picture emerges. Work undertaken for Rethinking Crime and Punishment has shown that when given options, the public does not rank prison highly as a way of dealing with crime. Most think that offenders come out of prison worse than they go in, only two percent would choose to spend a notional £10 million on prison places, and when asked how to deal with prison overcrowding, building more prisons is the least popular option, with the support of only a quarter of people. Over half think residential drug treatment and tougher community punishments are the way forward. Only one in ten people think putting more offenders in prison would do most to reduce crime in Britain. Better parenting, more police, better school discipline and more constructive activities for young people all score much more highly. This suggests that at one level public punitiveness is largely a myth and public confidence need not stand in the way of a bolder strategy of replacing imprisonment with more constructive alternatives. It is however true that community alternatives do not enjoy the level of confidence that they could and should. The Lord Chief Justice said 'neither the public nor sentencers have sufficient confidence in the community alternative' and when the Home Affairs Select Committee published a report on Alternatives to Prison in 1998, they concluded that confidence was key. 'Unless the public has confidence, far from reducing the prison population there will be calls for increasing it.' This has to extent come to pass.

What we have to do is to achieve a situation where in the words of Lord Woolf 'our punishments in the community are ones which the public find more acceptable than they do at present'.

RCP's experience suggests that action is needed on a number of fronts. The first is public education. Members of the public given information about the criminal justice system are more likely than the general public to think probation, community service and fines effective in reducing offending. The Local Crime Community Sentence (LCCS) project funded by RCP found that presentations to community groups by magistrates and probation officers shifted attitudes. Other RCP funded projects found that:

- People can change their views as a result of absorbing factual information, when confronted with different perspectives or when they experience first hand the work of prisons and other penalties.
- The high cost of prison, rising prison numbers and humanitarian costs do not lead people to believe prison should be used less, but it is widely accept-

ed that some types of offender (e.g. those with mental illness, drug dependency and women with children) require a different approach.

More systematic awareness raising efforts and public education initiatives
along the lines of LCCS should be introduced nationally.

The second area for action concerns the way community sentences are actually organised. The Henley research concluded that to become supportive of
prison alternatives, the public need to see the benefits that these bring to their
communities in terms of enhanced safety, rehabilitation of offenders and satis-
fied victims. The public also needs to see that community sentences are serious
penalties for offenders. Community penalties with some element of community service are widely supported; in 1996 nearly three quarters of people told
Mori that offenders who are not a big threat should be made to spend a certain
amount of time helping in the community. There is a case therefore for all community penalties to include some element of reparation. The mechanisms for
more direct community involvement outlined in the previous section should
also help.

Third, efforts need to be made to improve media coverage of issues of crime
and punishment. It has been argued by Mike Hough that the media systematically distort the crime problem and are largely responsible for the widespread
misperceptions about crime and sentencing. Research conducted for RCP by
the Open University has looked at the way soap operas shape public attitudes in
this area. While there are no easy solutions here, the RCP funded 'Case Study
Project' has produced promising results. This project prepares ex-offenders to
appear on the news media. This enables real life stories to illustrate what alternatives such as drug treatment actually involve. The project should be extended
nationally. This should form part of a marketing campaign, which should drawing on work undertaken by RCP by Strathclyde University. This found that to
market alternatives to prison there is a need to

- create a strong, well understood and attractive brand that encapsulates
  non-custodial sentences
- reduce the 'price' associated with the use of non custodial sentences so it is
  the easiest option
- increase the availability and accessibility of non custodial sentences
- use marketing communications to increase demand for non-custodial sen-

tences and reposition them as tough and effective in reducing crime e.g. through work with sentencers, politicians, the public and media. Focus groups suggest that key message strategies to engage public support for non-custodial sentences include:

Instillation of responsibility and discipline

Having to work hard, emotionally and physically

Putting something back

Paying back to victims

Restriction of liberty and requirement to change behaviour.

Treatment of causes of offending

Whether these efforts are made depends on the prior commitment of the government to reduce the prison population and promote alternative approaches to offenders. The Decision to Imprison concluded that policies to restrict prison numbers should involve three levels of intervention:

a) Adjustment to the legal and legislative framework of sentencing so as to bring down custody rates and sentence lengths

b) Softening the climate of political and public opinion

c) Improving understanding of the range of non custodial penalties.

However, none of these interventions is likely to meet with much success unless there is clear political will to stop the uncontrolled growth in prison numbers, and visible consistent, political leadership in stressing the need to do so.

Index